Machine Reading Comprehension

T0296775

Machine Reading Comprehension
Algorithms and Practice

CHENGUANG ZHU
Microsoft Corporation, Redmond, WA, United States

ELSEVIER

Elsevier
Radarweg 29, PO Box 211, 1000 AE Amsterdam, Netherlands
The Boulevard, Langford Lane, Kidlington, Oxford OX5 1GB, United Kingdom
50 Hampshire Street, 5th Floor, Cambridge, MA 02139, United States

Copyright © 2021 Beijing Huazhang Graphics & Information Co., Ltd/China Machine Press.
Published by Elsevier Inc. All rights reserved.

No part of this publication may be reproduced or transmitted in any form or by any means, electronic or mechanical, including photocopying, recording, or any information storage and retrieval system, without permission in writing from the publisher. Details on how to seek permission, further information about the Publisher's permissions policies and our arrangements with organizations such as the Copyright Clearance Center and the Copyright Licensing Agency, can be found at our website: www.elsevier.com/permissions.

This book and the individual contributions contained in it are protected under copyright by the Publisher (other than as may be noted herein).

Notices
Knowledge and best practice in this field are constantly changing. As new research and experience broaden our understanding, changes in research methods, professional practices, or medical treatment may become necessary.

Practitioners and researchers must always rely on their own experience and knowledge in evaluating and using any information, methods, compounds, or experiments described herein. In using such information or methods they should be mindful of their own safety and the safety of others, including parties for whom they have a professional responsibility.

To the fullest extent of the law, neither the Publisher nor the authors, contributors, or editors, assume any liability for any injury and/or damage to persons or property as a matter of products liability, negligence or otherwise, or from any use or operation of any methods, products, instructions, or ideas contained in the material herein.

British Library Cataloguing-in-Publication Data
A catalogue record for this book is available from the British Library

Library of Congress Cataloging-in-Publication Data
A catalog record for this book is available from the Library of Congress

ISBN: 978-0-323-90118-5

For Information on all Elsevier publications
visit our website at https://www.elsevier.com/books-and-journals

Publisher: Glyn Jones
Editorial Project Manager: Naomi Robertson
Production Project Manager: Punithavathy Govindaradjane
Cover Designer: Mark Rogers

Typeset by MPS Limited, Chennai, India

Contents

Part I Foundation

About the author

Dr. Chenguang Zhu is a Principal Research Manager in the Microsoft Corporation. Dr. Zhu obtained his PhD in Computer Science from Stanford University, United States. He is leading efforts in the research and productization of natural language processing in Azure Cognitive AI. He is proficient in artificial intelligence, deep learning, and natural language processing, specializing in machine reading comprehension, text summarization, and dialogue understanding. He has led teams to win the first place in the SQuAD 1.0 Machine Reading Comprehension Competition held by Stanford University, and reach human parity in the CoQA Conversational Reading Comprehension Competition. He has 40 papers published in top AI and NLP conferences, such as ACL, EMNLP, NAACL, and ICLR, with more than 1000 citations.

Foreword by Xuedong Huang

There are two levels of intelligence. One is perceptual intelligence, which enables the computer to see, hear, and touch. In these areas, artificial intelligence has made many breakthroughs, such as speech recognition, speech synthesis, and computer vision. A higher level is cognitive intelligence, which requires computers to understand and analyze concepts, relationships, and logic. At this level, artificial intelligence is still in its infancy.

As an important medium for human communication and information dissemination, language is at the core of human intelligence. From the Turing Test in the 1950s to the deep learning era today, the understanding and application of natural language has always been a hot research topic. If AI is the crown, speech and language technologies are the jewels on top of the crown. It is fair to say that if computers can fully understand human language, we'll have achieved strong artificial intelligence.

In recent years, machine reading comprehension has become one of the most popular and cutting-edge directions in natural language processing research. It has significant scientific and practical values to enable computer models to read articles, analyze semantics, and answer questions like humans. Machine reading comprehension technology can automate plenty of time-consuming and laborious text analysis work and greatly improve the productivity of many applications, ranging from intelligent customer service to search engines, from automatic essay scoring to intelligent finance.

With the development of deep learning technology, the research of machine reading comprehension has made tremendous progress. In some specific tasks, the answers of computer models are already comparable to the human level. Some media reports have even claimed that the computer is superior to humans in reading comprehension. However, existing models are still far from a genuine and thorough understanding of text. In many cases, these models still rely on simple matching of words and phrases, rather than on a thorough understanding of the syntactic structure and semantics.

In general, there are three key factors to the success of an artificial intelligence system: platform, data, and algorithm. As the computing power and magnitude of data continue to soar, the exploration and improvement of algorithms have become a hotly contested spot for artificial intelligence research.

Currently there are very few books on the market which have a complete introduction to machine reading comprehension. Dr. Chenguang Zhu in our team has worked deeply in this direction for many years and has led the team to achieve top places in a number of international contests. The purpose of his book is to objectively show the field of machine reading comprehension to readers. The book includes a detailed introduction to the latest research results and thoughts on the future directions of machine reading comprehension. I hope this book will inspire readers to work together to achieve human–level machine reading comprehension.

Dr. Xuedong Huang
CTO of Artificial Intelligence, Microsoft,
Redmond, WA, United States

Foreword by Zide Du

Natural language processing aims to solve the problem of understanding and generating natural language. Natural language is the jewel in the crown of artificial intelligence. It is one of the most important abilities of computers, but is also a challenging direction to study. Every human language has its own grammar, but because of the different styles of usage, coupled with factors such as dialects and idioms, the resulting forms of language have a large variation. These variations usually do not interfere much with the communication between humans, but it is very difficult for computers to understand. This is because the current von Neumann computer architecture is good at handling information with clear rules, but is less capable of handling constantly evolving forms of information.

Over the years, researchers have proposed and developed many methods, ranging from rule-based linguistic techniques to models based on statistical machine learning. In recent years, researchers have developed end-to-end deep learning frameworks for natural language processing, including word embeddings, attention mechanisms, encoder—decoder architecture, and the recent, pretraining models. These techniques have greatly improved models' ability to understand text and brought new interesting ideas to natural language processing.

Machine reading comprehension is one of the most popular and cutting-edge research topics in natural language processing. Reading is the basic means for people to obtain information. Without reading there is no understanding, and without understanding one cannot communicate. There are already many chatbots in the market, but people often find them responding off the point. The reason is that the current technology is a black box approach based on text matching. So the chatbot does not really understand what people mean. As we know, humans communicate with context, so that we can easily understand what other people are talking about via referencing. However, it is very difficult to make machines understand the context. In order to solve these problems, researchers have proposed many ways to improve models' ability to understand dialog and articles. Moreover, the release of many reading comprehension datasets have played an important role in promoting the development of technology.

In addition to its research values, machine reading comprehension has many meaningful applications. For example, machine-generated article summaries can save a lot of time of reading the full text, and the QA system can accurately find answers to user questions from a large number of documents. Machine reading comprehension is also the basis for translation and dialog, which are of great value to computer-assisted services.

Chenguang's book systematically introduces the key technologies and progress in this area as well as existing challenges. I believe that readers will have a clear understanding of the research and application of this field after reading this book.

During high school, Chenguang participated in the National Olympiad in Informatics (NOI) organized by the China Computer Federation (CCF), winning gold medals in the national competition. He was also a candidate for the Chinese team for the International Olympiad in Informatics. As I was the chairman of NOI, I got to know him back then. He later went to Tsinghua University to study computer science, got a PhD at Stanford University, and now works at Microsoft on natural language processing. We rarely see each other, but constantly keep in touch. I think he is a talented young scholar with a rigorous and very sensible style. I am therefore very happy to discuss various issues with him. He asked me to write the foreword for his new book and I am very glad to see his research progress. I also want to express my congratulations to him.

Zide Du
Former Researcher at the Institute of Computing Technology,
Chinese Academy of Sciences, Beijing, China;
Secretary General of the Chinese Computer Federation, Beijing, China

Preface

Reading is an important means for humans to acquire knowledge and understand the world. For thousands of years, language has been the carrier of human civilization, containing a wealth of information, experience, and wisdom. Language's nature of high concentration makes reading ability a vital intelligence. The famous science fiction writer, Mr. Liu Cixin, described the efficiency of human language communication in his novel *The Rural Teacher*:

> *You're trying to tell us that a species that has no memory inheritance, communicates with each other in sound waves at an incredible rate of 1 to 10 bits per second, can create a 5B-level civilization?! And this civilization has evolved on its own without any cultivation from external advanced civilization?!*

It is estimated that the average reading speed of humans is about two to three times the speed of speech. Thus, under a rough estimate, even if a person reads for 8 hours a day for 50 years, he or she can only get about 1.5 GB of information out of reading. However, human civilization has far exceeded this magnitude. Therefore reading is a complex process of abstracting text into concepts, ideas, and derived knowledge through understanding.

In today's wave of artificial intelligence, it is very important to enable the computer learn to read. On the one hand, reading ability lies at the core of human intelligence, which is indispensable in the ultimate form of artificial intelligence. On the other hand, with the explosion of text data, computer models can automate the process of text understanding, save a lot of cost and time, and have a wide range of applications in many industries.

Thus in recent years machine reading comprehension (MRC) has been one of the most cutting-edge research topics in natural language processing. The goal of the study is to teach computers to read articles and answer related questions like humans. Lots of AI technologies have been applied to this field, and there have emerged many MRC tasks. I was fortunate enough to be among the first group of researchers in this field, designing and implementing several models to win the first place in the SQuAD competition hosted by Stanford University, and surpass human level performance for the first time in the conversational MRC competition CoQA.

However, as computer models outperform humans on more datasets, many media reports use headlines like *Computer has beaten humans in reading*, which contributes to the so-called claim that AI has replaced humans. As a researcher in this area, I deeply feel that computers are far from humans' ability of reading and understanding. Although current reading comprehension models have achieved huge progress compared with a decade ago, they are above the human level only in specific datasets under various constraints. Studies have shown that the performance of these models will significantly drop when a confusing sentence is appended to the article, while humans find it very easy to judge.

In contrast to the boom of machine reading comprehension research, there are so far no books on the market in this field. Most progress is published in the form of academic papers, and little information can be found about the application of MRC in industry. Therefore the purpose of this book is to objectively show the status quo of machine reading comprehension research. Starting from the basic modules, the architecture of models, and to cutting-edge algorithms, the book details the design and implementation of machine reading comprehension models. There are numerous code examples in Python and PyTorch by the author, showcasing the model building process, which has a high practical value. All the code is available at https://github.com/zcgzcgzcg1/MRC_book_en. In addition, the book introduces the landing of machine reading comprehension technology in various industrial applications, such as intelligent customer service and search engines, and points out the challenges and future directions of MRC research.

Although currently machines are still inferior to humans in terms of reading ability, we can leverage the high speed and large storage of computers to overtake humans. As said in the ancient Chinese proverb, *When one learns 300 poems of the Tang Dynasty by heart, he is sure to be able to write poetry*. Nowadays, computers can read a million poems in a split second. So there is every reason to expect a breakthrough in machine reading comprehension. For example, the BERT model combines the merits of massive data and large models to make breakthroughs in many areas of natural language processing including machine reading comprehension. I hope that this book can inspire readers to make computers achieve and exceed the reading ability of humans in the near future.

The book is divided into three parts, with a total of eight chapters.

The first part is Foundation (Chapters 1–3), which introduces the basics of machine reading comprehension and key technologies. These include the definition of the MRC task, natural language processing techniques used in MRC models, and related deep learning network modules, such as how to represent articles and questions in computers, how to answer multiple-choice questions, and how to generate freestyle answers.

The second part is Architecture (Chapters 4—6), which introduces the basic model architecture and popular models for machine reading comprehension. It also analyzes the state-of-the-art pretrained models, for example, GPT and BERT, that have had a revolutionary impact on machine reading comprehension research.

The third part is Application (Chapter 7: Code Analysis of SDNet Model and Chapter 8: Applications and Future of Machine Reading Comprehension), including the code analysis of the SDNet model which won first place in the CoQA MRC competition in 2018, the process of landing machine reading comprehension technology in various industrial applications, as well as challenges and future directions of MRC research.

The errata information of this book is available in the code link above. If you have any comments, please contact me at zcg.stanford@gmail.com. I look forward to receiving feedback and communicating with dear readers.

Acknowledgment

Many thanks to Dr. Xuedong Huang and Mr. Nanshan Zeng from Microsoft Cognitive Services for their guidance and help.

Many thanks to Mr. Zide Du, Secretary-General of the China Computer Federation, for his long-time encouragement and support.

Thanks to Prof. Maosong Sun of Tsinghua University, Prof. Jiajun Wu of Stanford University, Prof. Meng Jiang of the University of Notre Dame, and Principal Scientist Quoc V. Le of Google for writing recommendations for this book.

Special thanks to my wife Mengyun and daughter. I sacrificed a lot of family time in writing this book. Without their love and support, I could not finish this book.

Thanks to my parents who helped to take care of my daughter to support me to finish writing.

I would like to dedicate this book to my dearest family, as well as to all my friends who love machine reading comprehension!

Chenguang Zhu

Recommendation

The last several years can be seen as a golden era of natural language processing, especially machine reading comprehension. The rapid progress has the potential to enable many applications that we could only imagine before. Both beginners and experts in machine reading comprehension will enjoy this book because it is comprehensive and it explains difficult concepts in an easy-to-understand manner. I highly recommend it!

Quoc Le
Principal Scientist, Google Brain, Mountain View, CA, United States

We have witnessed rapid progress in natural language processing in the past few years. Dr. Zhu's book is a very good introduction to this field. Through both hands-on code samples and the author's deep understanding and analysis of the area, the book will be highly useful to readers at all levels.

Jiajun Wu
Assistant Professor in the Computer Science Department at Stanford University, Stanford, CA, United States

I love this book. It will help both beginners and long-term researchers. It can be used for teaching, research, and even self-study and experimentation. Thanks to the emergence of this book, I hope you will also start to love artificial intelligence and natural language processing.

Meng Jiang
Assistant Professor in the Department of Computer Science and Engineering, the University of Notre Dame, Notre Dame, IN, United States
Head of Data Mining Towards Decision Making Lab, Notre Dame, IN, United States

Machine reading comprehension is a frontier research topic in natural language processing and artificial intelligence. In recent years, there are many research results and international competitions in this field. However, there are very few books that comprehensively investigate machine reading comprehension. The publication of this book fills this gap at the right time. The author has an educational background at Tsinghua University and Stanford University, with extensive research and engineering experience in the world's leading IT companies. He has led teams to achieve first places in the Stanford Conversational Question Answering Challenge

(CoQA), the Stanford Question Answering competition (SQuAD v1.0), and the AI2 Reasoning Challenge (ARC). Therefore this book has a great combination of both cutting-edge research results and practical applications. At present, the study of machine reading comprehension is rapidly rising, so I believe you will like reading this book.

Maosong Sun

Professor in the Department of Computer Science at Tsinghua University, Beijing, China

Executive Vice President of the Institute of Artificial Intelligence at Tsinghua University, Beijing, China

This book provides an in-depth introduction to the basics of natural language processing, various model architectures, the applications, and challenges of machine reading comprehension, coupled with detailed examples. The author also shares his leading research results on machine reading comprehension and in-depth thinking on the future direction. I recommend this book to students, researchers, and engineers who specialize in natural language processing, especially machine reading comprehension.

Michael Zeng

Partner Research Manager, Head of AI Cognitive Services Group, Microsoft, Redmond, WA, United States

PART I

Foundation

CHAPTER 1

Introduction to machine reading comprehension

1.1 The machine reading comprehension task

Since the advent of computers, we have dreamed of enabling machines to acquire human-level intelligence. Among the various forms of intelligence, understanding language is essential in human life, including daily communication, description of concepts, and propagation of ideas. As a famous example, the Turing Test proposed by Alan Turing in 1950 employed conversation as an important criterion for artificial intelligence.

Machine reading comprehension (MRC) is one of the most important tasks in language understanding. Snow defined reading comprehension in [1] as "the process of extracting and constructing article semantics from written text by interaction." The goal of MRC is to use artificial intelligence technology to enable computers to understand articles like humans.

1.1.1 History of machine reading comprehension

The history of MRC dates back to the 1970s, when researchers started to recognize the significance of text understanding in artificial intelligence. The first reading comprehension system, QUALM [2], was proposed in 1977. The system was built upon hand-coded scripts and focused on pragmatic issues of reading comprehension, including its relation to question answering.

Twenty years later, a reading comprehension dataset consisting of about 120 stories for 3rd–6th grade students was released in 1999, together with a rule-based model Deep Read [3]. The model leveraged low-level linguistic features and could achieve 30%–40% accuracy in question answering.

In 2013 the MRC problem was formally framed as a supervised learning task: given a passage and a related question, the model should give the answer in the required format. With the advent of larger datasets like McTest and ProcessBank, many machine learning models have been proposed. Most of these approaches leveraged linguistic tools such

Machine Reading Comprehension. DOI: https://doi.org/10.1016/B978-0-323-90118-5.00001-1
© 2021 Beijing Huazhang Graphics & Information Co., Ltd/China Machine Press.
Published by Elsevier Inc. All rights reserved.

as dependency parsers and named entity recognition to obtain features and build statistical models to maximize the probability of correctness of the generated answer.

From 2015 the vast majority of MRC algorithms have been built on deep learning and deep neural networks. These approaches utilize their immense model complexity to accurately characterize the semantic space and achieve higher answer accuracy. Moreover, these models typically don't require manually designed features. Instead, a robust and generalizable feature representation can be automatically learned from the data. This greatly reduces the dependence on expert knowledge and downstream linguistic tools. The success of deep learning models is also closely related to the emergence of various large-scale MRC datasets such as SQuAD, RACE, and MS MARCO. In this book, we will primarily focus on the MRC models based on deep learning.

1.1.2 Application of machine reading comprehension

With a plethora of text data generated from various industries, the traditional way of manually processing data has become the bottleneck of many applications due to its slow speed and huge cost. Therefore MRC technology, which can automatically process and analyze text data and extract semantic knowledge from it, is gaining more popularity.

For example, the traditional search engine can only return documents related to user queries, while an MRC model can pinpoint the answers in the document, thereby improving the user experience. MRC can also greatly improve the efficiency in customer service when searching for solutions to users' problems in product documentations. In the field of medical intelligence, a reading comprehension model can analyze the patient's symptoms and automatically consult huge piles of medical records and papers to find possible causes and give a diagnosis. MRC can help revise essays for students and offer suggestions for improvement, enabling students to improve their writing skills anytime, anywhere. Chapter 8, Applications and Future of Machine Reading Comprehension, will cover these applications of MRC in more details.

Thus MRC can help save tremendous manpower and time in scenarios that require automated processing and analysis of a large amount of text. Even if the quality of a reading comprehension model does not completely reach the level of humans, it can save cost by solving a part of the problem space. For instance, in customer service, the computer can focus on solving the most frequent problems with a high accuracy, while resorting to human agents for the remaining problems. Due to its widespread applications in various domains, MRC has become one of the most popular directions in cutting-edge AI research.

1.2 Natural language processing

MRC is an important direction in natural language processing (NLP). NLP analyzes the patterns and structures of human language, with the goal of designing computer models to understand language and communicate with humans. The history of NLP can be traced back to the birth of artificial intelligence. Over the decades, we have made huge progress in many NLP areas, such as understanding and generation, which has laid a solid foundation for MRC research. Thus in this section we will introduce the status quo of NLP research and its impact on MRC.

1.2.1 The status quo of natural language processing

NLP has evolved over 70 years, with many refined subtasks in the field. Here is an introduction to those important research directions related to MRC:

1. *Information retrieval* studies how to find results related to user queries in a massive number of documents or webpages. The research on information retrieval is relatively mature and widely used in products like search engines. It greatly promotes the dissemination and acquisition of information. When a reading comprehension task involves a large-scale text corpus, information retrieval is usually employed as the first module to extract relevant information.

2. *Question and answering system* establishes a system that automatically answers a user's question. The difference between a QA system and an information retrieval system is that a QA system needs to understand the semantics of complex questions and often support multiple turns of question answering. In a conversational reading comprehension task, the model should analyze the information from both the article and previous rounds of conversation to answer the question.

3. *Text classification* refers to the task of classifying articles, paragraphs, and statements, such as categorizing webpages by content and subject. In MRC, some models build a text classification module to check whether the question is about time, location, or other category of information. This can help improve the accuracy of answers.

4. *Machine translation* studies how to let the computer automatically translate text into other languages. This can be applied to cross-lingual reading comprehension tasks. For example, we can use machine translation to generate training data from popular languages to train a MRC model on low-resource languages.

5. *Text summarization* studies how to summarize an article's salient information in an abridged version. Because text summarization involves a deep analysis of the article semantics, many of its techniques have been applied to MRC, including the encoder—decoder architecture and the pointer—generator network.

1.2.2 Existing issues

Although we have made remarkable achievements in many NLP tasks, there are still many problems that have not yet been well addressed, including the understanding of language structure and semantics. Many of these unsolved problems are also closely related to MRC.

1.2.2.1 The ambiguity of language

One of the characteristics of language is that it can express complex ideas with succinct statements. Thus it is common to have ambiguity in a sentence, that is, there are many reasonable interpretations. Here are some examples.

Example 1: *The fish is ready to eat.*

It can mean that the fish can start eating or the fish can be provided to someone to eat. The ambiguity comes from the different interpretations of the thematic role of the fish: whether it is the agent or patient of the action "eat."

Example 2: *David solved the problem too.*

Without context, it is hard to determine what fact "too" refers to. It can be that someone else solved the problem and David also did it. It can also be that David designed the problem and also solved it.

Example 3: *I saw a man on the hill with a telescope.*

The telescope could be in my hand (which I used to see the man) or with the man (I saw the man and his telescope), since both are valid under grammatic rules.

These are just some of the numerous examples of ambiguity in language. Even for humans, it is difficult to judge the true intentions of the speaker. However, if there is enough contextual information, most ambiguity can be eliminated. For example, if a cook says "the fish is ready to eat" before dinner, we know that this dish is ready for dining.

Nevertheless, many NLP models still struggle to understand the semantics of context. By analyzing the results of various models on tasks such as MRC, the researchers find that existing models are largely dependent on keyword or phrase matching, which greatly limits their capability to understand context and handle ambiguity.

1.2.2.2 Common sense and reasoning skills

In many cases, humans can reason from conversations to draw conclusions without explicit explanation. Here is an example dialogue of a customer booking tickets through customer service:

> Agent: Hello, how can I help you?
>
> Customer: I'd like to book a flight from San Francisco to New York in early May.
>
> Agent: OK, when do you want to fly?
>
> Customer: Well, I'm going to New York for a conference, which is from the 4th to 7th.
>
> Agent: OK, here's the direct flight information from San Francisco to New York on May 3,...

Here, the customer does not directly answer the agent's question about the departure date. Instead, he gives the start and end date of the conference he will attend. As the flight must arrive in New York before the meeting starts, the agent infers that the departure date is May 3. And if the customer also needs a flight back to San Francisco from New York, the agent should give information about flights departing in the evening of May 7 or on May 8.

Therefore an automatic customer service model needs to infer information like the departure date from previous conversations. This inference requires the model to carry the common sense that the flight must reach its destination before the conference.

In recent years, there have been many efforts in applying common sense and reasoning to NLP. However, it remains an open question on how to equip a model with large-scale common sense and conduct effective reasoning.

1.3 Deep learning

Deep learning is currently one of the hottest areas of research in AI. Models based on deep learning play major roles in image recognition, speech recognition, NLP, and many other applications. The vast majority of MRC models nowadays are based on deep learning as well. Therefore this section will describe the characteristics of deep learning and the successful use cases.

1.3.1 Features of deep learning

Why can deep learning, as a branch of machine learning, stand out from the numerous directions? There are several important reasons as follows.

First, most deep learning models have a large model complexity. Deep learning is based on artificial neural networks (ANN), and one of the characteristics of ANN is that its model size is controllable: even with a fixed input dimension, the number of model parameters can be regulated by adjusting the number of network layers, number of connections, and layer size. As a result, deep learning makes it easy to increase model complexity to make a more efficient use of massive data. At the same time, studies have shown that the accuracy of deep learning models can increase with a larger size of data. As the field of MRC continues to evolve, more and more datasets emerge, making deep learning the most common machine learning architecture in reading comprehension.

Second, deep learning has a powerful **feature learning ability**. In machine learning, the performance of a model largely depends on how it learns a good representation of the data, that is, representation learning. Traditional machine learning models require a predefined procedure of extracting task-specific features. Prior to the advent of deep learning, feature extraction was often manual and required knowledge from domain experts. On the contrary, deep learning relies on neural networks to automatically learn effective feature representations via a nonlinear transformation on the primitive data features, for example, word vectors, picture pixels. In other words, deep learning can effectively obtain salient features that are helpful to the target task, without the need for model designers to possess special domain knowledge. As a result, it greatly increases the efficiency of designing deep learning models for tasks from various applications.

Third, deep learning enables **end-to-end learning**. Previously, many machine learning models proposed multistep solutions in the form of pipelines, such as feature learning $\rightarrow$ feature categorization $\rightarrow$ modeling each category $\rightarrow$ model ensembling. However, since each step can only be independently optimized, it is difficult to simultaneously optimize the whole system to improve its performance. Moreover, if any step within the model is updated, it is likely that all downstream steps have to be adapted as well, which greatly reduces the efficiency. One advantage of deep learning is that it enables end-to-end learning via the featurization ability of neural networks: feed in the raw data as input, and output the required result. This approach can optimize all parameters in an orchestrated manner to boost accuracy. For example, in MRC, the model takes in the article and question text, and outputs the answer text. This greatly simplifies the optimization and is also easy to use and deploy.

Fourth, the hardware for deep learning, especially **Graphics Processing Unit (GPU)**, is being continuously upgraded. As deep learning models are usually large, computational efficiency has become a very important factor for the progress of deep learning. Fortunately, the improved design of GPU has greatly accelerated the computation. Compared with CPU, GPU has greater floating-point computing power, faster read—write speed, and better parallelism. The development of GPUs over the last decade follows the Moore's law of early day CPUs, where computing speed and device complexity grow exponentially over time. The GPU industry, represented by companies such as NVIDIA, Intel, and Google, continues to evolve and develop specialized GPUs for deep learning, contributing to the development and application of the entire deep learning field.

Fifth, the emergence and prosperity of deep learning frameworks and community immensely help prompt the booming of deep learning. With the advent of frameworks, such as TensorFlow, PyTorch, and Keras, neural networks can be automatically optimized and the most commonly used network modules are predefined, making deep learning development much simpler. Meanwhile, deep learning communities quickly thrive. Every time a new research result appears, there will be developers who immediately implement, validate, and open source models, making the popularization of new technologies to be at an unprecedented level. Academic paper repositories (e.g., arXiv) and open-source code platforms (e.g., GitHub) greatly facilitate the communication between researchers and developers, and considerably lower the threshold for participation in deep learning research. For example, within a few months of the publication and open source of the breakthrough Bidirectional Encoder Representations from Transformers (BERT) model in 2018 (more details in Chapter 6, Pretrained Language Model), models utilizing BERT had taken top places in MRC competitions such as SQuAD and CoQA (Fig. 1.1).

1.3.2 Achievements of deep learning

Since the advent of deep learning, it has achieved many remarkable results in various fields such as speech, vision, and NLP.

In 2009 the father of deep learning, Geoffrey Hinton, worked with Microsoft Research to significantly improve the accuracy of speech recognition systems through the Deep Belief Network, which was quickly

Leaderboard

SQuAD2.0 tests the ability of a system to not only answer reading comprehension questions, but also abstain when presented with a question that cannot be answered based on the provided paragraph. How will your system compare to humans on this task?

Rank	Model	EM	*F*1
	Human Performance *Stanford University*	86.831	89.452
1 Mar 20, 2019	BERT + DAE + AoA (ensemble) *Joint Laboratory of HIT and iFLYTEK Research*	87.147	89.474
2 Mar 15, 2019	BERT + ConvLSTM + MTL + Verifier (ensemble) *Layer 6 AI*	86.730	89.286
3 Mar 05, 2019	BERT + *N*-Gram Masking + Synthetic Self-Training (ensemble) *Google AI Language* https://github.com/google-research/bert	86.673	89.147

Figure 1.1 The top three models in the machine reading comprehension competition SQuAD 2.0 are all based on BERT.

reproduced by IBM, Google, and HKUST. This is also one of the earliest success stories of deep learning. Seven years later, Microsoft further used a large-scale deep learning network to reduce the word error rate of speech recognition to 5.9%. This is the first time ever a computer model achieved the same performance as a professional stenographer.

In 2012 the deep learning model AlexNet achieved 84.6% in Top-5 accuracy in the large-scale image recognition contest ILSVRC2012, outperforming the second place by over 10%.

In 2016 Stanford University introduced the MRC dataset SQuAD, which includes 500 articles and over 100,000 questions. Just 2 years later, Google's pretrained deep learning model BERT reached an accuracy of 87.4% in exact match and 93.2% in *F*1 score, surpassing the human performance (82.3% in exact match and 91.2% in *F*1 score), which impressed the whole industry.

In 2018 Microsoft developed a deep learning translation system which for the first time achieved the same level of translation quality and accuracy as a human translator on the Chinese—English News dataset.

These achievements manifest the power of deep learning from different aspects, and also lay a solid foundation for its landing in the industry. However, we also observe that deep learning has some unresolved issues. For example, many deep learning models are still a "black box," making it impossible to explain how the model produces output for a particular input instance, and very hard to correct specific errors. In addition, most deep learning models lack the ability of reasoning, induction, and common sense. There are many ongoing researches to solve these issues. Hopefully, in the near future, deep learning will solve these problems and enable computers to have the same level of intelligence as humans.

1.4 Evaluation of machine reading comprehension

MRC is similar to the human reading comprehension task. Therefore it needs to be evaluated by the model's ability to understand the content of the article. Unlike mathematical problems, reading comprehension requires specific evaluation metrics for semantic understanding. It is well-known that the assessment of reading comprehension for humans is usually in the form of question and answer, in which the reader is asked to answer questions related to the article. Therefore the evaluation of MRC models can take the same form: the model answers relevant questions of the article and is evaluated by the answer quality. In this section, we will describe commonly used methods to evaluate a MRC model.

1.4.1 Answer forms

Most MRC tasks are assessed by the quality of their answers to given questions related to articles. The evaluation criteria depends on the form of answer. Here are some common answer forms:
- Multiple choice, that is, the model needs to select the correct answer from a number of options.
- Extractive, that is, the answer is bound to be a segment of text within the article, so the model needs to mark the correct starting and ending position of the answer in the article.
- Freestyle, that is, there is no limitation on the answer's text, which allows the model to freely generate answers.
- Cloze test, that is, certain keywords are removed from the article and the model needs to fill in the blanks with correct words or phrases.

In addition, some datasets design "unanswerable" questions, that is, a question that may not have a suitable answer given the article. In this case, the model should output "unanswerable" as the answer.

In the above forms, multiple choices and cloze tests can be objectively evaluated by directly comparing with the ground truth. Thus the accuracy can be used as the evaluation criterion. Extractive answers are of a semi-objective type. We can compare the model's output with the correct answer, and give a score of 1 when they are exactly the same, and 0 otherwise. This metric is called **Exact Match**. However, this will treat partially correct answers as wrong ones. For example, if the correct answer is "eight o'clock" and the model's output is "It's eight o'clock," the exact match score will be 0, although the model's output is very close to the correct answer. Therefore for extractive answers, the $F1$ metric is also often used, which is the harmonic mean of the precision and recall:

$$F_1 = 2 \times \frac{Precision \times recall}{Precision + recall}$$

Precision refers to the ratio of words in the model's output that also appear in the correct answer, and recall is the ratio of words in the correct answer that appear in the model's output. Thus the $F1$ metric can give a partial score when the model's output is partially correct. Table 1.1 shows an example of computing the Exact Match and $F1$ scores.

Freestyle answer is the most flexible form. The ideal metric should give full credit when the model's output has exactly the same meaning as the correct answer, and partial credit otherwise. However, it is a complex and unsolved problem to automatically judge whether two statements express the same meaning. On the other hand, human evaluation is very time-consuming and labor-intensive, while suffering from a high variance. Thus most widely used metrics for freestyle answers are based on the ratio of matched words/phrases between the model's output and the correct answer. These metrics include ROUGE, BLEU, and METEOR. We introduce the ROUGE metric in the next section.

Table 1.1 Exact match and $F1$ metrics.

Correct answer	Model's output	Exact match	Precision	Recall	$F1$
20 miles	is 20 miles	0	2/3 = 0.66	1/1 = 1	0.8
20 miles	20 miles	1	1	1	1

1.4.2 Recall-oriented understudy for gisting evaluation: metric for evaluating freestyle answers

ROUGE (Recall–Oriented Understudy for Gisting Evaluation) is a set of text similarity metrics based on recall [4]. It is used to measure the proportion of words and phrases in the correct answer that appear in the model's output. Because one question may have different expressions for the correct answer, ROUGE allows a set of reference answers for the same question.

ROUGE includes metrics such as ROUGE-N, ROUGE-S, and ROUGE-L. ROUGE-N measures the recall for N-grams, which is computed as follows:

$$ROUGE - N(M) = \frac{\sum_{A \in references} \sum_{s \in N-\text{grams in } A} \min\{count_s(A), count_s(M)\}}{\sum_{A \in references} \sum_{s \in N-\text{grams in } A} count_s(A)},$$

where M is the model's output, an N-gram is a phrase that consists of N neighboring words in the text, and $count_s(A)$ is the number of appearances of the N-gram s in A.

ROUGE-S is similar to ROUGE-2 ($N = 2$), but does not require the two words to be neighboring. Instead, the two words can be at most Skip words apart, where Skip is a parameter. For example, in "I like to run at night," if Skip $= 2$, "I like," "I to" and "I run" are all 2-grams in ROUGE-S.

ROUGE-L computes the longest common subsequence (LCS) between the model's output and the reference answer. The subsequence does not need to be contiguous in the original sequence. For instance, the LCS between "I want to have lunch" and "I forget to bring lunch to school" is "I to lunch" with a length of $L = 3$. Then, the ROUGE-L score is defined to be F_{LCS}, computed as follows:

$$R_{LCS} = \frac{LCS(correct\ answer, model's\ output)}{Length\ of\ correct\ answer}$$

$$P_{LCS} = \frac{LCS(correct\ answer, model's\ output)}{Length\ of\ model's\ output}$$

$$F_{LCS} = \frac{(1 + \beta^2)R_{LCS}P_{LCS}}{R_{LCS} + \beta^2 P_{LCS}}$$

where β is a parameter. Table 1.2 shows an example of ROUGE-N, ROUGE-S, and ROUGE-L.

Table 1.2 Different ROUGE metrics.

Correct answer Model's output	I like this school I also like that school		
ROUGE-1 ROUGE-2 ROUGE-S Skip $= 1$	$3/4 = 0.75$ (I, like, school) $0/3 = 0$ $2/5 = 0.4$ (I like, like school)		
ROUGE-L $\beta = 1$	Longest common subsequence (LCS): I like school		
	$R_{LCS} = 3/4 = 0.75$	$P_{LCS} = 3/5 = 0.6$	$F_{LCS} = 0.67$

There is a certain level of correlation between the ROUGE metric with human evaluation. However, there also exist discrepancies as it only measures lexical overlapping. Thus in addition to automatic metrics like ROUGE, freestyle answers are often manually evaluated on their correctness and naturalness.

1.5 Machine reading comprehension datasets

There are many public datasets in various NLP areas. Through the evaluation on these datasets, one can test the quality of models and compare the pros and cons. As a result, these datasets have greatly contributed to the development of related researches.

In MRC, there are also many datasets and competitions. Depending on the form of articles, we categorize these datasets into three types: single-paragraph, multiparagraph, and corpus. For single-paragraph and multiparagraph articles, the model can directly look for the answer within the article. For corpus-based articles, an information retrieval module is required. This module looks for the most relevant paragraphs or statements in the corpus based on the question, and then the model gets the answer within the retrieved results. In the following, we will describe the three types of MRC datasets with examples.

1.5.1 Single-paragraph datasets

A single-paragraph MRC dataset requires the model to answer questions about a given paragraph. During this process, the model does not need to refer to any external information. Thus this kind of dataset inspects the core reading comprehension ability of a model. As the construction of a single-paragraph dataset is relatively simple, it is the most common type in MRC.

1.5.1.1 RACE

RACE [5] is a large-scale English MRC dataset introduced by CMU in 2017. The dataset comes from the English tests for Chinese students. RACE contains 28,000 articles and nearly 100,000 multiple-choice questions. The model needs to select the correct answer from the options. The RACE dataset is divided into RACE-M, which is for middle school students, and RACE-H, which is for high school students. It is worth mentioning that in the process of answer collection, RACE uses an optical character recognition system to identify the answers from publicly available images.

1.5.1.2 NewsQA

NewsQA [6] is a news reading comprehension dataset from Maluuba in 2016, with more than 12,000 convolutional neural network (CNN) news articles and nearly 120,000 manually edited questions with extractive answers. One of the key goals of the NewsQA dataset is to access the model's reasoning and induction abilities, that is, to get the final answer based on information from different places in the article. Also, it provides "unanswerable" questions.

1.5.1.3 CNN/DailyMail

CNN/DailyMail [7] is a reading comprehension dataset by DeepMind in 2015, where the articles come from CNN and DailyMail. This dataset contains approximately 1.4 million instances, each containing an article, a question, and an answer. The CNN/DailyMail dataset adopts a cloze-style design. In order to let models focus on semantic understanding, the entities in the articles such as persons and places are replaced by ids. Therefore the model only needs to select the correct entity ids from the article to fill in placeholders in the question.

1.5.1.4 SQuAD

SQuAD [8] is the most influential and popular MRC contest, launched by Stanford University in 2016. The SQuAD dataset comes from 536 Wikipedia articles with more than 100,000 questions and extractive answers. SQuAD v2.0, which was launched in 2018, includes a large number of "unanswerable" questions which makes a total of 150,000 questions. The SQuAD dataset receives a lot of attention from both academia and industry for its massive size and high quality. As of December 2019, there are 294 submissions to SQuAD from teams around the world.

On October 5, 2018 Google's BERT model scored above the human level in SQuAD v1.1 for the first time, making headlines in the field of MRC.

1.5.1.5 CoQA

CoQA [9] is a multiturn conversational MRC competition introduced by Stanford University in 2018. Its distinguishing feature is the inclusion of context in QA dialogues, that is, multiple turns of questions and answers for each article. One needs to understand both the article and previous rounds of questions and answers to answer each question. This requires the model to have the ability to understand the context. There are more than 8000 articles and more than 120,000 questions in this dataset, with an average of 15 rounds of questions and answers per article. In addition, the test set of CoQA includes questions from domains unseen in the training set (Reddit forum and scientific questions) to test the generalization capability of models. CoQA contains extractive, "yes/no," "cannot answer," and a small number of freestyle answers. In March 2019 Microsoft's MMFT model achieved an $F1$ score of 89.4%, surpassing the human level of 88.8% for the first time, once again proving the effectiveness of MRC models.

1.5.2 Multiparagraph datasets

A multiparagraph MRC dataset requires the model to read multiple paragraphs and answer related questions. The correct answer may be in one paragraph, so the model needs to compute the correlation between the question and each paragraph; or the answer is obtained by collecting clues from multiple paragraphs, so the model must conduct multistep reasoning.

1.5.2.1 MS MARCO

MS MARCO [10] is a large MRC dataset launched by Microsoft in 2016, containing more than 1 million questions and more than 8 million articles. The questions in this dataset come from queries submitted by real users, while the relevant paragraphs are from Bing's search results for the query. MS MARCO adopts freestyle answers, and it has three tasks:
- determine whether the answer can be obtained from the given paragraph;
- generate the answer text; and
- sort multiple given paragraphs by their relevance to the question.

1.5.2.2 DuReader

DuReader [11] is a Chinese MRC dataset launched by Baidu in 2017. DuReader uses data from user queries and retrieved documents from Baidu search engine. In DuReader, the articles are full text from the webpages, instead of extracted paragraphs like in MS MARCO, making the task more challenging. In addition, due to the different standpoints of various articles, DuReader provides several candidate answers to some questions, which better aligns with real scenarios. DuReader contains 200,000 questions and 1 million documents, with both freestyle and yes/no types of answers.

1.5.2.3 QAngaroo

QAngaroo [12] is a multidocument reasoning MRC dataset introduced by University College London in 2017. It consists of two subsets: WikiHop from Wikipedia and MedHop from the abstract of the medical paper archive PubMed. The biggest feature of QAngaroo is that the answer cannot be drawn from a single paragraph. One must collect clues scattered across multiple paragraphs. As a result, QAngaroo requires the model to analyze multiple paragraphs and use multihop reasoning to get the answer. The dataset contains more than 50,000 questions and related documents, with multiple-choice answers.

1.5.2.4 HotpotQA

HotpotQA [13] is a multiparagraph reasoning MRC dataset introduced by Carnegie Mellon University, Stanford University, the University of Montreal, and Google in 2018. Similar to QAngaroo, HotpotQA requires the model to search for clues in multiple paragraphs and use multistep reasoning to get the answer. HotpotQA contains 110,000 questions and related Wikipedia paragraphs with extractive answers.

1.5.3 Corpus-based datasets

Corpus-based MRC datasets typically provide a large text corpus. The model should first find relevant paragraphs/articles in the corpus given the question, and then analyze the retrieved results to obtain the answer. Among the three types of MRC datasets, corpus-based dataset is closest to real applications such as QA in online search. Because corpus-based dataset does not limit the source of answers, it is also known as **Open Domain Machine Reading Comprehension**.

1.5.3.1 AI2 reasoning challenge

AI2 reasoning challenge (ARC) [14] is a corpus-based MRC dataset on sciences, launched by the Allen Institute of Artificial Intelligence in 2018. The questions in ARC come from 7800 scientific questions for US students in grades 3−9. All answers are in the form of multiple choices. ARC provides a large corpus of scientific text with 14 million sentences, which are the retrieved results by a search engine on scientific queries. Models are allowed to use both the corpus and external information to answer questions.

1.6 How to make an machine reading comprehension dataset

The previous section describes popular datasets and competitions for MRC. To ensure the quality of data, the generation of datasets and the acquisition of answers are often manually processed and verified. One common approach is **crowdsourcing**, that is, labelers are hired to generate and annotate data.

1.6.1 Generation of articles and questions

The three core concepts in any machine reading understanding dataset are articles, questions, and answers. Because the answer can be reasoned from the article based on the question, we often focus on how to collect articles and questions. It is not very common that both articles and questions can be automatically generated (e.g., a cloze dataset by randomly deleting keywords, or a QA dataset by converting reading comprehension tests for students). In most cases, only the articles or the questions are available for dataset makers. Thus one needs to employ labelers or use algorithms to get the other part of information, either generating questions from articles or generating articles from questions.

1.6.1.1 Generating questions from articles

MRC datasets often leverage publicly available corpora as article sources, such as Wikipedia and news reports. However, most of these articles are without related questions. Therefore the dataset makers need to employ labelers to generate questions relevant to the articles. These labelers can decide the question language, but must ensure the quality and difficulty, as well as the relevance to the article. For example, the SQuAD dataset uses paragraphs from Wikipedia as articles and leverages the crowdsourcing platform Amazon Mechanical Turk to hire labelers to generate up to five questions per article. To ensure label quality, each labeler should have a minimum of 97% approval rate for their historical labeling tasks with at least 1000 labels. Labelers are exposed to detailed instructions with examples of high-quality and low-quality questions. For instance, they must use their own language to formulate questions, rather than directly copying statements from the article. Each labeler's compensation is calculated by the time spent and the number of generated questions. In SQuAD dataset, each labeler is paid $9/hour to generate questions for at least 15 paragraphs.

The advantage of generating questions from articles is that the question is very relevant to the article and does not include external information. So this method is suitable for generating single-paragraph and multiparagraph MRC datasets. However, because the questions are artificially produced, it is inevitable that some questions are unnatural. This may cause discrepancies in focus points and language patterns between the generated questions and the questions raised by users in real applications.

1.6.1.2 *Generate articles from questions*
With the popularity of forums and search engines, online users issue a large number of questions and queries every day. By filtering appropriate questions from the history logs, one can collect a massive repository of questions for MRC tasks. Next, related articles are obtained by searching the web or large text corpora. The top retrieved documents and paragraphs can be used in the dataset.

The advantage of generating articles from questions is that all the questions come from real user queries, which are similar to questions in real applications. However, this approach cannot guarantee that the correct answer exists in the retrieved article, so a crowdsourced validation is required.

1.6.2 Generation of correct answers

Most MRC comprehension datasets employ manual answer generation, often in the form of crowdsourcing. The labelers need to provide concise answers in the required form, for example, extractive and freestyle. To ensure the quality of the answer, it is often necessary for multiple labelers to annotate the answer to the same question. However, due to subjective bias of the labelers, it is difficult to guarantee consistency among all answer candidates. One solution is majority voting, that is, use the answer that most people agree with. However, if there is too much disagreement among labelers, the answer has to be relabeled. Here, the degree of agreement between answers can be estimated by exact match, $F1$ score, or ROUGE, introduced in Section 1.4.

Labelers are typically given a software or web environment to annotate answers in the specified format. For example, the labeling interface for the conversational MRC dataset CoQA includes articles, questions, and answers in previous rounds, answer specifications (e.g., prefer shorter answers, reuse words from the article), and compensation information.

Since MRC datasets are labeled by humans, we often see descriptions like "human performance" or "human level" in related reports. In some datasets such as SQuAD and CoQA, the best machine learning models have already achieved performance beyond human levels. So, how is the human level defined?

First of all, we can never get absolutely correct answers to all questions, since each labeler has subjective bias and it is impossible to unify the length and variation of all answers. Even if multiple labelers vote, there is no guarantee that the answer will be accurate. Therefore the absolutely correct answers, that is, results with a true accuracy of 100%, are unattainable.

Therefore in datasets that require manual labeling, the set of answers or voting results from multiple labelers are deemed as correct answers with an accuracy of 100%. And **the human level refers to the accuracy of a single labeler**. For example, in SQuAD v1.1, three labelers write answers for each question, and the human level refers to the accuracy of the second labeler's answers, compared against the answers from the first and third labeler.

Because a single labeler is more likely to make mistakes in answers than multiple labelers, the human level score is generally less than 100%, which means that it is possible for a good machine learning model to exceed the human level. Fig. 1.2 shows the accuracy of computer models and human-level accuracy. Note that if a different group of labelers are employed, the correct answers may change, and the defined accuracy of computer models and human-level accuracy will alter accordingly.

1.6.3 How to build a high-quality machine reading comprehension dataset

A successful MRC dataset should be able to accurately assess whether a model has reading ability comparable to humans. It should also effectively identify and compare the strengths and weaknesses of different models. A high-quality dataset can greatly boost the development of MRC research.

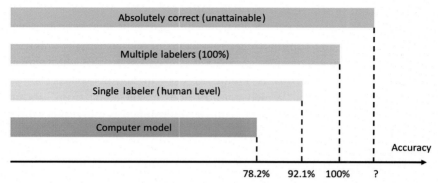

Figure 1.2 Comparison between the accuracy of computer model and human-level accuracy.

In this section, we will analyze what features a high-quality MRC dataset should have.

1.6.3.1 Distinguishing comprehension-based and matching-based models

After models achieved excellent results in various MRC competitions, researchers analyzed the mechanism by which the model generated the answers. The results reveal that the most models heavily rely on lexical matching between the question and the article, rather than understanding of the content, which often leads to comprehension errors. These errors indicate that MRC models are overdependent on the text matching between the question and the article when seeking answers.

The researchers further found that if a misleading sentence containing question keywords yet semantically irrelevant with the question is appended to each article in the SQuAD dataset, the $F1$ scores for all models drop by as much as 20%—40% [15]. However, this misleading statement has little effect on human performance.

Therefore if a dataset mostly contains questions that can be answered by simple text matching, it is hard to distinguish high-quality models from text-matching algorithms. It follows that a high-quality MRC dataset should punish text-matching models in the evaluation. For example, when building the SQuAD v2.0 dataset, the labelers were asked to generate "unanswerable" questions using a combination of keywords in the article. These questions account for 35% of all the questions in the dataset, which effectively reduces the accuracy of text-matching models. This design has been adopted as a new standard in many MRC datasets.

1.6.3.2 Evaluate the reasoning capability

Humans can reason and induct when reading articles. One example is that they can collect and summarize various clues in the article and infer the answer. For instance, an article mentions "David is from California" in one place, and "California is a state in US" in another place. So the answer to the question "Which country does David come from" should be "US." This type of question requires multistep reasoning and cannot be inferred by matching-based models. Thus reasoning is one of the key factors that MRC datasets should assess the models on.

In current MRC datasets that promote reasoning, for example, HotpotQA in Section 1.5, most questions are manually generated by labelers to include information from multiple paragraphs. However, questions created in this way may be unnatural and very different from those of real users. Another possible approach is to pick questions that require reasoning among real user queries, retrieve relevant documents, and then divide the text into paragraphs for multistep reasoning.

1.6.3.3 Assess common sense

Common sense is one of the most important cognitive abilities of humans. Common sense includes spatial knowledge like "big objects can't be put into a smaller space," temporal knowledge like "the year of 2016 is before 2019," and physical knowledge like "under normal conditions, the water will boil when heated to 212°F." The understanding and application of common sense is so far the weak point of NLP and machine learning. The reasons are that (1) common sense knowledge is massive in scale, vaguely defined, and difficult to summarize in its entirety, and (2) it is difficult to effectively express and apply common sense.

In reading comprehension, many questions involve common sense logic. For example, suppose the article is "David is having fun with Mary and Tom at home. After a while Tom left," and the question is "How many people are now in David's home?" To answer the question, the model should understand that "left" means that Tom is no longer in David's home, and it needs to do some math to figure out the answer is "two people." In another example, the article is "Kevin needs to go to the company for an interview at 9:00 a.m. It is lunchtime now, but he's still at home," and the question is "Did Kevin go to the interview?" Clearly, the model has to understand that "lunchtime" is after "9:00 a.m." and "at home" indicates that Kevin has not visited the company. Therefore the correct answer is "No."

Although common sense is commonly used in reading comprehension, few MRC datasets exist to investigate this area. In 2018 researchers from Tel

Aviv University and Allen Institute of Artificial Intelligence launched a common sense MRC dataset CommonsenseQA with 12,000 questions, based on the knowledge graph ConceptNet. Thus CommonsenseQA examines a model's understanding of structured knowledge.

MRC datasets for common sense also need to discern and punish simple text-matching methods. One possible approach is to let the model give the employed common sense when giving answers.

1.6.3.4 Other comprehension skills

In 2017 some researchers pointed out that MRC models should have 10 basic skills, such as understanding coreference, logical reasoning, common sense, and mathematical knowledge. A comprehensive list is given in Table 1.3.

1.6.3.4.1 List/enumeration

Models need to identify, summarize, and sequentially output related concepts in the article, such as the answer to the question "What are the categories of organisms on Earth?"

1.6.3.4.2 Mathematical operations

Some MRC questions necessitate basic math knowledge. For example, suppose the article is "Brian was playing basketball when James and Linda joined. Then

Table 1.3 Ten skills of machine reading comprehension models [16].

Skills	Details
List/enumeration	Tracking, retaining, and list/enumeration of entities or states
Mathematical operations	Four arithmetic operations and geometric comprehension
Coreference resolution	Detection and resolution of coreference
Logical reasoning	Induction, deduction, conditional statement, and quantifier
Analogy	Trope in figures of speech, for example, metaphor
Spatiotemporal relations	Spatial and/or temporal relations of events
Causal relations	Relations of events expressed by why, because, the reason for, etc.
Commonsense reasoning	Taxonomic and qualitative knowledge, action, and event changes
Schematic/rhetorical clause relations	Coordination or subordination of clauses in a sentence
Special sentence structure	Scheme in figures of speech, constructions, and punctuation marks

Linda left with her mom." and the question is "How many people are playing basketball now?" Obviously, the answer cannot be simply extracted from the text but has to be obtained via mathematical computing.

1.6.3.4.3 Coreference resolution
Coreference resolution is an important task in NLP. Its goal is to understand the referred object of pronouns, for example, this, that, he, and she, to answer the questions.

1.6.3.4.4 Logical reasoning
The model needs to derive inferred facts from the article to get answers via reasoning. For example, from the statement "I asked Wendy whether she wanted to eat at home or at the restaurant, and she said she'd like to have a walk," we can infer that Wendy chose to eat at the restaurant.

1.6.3.4.5 Analogy
To answer certain questions, the model should understand common rhetorical techniques like metaphors and analogies.

1.6.3.4.6 Spatial—temporal relations
Spatial—temporal relations are common topics of questions. For instance, suppose the article is "I ask Bob to come to the company on Wednesday. Since he had some personal errands, Bob came the next day." The model should infer that Bob came to the company on Thursday.

1.6.3.4.7 Causal relations
Understanding causality is important to answer questions of why.

1.6.3.4.8 Common sense reasoning
Questions involving common sense and logic require the model to conduct common sense reasoning.

1.6.3.4.9 Schematic/rhetorical clause relations
Language structures like clauses contain rich semantic information, such as descriptions of entities and references, which are challenging for MRC models.

1.6.3.4.10 Special sentence structure
Some less frequent language structures such as inverted order and subjunctive make it difficult to understand the article.

These reading comprehension skills cover many reading skills that humans acquire, in the aspects of language, rhetoric, and external knowledge. Therefore an MRC task should evaluate the model's skills from all these aspects. Current researches, especially those related to deep learning, still heavily rely on statistical pattern recognition and matching. Thus most models lack many of the above skills and hence the ability to give reasonable explanations of the given answer. These are important topics to address in MRC research.

1.7 Summary

- **Machine reading comprehension (MRC)** is similar to the reading comprehension task for humans, where a model's ability to understand an article is assessed by answering related questions.
- MRC can be applied in scenarios where it is desired to automatically process a large amount of text data and understand the semantics.
- **Natural Language Processing** has many subfields closely related to MRC, such as information retrieval and question-and-answer systems.
- **Deep learning** is one of the hottest research directions in artificial intelligence. It greatly improves the accuracy of models in many areas. The majority of current MRC models are based on deep learning.
- In MRC, the answer types include multiple-choice, extractive, free-style, and cloze test.
- Depending on the form of articles, MRC datasets can be categorized into three types: **single-paragraph**, **multiparagraph**, and **corpus**.
- To build an MRC dataset, one can manually generate questions based on articles from public sources. Another way is to retrieve articles using questions from search engines and forums.
- **Human level** refers to the accuracy of a single labeler, judged by the set of annotated answers from multiple labelers.
- A high-quality MRC dataset should effectively distinguish between understanding-based and matching-based models. It should also access models' reasoning and common sense ability.

References

[1] Snow C. Reading for understanding: toward an R&D program in reading comprehension. Rand Corporation; 2002.
[2] Lehnert WG. The process of question answering (No. RR-88). New Haven, CT: Yale University, Department of Computer Science; 1977.

[3] Hirschman L, Light M, Breck E, Burger JD. Deep read: a reading comprehension system. In: Proceedings of the 37th Annual Meeting of the Association for Computational Linguistics; June 1999. pp. 325–32.

[4] Lin CY. Rouge: a package for automatic evaluation of summaries. Text summarization branches out July 2004;74–81.

[5] Lai G, Xie Q, Liu H, Yang Y, Hovy E. Race: large-scale reading comprehension dataset from examinations. arXiv Preprint arXiv 2017;1704:04683.

[6] Trischler A, Wang T, Yuan X, Harris J, Sordoni A, Bachman P, et al. NewsQA: a machine comprehension dataset. arXiv Preprint arXiv 2016;1611:09830.

[7] Hermann KM, Kocisky T, Grefenstette E, Espeholt L, Kay W, Suleyman M, et al. Teaching machines to read and comprehend. Adv Neural Inf Process Syst 2015;1693–701.

[8] Rajpurkar P, Zhang J, Lopyrev K, Liang P. Squad: 100,000 + questions for machine comprehension of text. arXiv Preprint arXiv 2016;1606:05250.

[9] Reddy S, Chen D, Manning CD. CoQA: a conversational question answering challenge. Trans Assoc Comput Linguist 2019;7:249–66.

[10] Nguyen T, Rosenberg M, Song X, Gao J, Tiwary S, Majumder R, et al. Ms marco: a human-generated machine reading comprehension dataset; 2016.

[11] He W, Liu K, Liu J, Lyu Y, Zhao S, Xiao X, et al. Dureader: a chinese machine reading comprehension dataset from real-world applications. arXiv Preprint arXiv 2017;1711:05073.

[12] Welbl J, Stenetorp P, Riedel S. Constructing datasets for multi-hop reading comprehension across documents. Trans Assoc Comput Linguist 2018;6:287–302.

[13] Yang Z, Qi P, Zhang S, Bengio Y, Cohen WW, Salakhutdinov R, et al. Hotpotqa: a dataset for diverse, explainable multi-hop question answering. arXiv Preprint arXiv 2018;1809:09600.

[14] Clark P, Cowhey I, Etzioni O, Khot T, Sabharwal A, Schoenick C, et al. Think you have solved question answering? try arc, the ai2 reasoning challenge. arXiv Preprint arXiv 2018;1803:05457.

[15] Jia R, Liang P. Adversarial examples for evaluating reading comprehension systems. arXiv Preprint arXiv 2017;1707:07328.

[16] Sugawara S, Yokono H, Aizawa A. Prerequisite skills for reading comprehension: multi-perspective analysis of mctest datasets and systems. In: Thirty-first AAAI conference on artificial intelligence; February 2017.

CHAPTER 2

The basics of natural language processing

2.1 Tokenization

A word is an important basic element in language. As an information unit, a word can refer to names, functions, actions, etc. In the history of language, hundreds of thousands of words have emerged, and many more words have been marginalized until extinction with the changing of the times. The Oxford English Dictionary contains about 170,000 words. The understanding of words plays an important role in analyzing linguistic structure and semantics. Therefore an machine reading comprehension (MRC) model usually has a dedicated module to recognize and understand words as its first component.

Word tokenization refers to the process of splitting a piece of text into a list of words, or tokens. Tokenization in English is relatively simple compared with other languages like Chinese, because the English grammar requires the separation of words with spaces. Therefore one of the easiest ways is to remove all punctuations and divide the sentence into words using spaces. However, there are many exceptions to this approach:

- Sometimes punctuations should be retained as part of a word, for example, http://www.stanford.edu, Ph.D.
- Comma and period in numbers, for example, 123,456.78
- Contraction, for example, you're = you are, we'll = we will
- Multiword proper nouns, for example, New York, San Francisco

To tackle these exceptions, one can employ regular expressions and a proper noun list for special handling.

In addition, many words in English have variations, such as the plural form (-s, -es) for nouns and past-tense form (-ed) for verbs. In order for downstream processing to identify different variations of the same word, it is generally necessary to conduct word stemming during tokenization. For example, the three words *do*, *does*, and *done* are converted into the same stem *do*. A word stemming algorithm can be based on manually designed rules, for example, the Porter Stemmer employs a complex set of rules to extract stems (Table 2.1).

Machine Reading Comprehension. DOI: https://doi.org/10.1016/B978-0-323-90118-5.00002-3
© 2021 Beijing Huazhang Graphics & Information Co., Ltd/China Machine Press.
Published by Elsevier Inc. All rights reserved.

Table 2.1 Examples of stemming by the Porter Stemmer.

Rules	Words	Stem
sses → ss	Classes	Class
ies → i	Ponies	Pony
ative →	Informative	Inform

In Python, a piece of text can be tokenized via the spaCy package:

```
# Install spaCy
# pip install spacy
# python -m spacy download en_core_web_sm
import spacy
nlp = spacy.load('en_core_web_sm')
text = ('Today is very special. I just got my Ph.D. degree.')
doc = nlp(text)
print([e.text for e in doc])
```

Output:

```
['Today', 'is', 'very', 'special', '.', 'I', 'just', 'got', 'my',
'Ph.D.', 'degree', '.']
```

2.1.1 Byte pair encoding

After tokenization, a model needs to represent each word/token with an ID. Therefore it requires a vocabulary to store all the words. However, no matter how large the vocabulary is, it is inevitable that OOV (Out-Of-Vocabulary) words will appear in unseen text. For example, many articles in reading comprehension tasks contain novel person or location names. A simple method to represent these OOV words is to replace them with a special symbol, <OOV>. Nevertheless, this can result in a significant loss of information contained in the words and reduce the accuracy of MRC models.

Another type of tokenization method does not employ a word vocabulary. Instead, a set of frequent subwords are determined and each word is split into subwords from the set. As the list of subwords contains all single characters, any word can be represented. Table 2.2 compares tokenization methods with and without a vocabulary.

Table 2.2 Tokenization methods with and without a vocabulary.

Original sentence	Richard is visiting Facebook homepage.
Tokenization with a vocabulary	<OOV> | is | visiting | <OOV> | homepage |.
Tokenization without a vocabulary	Rich | #ard | is | visit | #ing | Face | #book | homepage |.

means that the subword and its predecessors form one word together.

Byte Pair Encoding (BPE) is a commonly used tokenizer that does not depend on a vocabulary of words [1]. BPE works by finding common substrings that can make up words, also known as subwords. It then represents each word as the concatenation of one or more subwords.

In detail, BPE starts from the most basic subword set, for example, {a, b, ..., z, A, B, ..., Z}. Next, it counts the occurrences of all two adjacent subwords in the training text, and selects the most frequent pair (s_1, s_2). The two subwords in this pair are then concatenated to form a new subword and added to the set. This is called a *merge* operation. After several merges, BPE returns the set of common subwords. For a new word, BPE follows the merging order to get its representation, which is illustrated in the following example.

```
// Training text
wonder ponder toner
// Tokenized by the current set of sub-words of single letters
w o n d e r
p o n d e r
t o n e r
```

Among the two neighboring subwords, **e r** is the most frequent, occurring three times. Therefore a new subword **er** is made.

```
// Tokenized by the current set of sub-words
w o n d er
p o n d er
t o n er
```

Among the two neighboring subwords, **o n** is the most frequent, occurring three times. Therefore a new subword **on** is made.

```
// Tokenized by the current set of sub-words
w on d er
p on d er
t on er
```

Among the two neighboring subwords, **on d** is the most frequent, occurring two times. Therefore a new subword **ond** is made.

```
w ond er
p ond er
t on er
```

After three merges, the set of subwords is {a, b,..., z, er, on, ond}. To decode a word, BPE follows the same order of merge operations.

```
// Decode a new word fond
Merge e and r: f o n d
Merge o and n: f on d
Merge on and d: f ond
```

There are several advantages of using Byte Pair Encoding as the tokenizer. First, since the subword list of BPE contains all single characters, any word can be broken down into BPE subwords, that is, there is no OOV problem. Second, BPE can flexibly control the size of the subword list by adjusting the number of merges. As a result, BPE is widely used in many natural language processing (NLP) fields such as machine translation and language models.

However, BPE also has some limitations. The subword lists of BPE trained on different corpora may be different, making the corresponding models impossible to share. Moreover, the subwords generated by BPE are entirely based on frequency, which may be inconsistent with word roots that carry semantic information.

In real applications, BPE or other vocabulary-independent tokenizers are usually applied when the model needs to generate text, for example, freestyle answers in MRC; while vocabulary-based tokenizer are used in classification tasks, for example, multiple-choice and extractive answers in MRC.

2.2 The cornerstone of natural language processing: word vectors

The input to a machine reading comprehension model is the text of article and question. However, computers conduct numerical operations and cannot directly manipulate on characters or strings. Therefore the text needs to be converted into numeric representations. A common approach is to represent each word by a list of numbers, that is, word vector. This section describes several methods to generate word vectors.

2.2.1 Word vectorization

In computers, any string needs to be converted into the binary format for computation and storage. For example, in C language, it takes 1 byte (8 bits) to store a character in ASCII code, for example, the letter A is represented by the 8-bit binary code 01000001.

Since words are strings, it is convenient to store a word by concatenating the numeric representations of its characters into a vector, that is, word embedding. However, this approach has two drawbacks. First, this vector only represents the spelling, not the semantic meaning of the word. But it is essential to make the computer understand the meaning of words, sentences, and paragraphs. Second, the word embedding becomes longer when the word has more characters, making it difficult to understand long and complex words. Also the nonuniform length of representation for different words can cause problems for subsequent processing.

To solve the above problems in word vectorization, researchers propose one-hot embedding and distributed representation.

2.2.1.1 One-hot embedding

In **One-hot Embedding**, the embedding of a word is a vector of the same size of the dictionary. The vector contains zero everywhere except one at the position of the word in the dictionary. For example, suppose the dictionary is [apple, pear, banana, peach]. Because the size of the dictionary is 4, the one-hot embedding is a vector of length 4. As *pear* is the

Table 2.3 One-hot embedding for words in the dictionary [apple, pear, banana, peach].

Word	One-hot embedding
Pear	(0, 1, 0, 0)
Peach	(0, 0, 0, 1)

second word in the dictionary, its one-hot embedding vector has 1 in the second bit and 0 in all other bits, as shown in Table 2.3.

The advantage of one-hot embedding is that the embedding is easily obtained without any computation after the dictionary is determined. Moreover, one-hot embedding solves the problem of varying word vector sizes, since any word in the vocabulary, regardless of its length, can be represented by a vector of uniform length.

However, one-hot embedding does not carry semantic meanings of words. Thus it is impossible to draw any conclusion to the similarity of two words by observing their embeddings. Actually, the internal product of the one-hot embeddings of any two different words is 0. Furthermore, when the dictionary becomes larger, the length of one-hot embedding grows, which increases the complexity of subsequent processing.

2.2.1.2 Distributed representation

In mathematics, the concept of vector is closely related to geometry. For example, in a 2D plane, a vector (x, y) represents the coordinate of a point. More generally, the vector $(a_1, a_2, \ldots, a_n)$ represents a point in the n-dimensional space. Therefore in a distributed representation, each word is represented by a vector of length n, which corresponds to a point in the n-D space.

Since word semantics are quite complex, it is very difficult to partition different regions in the n-D space to represent different types of words. But we can leverage an important concept in geometry: distance. A reasonable word embedding should map two semantically similar words to two close-by points, and map two irrelevant words to two points far apart. It follows that in the distributed representation, searching for synonyms of a word entails looking for word vectors near its embedded point.

In addition to incorporating semantic information, distributed representation has a fixed length of word vector, which makes following procedures more convenient. As a result, most NLP methods employ the distributed representation for word vectors.

However, it is not always easy to obtain a distributed representation of high quality. It often requires careful mathematical modeling and a large text corpus. In the next section, we will describe in detail a popular distributed representation method: word2vec.

2.2.2 Word2vec

Word2vec [2] is a distributed representation model proposed by Google in 2013. It has been very widely used ever since. Word2vec computes word embeddings by leveraging the context of a word, since the meaning of a word is often associated with the words around it in text. To precisely characterize the relation between a word and its context, word2vec uses the following skip-gram model.

2.2.2.1 Skip-gram

In sentences, each word is semantically closely related to its surrounding words, that is, context. Therefore the word vectors should reflect this relationship between each word and its context. The skip-gram model tries to maximize the probability of context words given a central word w.

The context is defined to be a window centered at w. Fig. 2.1 gives an example of a window of length 5 centered at the word *to*. The skip-gram model tries to maximize the conditional probability of every context word given the word *to*, that is, $P(shop|to)$, $P(yesterday|to)$, $P(meet|to)$, $P(a|to)$.

These conditional probabilities are computed via the word vectors. The skip-gram model uses word vectors to score all words in the vocabulary and a larger score indicates a higher chance that the corresponding word appears in the window around w. The score is computed by an inner product between word vectors. For instance, given the central word *to*, the word *meet* has a score of $s_{meet} = v_{meet}^T v_{to}$, while the word *shop* has a score of $s_{shop} = v_{shop}^T v_{to}$.

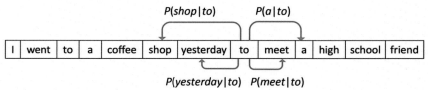

Figure 2.1 Skip-gram with a window size of 5. The center word is **to**.

However, these scores don't necessarily add up to 1, and the score may lie outside of the range of [0, 1]. In other words, we cannot use these scores as probabilities. Therefore skip-gram employs the softmax function, which turns a set of input numbers into legitimate probability values while keeping the size relationship. The softmax function is defined as follows:

$$\text{Given } a_1, a_2, \ldots, a_n, softmax(a_1, a_2, \ldots, a_n) = \left(\frac{e^{a_1}}{Z}, \frac{e^{a_2}}{Z}, \ldots, \frac{e^{a_n}}{Z}\right),$$
$$\text{where } Z = e^{a_1} + e^{a_2} + \ldots + e^{a_n}$$

The result of the softmax function is the conditional probability of each word appearing in the window of the central word: $P(shop\,|\,to)$, $P(yesterday\,|\,to)$, . . .

Then, skip-gram needs to adjust the word vectors to maximize these conditional probabilities on a real corpus containing natural sentences. We describe this process in the next section.

2.2.2.2 Implementation details of word2vec

In the implementation of word2vec, each word w is represented by two vectors: c_w is used when w is the central word, and v_w is used when w is a context word. The score of a context word u given the central word w is $s_u = v_u^T c_w$. And the final word vector for u is given by the average of v_u and c_u.

Then, the computation of $P(context\ word\,|\,central\ word)$ is framed as a binary classification problem, that is, compute $P(u\ appears\ in\ the\ w's\ context\ window\,|\,u,\ w) \in [0,1]$. This can be calculated by the Logistic Regression model:

$$P(u\ appears\ in\ w's\ context\ window\,|\,u, w) = \frac{1}{1 + e^{-v_u^T c_w}}$$

However, there is a trivial yet unwanted solution to maximize this binary classification probability: all words vectors are the same: [1,1,. . .], and the length goes to infinite. Then the classification probability is always 1. Therefore word2vec employs the negative sampling method.

In detail, for each context word u and center word w, word2vec randomly selects K noncontext words from the vocabulary. The model needs to minimize the probability of these noncontext words appearing in the window. Equivalently, the model maximizes the following probability:

$$\Pi_{\text{context word } u, \text{central word } w} \left[P(u \text{ in the window} | u, w) * \Pi_{i=1}^{K} P \right.$$
$$\left. (u_i' \text{ not in the window} | \text{randomly chosen } u_i', w) \right]$$

For instance, if $K = 3$, word2vec needs to maximize $P(shop \,|\, to)(1 - P(apple \,|\, to))(1 - P(egg \,|\, to))(1 - P(book \,|\, to))$. The optimization can be conducted by gradient descent to obtain the final word vectors.

The paper of word2vec has a detailed description of the model specifications. The probability of a word u_i' to be selected as a noncontext word is proportional to $f^{0.75}$, where f is the frequency of u_i' in the corpus. The value of K is 5—20 for small-scale data and 2—5 for large-scale data. The word2vec model is trained on the Google News corpus of 3 billion words, and a 300-dim vector representation is obtained for a dictionary of 3 million words.

The advantage of word2vec is that it is unsupervised, without using any human-labeled data. Thus high-quality word vectors can be automatically learned from large-scale unlabeled corpus.

2.3 Linguistic tagging

While the word embedding can depict the meaning of a word, some words may carry different meanings. Also, the inherent ambiguity of language makes it hard to comprehend a piece of text only based on the understanding of each single word. Linguistic tagging can provide additional information of a word such as word class and syntactic category, which can help reveal the exact meaning of a word and its relationship with its context.

In machine reading comprehension, the category information of words can often improve the answer accuracy. For example, if the question is *When was Madame Curie born*, then the words and phrases related to dates in the article should be the focus of attention. If the question is *Which drugs are mentioned in this article*, then the noun entities are more likely to be the answer. In MRC, there are two types of commonly used linguistic tagging: named entity recognition and part-of-speech tagging.

2.3.1 Named entity recognition

Named entities refer to proper nouns, which are generally divided into three categories: names of person, location, and organization. There are also extended categories such as time and date. **Named Entity Recognition (NER)** is the task of tagging and classifying words into these categories. Here is an example of NER on a sentence, where ORG means organization, LOC means location, and PER means person name.

```
[ORG Stanford University] is in [LOC California], currently led by
President [PER Marc Tessier-Lavigne].
```

NER plays an important role in examining text structure, extracting information, and analyzing semantics. Since many new entities emerge every day, it is not possible to cover all proper nouns solely by a predefined list. There are several general NER methods introduced as follows.

2.3.1.1 Rule-based named entity recognition

One can manually edit rules to recognize usage of names of person, location, and organization. For example, the word after *Prof.* or *Dr.* is very likely to be a person name, and the word after *We have arrived at* is likely to be a location name. Generally, rule-based NER has a high precision but low recall rate because the language usage is very diverse and a set of rules cannot cover all possible patterns. However, under specific domains where the format of language is relatively fixed, for example, earning reports and law articles, rule-based NER can be a viable approach.

2.3.1.2 Feature-based named entity recognition

Since NER is essentially a word classification task, it belongs to supervised machine learning when labeled data is available. Also, NER is a sequence labeling task as tags are predicted for a sequence of words. Therefore the label of a word depends not only on the word but also on neighboring words and labels. Feature-based NER extracts features for various aspects of a word and its context, like the following examples:

1. whether it is a noun;
2. whether the word is a predictive word (for example, *Dr.*, *Prof.*);
3. whether the previous word is a predictive word;
4. whether the word is quoted;

5. whether the word is at the end of the sentence; and

6. the word prefix and suffix.

Once the features of each word are obtained, NER can be carried out by context-independent models (for example, Logistic Regression) or context-dependent models (for example, Conditional Random Field).

2.3.1.3 Named entity recognition based on deep learning

We present a brief introduction to the application of deep learning in NER while more details about deep learning are present in the next chapter. Deep learning builds neural networks which take in word vectors and use a multiclass classifier layer to output the likelihood scores of each word being a named entity of certain types. For example, the scores of *Stanford* may be 0.25 for person name (PER), 1.26 for location name (LOC), 15.33 for organizational name (ORG), and 0.98 for nonnamed entity (O). These scores are then normalized using softmax and compared against ground-truth labels. The error signal is transmitted back to each network layer to adjust parameters so that the whole network can be improved in recognition accuracy.

One advantage of this approach is that all model parameters can be simultaneously optimized to improve the NER performance in an end-to-end fashion. This is a great advantage over pipelined approaches, such as collecting predicative words → adjusting feature list → feature-based learning, where errors can easily accumulate over multiple steps. Moreover, deep learning can flexibly adjust its network size to improve the performance on large-scale datasets. As a result, the best NER models are currently based on deep learning.

2.3.2 Part-of-speech tagging

Part-of-Speech Tagging (POS Tagging) is the process of identifying the part-of-speech of words in the text. Part of speech is a linguistic concept based on grammatical properties and syntactic behaviors. There are nine parts of speech in English: noun, verb, adjective, adverb, pronoun, preposition, conjunction, interjection, and article/determiner.

If each word had a fixed part of speech, POS tagging would be easily solved by a word-POS table. However, it is very common for the same word to have multiple parts of speech, causing ambiguation. For instance, the word *book* can be a noun in *This is a book* but a verb in *I want to book a flight*. According to statistics, 40% of the words in the Brown corpus are ambiguous in part of speech [3].

Similar to NER, POS tagging is a sequence labeling task, that is, each word in a statement should be assigned a part of speech. One of the most popular and effective POS tagging algorithms is the **Hidden Markov Model (HMM)**.

The input to HMM is a list of tokenized words, $w_1, w_2, \ldots, w_n$, and the output is their parts of speech, $q_1, q_2, \ldots, q_n$. As part of speech is unobservable, it is considered as a hidden state in HMM, while words are observed information. Therefore the goal of HMM is to maximize the probability of the hidden parts of speech conditioned on the observed words, that is, $P(q_1, q_2, \ldots, q_n | w_1, w_2, \ldots, w_n)$.

According to the Bayes' theorem,

$$P(q_1, q_2, \ldots, q_n | w_1, w_2, \ldots, w_n)$$

$$= \frac{P(w_1, w_2, \ldots, w_n | q_1, q_2, \ldots, q_n)P(q_1, q_2, \ldots, q_n)}{P(w_1, w_2, \ldots, w_n)}$$

As our goal is to find the most probable parts of speech $\{q_i\}$,

$$\underset{q_1, q_2, \ldots, q_n}{\mathrm{argmax}} P(q_1, q_2, \ldots, q_n | w_1, w_2, \ldots, w_n)$$

$$= \underset{q_1, q_2, \ldots, q_n}{\mathrm{argmax}} \frac{P(w_1, w_2, \ldots, w_n | q_1, q_2, \ldots, q_n)P(q_1, q_2, \ldots, q_n)}{P(w_1, w_2, \ldots, w_n)}$$

$$= \underset{q_1, q_2, \ldots, q_n}{\mathrm{argmax}} P(w_1, w_2, \ldots, w_n | q_1, q_2, \ldots, q_n)P(q_1, q_2, \ldots, q_n)$$

According to HMM's assumption, q_i only depends on q_{i-1}, that is, it is a bigram model. Thus $P(q_1, q_2, \ldots, q_n) \approx \prod_{i=1}^{n} P(q_i | q_{i-1})$. Moreover, HMM assumes that there is conditional independence between words, that is, $P(w_1, w_2, \ldots, w_n | q_1, q_2, \ldots, q_n) \approx \prod_{i=1}^{n} P(w_i | q_i)$. It follows that one only needs to maximize the following probability to infer the most probable parts of speech:

$$\prod_{i=1}^{n} P(w_i | q_i)P(q_i | q_{i-1})$$

For example, in the sentence *book the flight*, the equation above becomes:

$$P(book | q_1)P(the | q_2)P(q_2 | q_1)P(flight | q_3)P(q_3 | q_2)$$

However, there are two more unsolved questions: (1) how to estimate probabilities like $P(book | q_1)$ and $P(q_2 | q_1)$; and (2) how to obtain the optimal sequence of parts of speech. We deal with each of them in the following sections.

2.3.2.1 Estimate probabilities in hidden Markov model
Statistical methods can be used to estimate the probabilities involved in
HMM. Given text corpus with part of speech labels for each word, the
probability $P(w|q)$ can be estimated via the frequency of w with each
POS tag:

$$P(w|q) = \frac{C(w; q)}{C(q)}$$

$C(w; q)$ is the number of times w appears with the POS q in the training corpus, and $C(q)$ is the number of occurrences of POS q in the
corpus.

Similarly, the 2-gram probability $P(q_i|q_{i-1})$ can be estimated by the
follow frequency:

$$P(q_i|q_{i-1}) = \frac{C(q_{i-1}; q_i)}{C(q_{i-1})}$$

$C(q_{i-1}; q_i)$ is the number of times that a word with POS q_{i-1} is followed by a word with POS q_i in the corpus, and $C(q_{i-1})$ is the number
of occurrences of POS q_{i-1} in the corpus. Table 2.4 presents an example.

2.3.2.2 Maximize probabilities in hidden Markov model
Suppose a sentence has n words and there are K parts of speech, then
there are a total of K^n possible POS tag sequences. Therefore it is compu-
tationally very inefficient to enumerate all POS tag sequences. Recall that
in HMM, the POS tags should maximize the following probability:

$$P_{HMM}(q_1, \ldots, q_n) = \prod_{i=1}^{n} P(w_i|q_i)P(q_i|q_{i-1})$$

The Viterbi algorithm can compute the optimal POS tag sequence by
dynamic programming. The Viterbi algorithm defines the state $f(i,j)$ as

Table 2.4 Estimating probability in hidden Markov model (HMM).

C(book; noun)	20	C(noun)	500	P(book|noun)	20/500 = 0.04
C(book; verb)	10	C(verb)	300	P(book|verb)	10/300 = 0.03
C(verb; noun)	240	C(verb)	300	P(noun|verb)	240/300 = 0.8
C(verb; adverb)	50	C(verb)	300	P(adverb|verb)	50/300 = 0.17

C(book; noun) is the number of times *book* appears as a noun in the corpus. C(noun) is the number of
occurrences of nouns in the corpus. C(verb; noun) is the number of times a verb is followed by a noun
in the corpus.

the maximum HMM probability for the first i words, given that $q_i = j$, that is, $f(i, j) = \max_{q_i = j} P_{HMM}(q_1, \ldots, q_i)$.

For initialization, $f(1, j) = P(w_1|j), 1 \leq j \leq K$. The state transition function is:

$$f(i + 1, j) = \max_{1 \leq k \leq K} f(i, k) P(w_{i+1}|j) P(j|k)$$

After all f values are computed, the maximum HMM probability is $\max_{1 \leq k \leq K} f(n, k) = f(n, k^*)$. And we can recover the best POS tag sequence by recording the best value of k that $f(i + 1, j)$ selects in the state transition function above. The time complexity of the Viterbi algorithm is $O(K^2 n)$.

In practice, trigram modeling is also often used in HMM, and the computation is similar:

$$P(q_1, q_2, \ldots, q_n) \approx \prod_{i=1}^{n} P(w_i|q_i) P(q_i|q_{i-1}, q_{i-2})$$

2.3.2.3 Named entity recognition and part-of-speech tagging in Python

In Python, both NER and POS tagging can be carried out by the spaCy software package:

```
# Named entity recognition and part-of-speech tagging
import spacy
nlp = spacy.load('en_core_web_sm')
doc = nlp(u"Apple may buy a U.K. startup for $1 billion")
print('-----Part of Speech-----')
for token in doc:
    print(token.text, token.pos_)
print('-----Named Entity Recognition-----')
for ent in doc.ents:
    print(ent.text, ent.label_)
```

Results:

```
-----Part of Speech-----
Apple PROPN # proper noun
may AUX      # auxiliary verb
buy VERB     # verb
```

(Continued)

(Continued)
```
a IT           # article
U.K. PROPN     # proper noun
startup NOUN # noun
for ADP        # preposition
$ SYM          # symbol
1 NUM          # number
billion NUM  # number
-----Named Entity Recognition-----
Apple ORG           # organization
U.K. GPE            # geopolitical entity
$1 billion MONEY # money
```

2.4 Language model

With thousands of years of development, the human language has established a mature grammar system to constrain possible language combinations. Assuming there are 10,000 words in the dictionary, there could be $10,000^{10}$ possible sentences of only 10 words. However, most of these combinations are meaningless. Instead, only a small number of them are grammatical, and an even smaller portion conforms to logic and common sense. If we can assign each possible sentence a probability of occurrence, these $10,000^{10}$ sentences are not of equal probabilities. Therefore a language model assigns legitimate text a high probability, while giving rare or ungrammatical text a small probability. Once the probabilities are properly defined, machines can recognize and generate grammatically correct and reasonable statements like humans.

For example, some machine reading comprehension tasks require models to produce freestyle answers. If a model ignores language usage rules, it will generate ungrammatical sentences like *Lunch for to I go want.* Therefore any MRC algorithm that generates freestyle answers must establish a language model to regulate the produced answers.

In a language model, if a piece of text consists of m words, its probability, that is, $P(w_1 w_2...w_m)$, is calculated by the chain rule of conditional probability:

$$P(w_1 w_2...w_m) = P(w_1)P(w_2|w_1)...P(w_n|w_1...w_{m-1}) = \prod_{i=1}^{m} P(w_i|w_1...w_{m-1})$$

Here, $P(w_i|w_1...w_{i-1})$ is the probability that the ith word is w_i given the first $i-1$ words.

2.4.1 *N*-gram model

If the language model directly uses $P(w_i|w_1...w_{i-1})$ to compute the probability distribution of the ith word, it needs to know all the previous $i-1$ words, which makes the computation very expensive. To alleviate this problem, the **n-gram model** assumes that each word is only dependent on the previous $n-1$ words. For example:

- unigram: $P(w_i|w_1...w_{i-1}) \approx P(w_i)$
- bigram: $P(w_i|w_1...w_{i-1}) \approx P(w_i|w_{i-1})$
- trigram(triple model): $P(w_i|w_1...w_{i-1}) \approx P(w_i|w_{i-2}w_{i-1})$
- n-gram: $P(w_i|w_1...w_{i-1}) \approx P(w_i|w_{i-n+1}...w_{i-1})$

Take bigram as an example, $P(I\ am\ very\ happy) = P(I) \times P(am|I) \times P(very|am) \times P(happy|very)$. To compute these probabilities, we can reuse the statistical method in HMM.

Suppose the language model is trained on a given corpus. Then, the unigram probability such as $P(I)$ is estimated by the ratio of occurrences of the word I among all words, while the bigram probability $P(am|I)$ is estimated by the ratio of the word am being the next word to I. Define $C(text)$ as the number of occurrences of $text$ in the corpus, then:

$$P(am|I) = \frac{C(I\ am)}{C(I)}$$

Note that the denominator, $C(I) = \sum_{w \in all\ words} C(I\ w)$. So it is computing the frequency of each word immediately following I in the corpus. Table 2.5 gives an example.

However, since sentences are not of equal lengths, the sum of probabilities for all sentences is not 1. For example, suppose the vocabulary contains two words: $P(we) = 0.3$, $P(today) = 0.7$. Then the sum of probabilities for one-word sentences is already $0.3 + 0.7 = 1$. It follows that the sum of all sentence probabilities is infinity, which violates the definition of probability. Thus n-gram prepends a special sentence start symbol and appends a special sentence end symbol to each sentence, for example, *Let's go out today* becomes $<s>$ *Let's go out today* $</s>$. $<s>$ and $</s>$ are also included in the vocabulary. It can be proved that the sum of probabilities of sentences of all lengths become 1 after $</s>$ is added.

Another problem is that any training corpus cannot cover all legitimate sentences and word combinations. For example, since Table 2.5 does not contain the phrase *we have*, $P(have|we) = 0$. Then, a trained bigram model will assign the legitimate sentence *We have dinner* a probability of 0. Furthermore, the

Table 2.5 Compute the probabilities in bigram language model.

Text

Today we will have dinner. Today he will meet Mr. James. Today we are going to the cinema.

Count		Probability	
C(today)	3	P(today)	4/18 = 0.22
C(today we)	1	P(we | today)	2/3 = 0.67
C(today he)	2	P(he | today)	1/3 = 0.33

We lowercase all letters and ignore punctuations and in counting.

word *she* is a valid word but does not appear in the text, so a phrase like *she will* has ill-defined probability since the denominator C(*she*) = 0.

Therefore **Laplace Smoothing** can be used for nonexistent words or phrases in the training corpus. It adds a smoothing item 1 (or a value K in add-k smoothing) to all the counting, which makes all the probabilities strictly bigger than zero. For example, if there are V words in the vocabulary, the bigram model with Laplace smoothing defines:

$$P(w_i) = \frac{C(w_i) + 1}{\sum_w C(w) + V}$$

$$P(w_i|w_{i-1}) = \frac{C(w_{i-1}w_i) + 1}{C(w_{i-1}) + V}$$

Table 2.6 gives an example of Laplace smoothing. As shown, probabilities like P(*sing*|*we*) become nonzero after the smoothing term is added.

Here is the Python implementation for a bigram language model using Laplace smoothing:

```
'''
Suppose the text A has been tokenized, and special symbols <s> and
  </s> are added. Each sentence is represented by a list of words.
  Vocab is the list of all words, and K is the parameter for Laplace
  Smoothing.
Example:
  Input:
  A=[[ '<s>', 'today', 'is', 'monday', '</s>'],
     [ '<s>', 'we', 'go', 'fishing', 'today', '</s>'],
```

(Continued)

(Continued)

```
    ['<s>', 'we', 'have', 'meetings', 'today', '</s>']]
vocab =['<s>', '</s>', 'today', 'we', 'is', 'go', 'have',
    'fishing', 'meetings', 'monday']
Call bigram(A, vocab, 1)
Output:
P(<s> | <s>) = 0.077
P(</s> | <s>) = 0.077
P(today| <s>) = 0.154
'''
def bigram(A, vocab, K):
    cnt = {word: 0 for word in vocab}
    cnt2 = {word:{word2: 0 for word2 in vocab} for word in vocab}
    # cnt[word] is the number of occurrences of word in the text, and
        cnt2[word][word2] is the number of occurrences of word word2
        in the text.
    for sent in A:
        for i, word in enumerate(sent):
            cnt[word] += 1
            if i+1 < len(sent):
                cnt2[word][sent[i+1]] += 1
    for word in cnt2:
        for word2 in cnt2[word]:
        # Laplace Smoothing
            prob = (cnt2[word][word2] + K) / (cnt[word] + K * len
            (vocab) + 0.0)
            print('P({0} |{1}) ={2}'.format(word2, word, prob))
```

Table 2.6 Laplace smoothing.

Vocabulary [we, you, today, play, sing], $V = 5$ Corpus We play today You sing today			
Count		Laplace smoothing ($K = 1$)	
$C(we)$	1	$P(we)$	$(1 + 1)/(6 + 5) = 0.182$
$C(we\ play)$	1	$P(play\,\|\,we)$	$(1 + 1)/(1 + 5) = 0.333$
$C(we\ sing)$	0	$P(sing\,\|\,we)$	$(0 + 1)/(1 + 5) = 0.167$
$C(we\ we)$	0	$P(we\,\|\,we)$	$(0 + 1)/(1 + 5) = 0.167$
$C(you\ play)$	0	$P(play\,\|\,you)$	$(0 + 1)/(1 + 5) = 0.167$

2.4.2 Evaluation of language models

The language model establishes the probability model for text, that is, $P(w_1w_2...w_m)$. So a language model is evaluated by the probability value it assigns to test text unseen during training.

In the evaluation, all sentences in the test set are concatenated together to make a single word sequence: $w_1, w_2, ..., w_N$, which includes the special symbols $<s>$ and $</s>$. A language model should maximize the probability $P(w_1w_2...w_N)$. However, as this probability favors shorter sentences, we use the **perplexity** metric to normalize it by the number of words:

$$Perplexity(w_1w_2...w_N) = P(w_1w_2...w_N)^{-\frac{1}{N}} = \sqrt[N]{\frac{1}{P(w_1w_2...w_N)}}$$

For example, in the bigram language model, $Perplexity(w_1w_2...w_N) = \sqrt[N]{\prod_{i=1}^{N}\frac{1}{P(w_i|w_{i-1})}}$.

Since perplexity is a negative power of probability, it should be *minimized* to maximize the original probability. On the public benchmark dataset Penn Tree Bank, the currently best language model can achieve a perplexity score around 35.8 [4].

It's worth noting that factors like the dataset size and inclusion of punctuations can have a significant impact on the perplexity score. Therefore beyond perplexity, a language model can be evaluated by checking whether it helps with other downstream NLP tasks.

2.5 Summary

- **Tokenization** is an important basic task in NLP. **Byte Pair Encoding (BPE)** is a popular tokenization method.
- **Word vector** represents a word by a vector of numbers. Common word vectors include **one-hot embedding** and **word2vec**.
- **Named Entity Recognition (NER)** models include rule-based, feature-based, and deep learning methods.
- **Hidden Markov Model (HMM)** is a standard algorithm for **Part-of-speech Tagging (POS Tagging)**.
- **Language model** characterizes the probability of natural language. *N*-gram model is a common language model. Language models can be evaluated by **perplexity**.

Reference

[1] Sennrich R, Haddow B, Birch A. Neural machine translation of rare words with sub-word units. arXiv preprint arXiv 2015;1508.07909.

[2] Mikolov T, Sutskever I, Chen K, Corrado GS, Dean J. Distributed representations of words and phrases and their compositionality. Advances in neural information processing systems 2013;3111–19.

[3] DeRose SJ. Grammatical category disambiguation by statistical optimization. Comput Linguist 1988;14(1):31–9.

[4] Radford A, Wu J, Child R, Luan D, Amodei D, Sutskever I. Language models are unsupervised multitask learners. OpenAI Blog 2019;1(8):9.

CHAPTER 3

Deep learning in natural language processing

3.1 From word vector to text vector

Suppose a sentence contains n words represented by n word vectors. If these word vectors go through a fully connected neural network, we will obtain n vectors with a new dimension; if the word vectors are processed by a recurrent neural network (RNN), we get n hidden state vectors. However, neither method gives us a single vector to represent the whole sentence. If the goal is to classify the sentence, one must first convert the n vectors into a single sentence vector. Therefore, in general, we need a way to turn multiple word vectors into one vector representing the text.

3.1.1 Using the final state of recurrent neural network

We note that data is generally processed in batches in deep learning to speed up computation. Therefore, the word vectors are represented by a **tensor** of size $batch \times seq\_len \times word\_dim$, that is, a 3D matrix, where the $batch$ is the number of data samples in the batch, seq_len is the length of the longest text/sentence in this batch, and each word is represented by a vector of $word\_dim$ dimensions. The goal is to have an output vector of dimension doc_dim for each text/sentence, that is, a tensor with size $batch \times doc\_dim$. Clearly, as seq_len varies from batch to batch, we cannot use a predefined fixed-size fully connected network to directly convert word tensor to text tensor.

In a **recurrent neural network (RNN)**, the word vectors sequentially enter RNN cells and the hidden states can transmit context information. In a forward RNN, the hidden state vector of the ith word h_i contains information about the first i words in the text. Thus the last hidden state, h_n, can be used to represent the meaning of the entire text. Moreover, a bidirectional RNN can be used to grasp semantic information from both directions to produce a better context-aware representation. The following code snippet exemplifies how to use a bidirectional RNN to get text representation from word vectors.

Machine Reading Comprehension. DOI: https://doi.org/10.1016/B978-0-323-90118-5.00003-5
© 2021 Beijing Huazhang Graphics & Information Co., Ltd/China Machine Press.
Published by Elsevier Inc. All rights reserved.

```
import torch
import torch.nn as nn
class BiRNN(nn.Module):
    # word_dim: dimension of word vector
    # hidden_size: dimension of RNN hidden state
    def __init__(self, word_dim, hidden_size):
        super(BiRNN, self).__init__()
    # Bi-directional GRU, where the first dimension is the batch size
        self.gru = nn.GRU(word_dim, hidden_size = hidden_size,
        bidirectional = True, batch_first = True)

# Input:
# Tensor x. Size: batch × seq_len × word_dim
# Output:
# The text tensor. Size: batch × (2 × hidden_size)
    def forward(self, x):
        batch = x.shape[0]
        # output is the hidden states in the last RNN layer for each
            word. Size: batch × seq_len × (2 × hidden_size)
        # last_hidden is the RNN's hidden state for the last word.
            Size: 2 × batch × hidden_size
        output, last_hidden = self.gru(x)
        return last_hidden.transpose(0,1).contiguous().view(batch, -1)
```

3.1.2 Convolutional neural network and pooling

The word vectors in one sentence are stored in a 2D tensor of size *seq_len × word_dim*. Thus we can borrow the idea of **convolutional neural network** (**CNN**) in image processing to use a filter on sliding windows. In detail, a filter tensor of dimension *window_size × word_dim* sweeps through the 2D word tensor, each time processing *window_size* neighboring words and obtaining one number using inner product, resulting in a final vector of size *seq_len-window_size* + 1. For example, suppose the *window_size* = 3, and the 5-word sentence is *I like sports very much*. Then, the filter computes $5 - 3 + 1 = 3$ convolution values for *I like sports*, *like sports very* and *sports very much*.

If there are *m* filters, that is, output channels, we can get *m* convolution values from each window. Thus, the final output of CNN is a tensor of size *batch × (seq_len-window_size* + 1) *× m*. However, each text is still represented by $L = seq\_len\text{-}window\_size + 1$ vectors. To get a single text vector, one way is to take the average of the *L* vectors: the *j*th dimension of the new vector is the average of the *j*th dimension of the *L* vectors. The resulting tensor has size *batch* × *m*, so each text is represented by a single *m*-dimension vector. This approach is called **average pooling**.

Another method is to take the maximum value of the *L* vectors: the *j*th dimension of the new vector is the maximum over the *j*th dimension of the *L* vectors. This method is called **maximum pooling (max-pooling)**. One advantage of max-pooling is that the text representation is independent of the location of the key words in the text. For example, in the sentence *I like sports very much*, *I* is a keyword and its information should be reflected in the text vector. Suppose in the window over *I like sports*, because of the occurrence of the word *I*, the third dimension of the convolution vector has a much greater value than the third dimension of convolution vectors produced by other windows. Max-pooling makes sure that no matter where *I like sports* lies in the sentence, the third dimension of the final text vector will be the same, reflecting the information from the keyword *I*.

Fig. 3.1 shows an example of CNN with max-pooling. The window size is 3 and there are four filters/output channels, so the input to max-pooling is $n - 3 + 1 = n - 2$ vectors of dimension 4. The final text vector has four dimensions, each of which may come from the convolution vector from different filters.

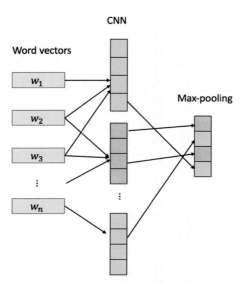

Figure 3.1 CNN with max-pooling. The window size is 3, and there are four output channels.

The following code snippet implements CNN with max-pooling. As the input to CNN in PyTorch requires a dimension for channels, but the word vector has only one channel, we use the function *tensor.unsqueeze* to add a dimension of size 1 to a specified location. Similarly, we apply *tensor.squeeze* to CNN's output tensor to remove that singleton dimension. The max-pooling operation is done via *tensor.max*.

```
import torch
import torch.nn as nn
import torch.nn.functional as F
class CNN_Maxpool(nn.Module):
    # word_dim: dimension of word vector
    # window_size: length of CNN window
    # out_channels: the number of output channels in CNN
    def __init__(self, word_dim, window_size, out_channels):
        super(CNN_Maxpool, self).__init__()
        # 1 input channel, out_channels output channels, and a filter
          with size window_size × word_dim
        self.cnn = nn.Conv2d(1, out_channels, (window_size, word_dim))

    # Input:
    # x is the text tensor. Size: batch × seq_len × word_dim
    # Output:
    # res is the output text vectors, each of which has out_channels
      dimensions
    def forward(self, x):
        # Convert input to single channel. Size: batch × 1 ×
          seq_len × word_dim
        x_unsqueeze = x.unsqueeze(1)
        # Go through CNN. Size: batch × out_channels × new_seq_len × 1
        x_cnn = self.cnn(x_unsqueeze)
        # Remove the last dimension, size: batch × out_channels ×
          new_seq_len
        x_cnn_result = x_cnn.squeeze(3)
        # max-pooling, which computes the maximum value in the last
          dimension. Size: batch × out_channels
        res, _ = x_cnn_result.max(2)
        return res
```

Another application of CNN and max-pooling in natural language processing (NLP) is the **Character Convolutional Neural Network (Character CNN)**, which will be introduced in Section 4.2.2. If each word is considered as a sequence of characters, the character embeddings can be aggregated into the one word embedding vector in the same way the text vector is obtained from word vectors.

Character CNN can effectively deal with spelling errors, because even if a few letters are misspelled in a word, most neighboring letters in the CNN window are still correct. So the word embedding generated by the CNN won't be very different from that of the correctly spelled word. In practice, word embeddings from both the dictionary and Character CNN are often concatenated as a most robust representation.

3.1.3 Parametrized weighted sum

Parametrized weighted sum is a commonly used method to turn multiple word vectors into a text vector. Assume the input contains n word vectors, $a_1, a_2, \ldots, a_n$. A simple *average pooling* is equivalent to the weighted sum $a = \sum_{i=1}^{n} w_i a_i$ where the weights are all $1/n$. However, if we want to dynamically tune these weights to reflect the relationship between the words, the parametrized weighted sum can be used.

The first step is to define a parameter vector b with the same dimension as the word vector a_i. Then, each word vector is assigned a weight score via the inner product $s_i = b^T a_i$. As the sum of weights in average pooling is 1, we can use the softmax operation in Section 3.2 to normalize these scores to sum up to 1:

$$(w_1, w_2, \ldots, w_n) = softmax\ (s_1, s_2, \ldots, s_n), w_i = \frac{e^{s_i}}{e^{s_1} + e^{s_2} + \cdots + e^{s_n}}$$

Finally, the weighted sum of all word vectors is used as the text vector:

$$a = \sum_{i=1}^{n} w_i a_i$$

The following code implements the parametrized weighted sum.

```
import torch
import torch.nn as nn
import torch.nn.functional as F
class WeightedSum(nn.Module):
    # word_dim: dimension of input word vector
    def __init__(self, word_dim):
        super(WeightedSum, self).__init__()
```

(Continued)

(*Continued*)
```
        self.b = nn.Linear(word_dim, 1) # the parameter vector

# Input:
# x is the input tensor. Size: batch × seq_len × word_dim
# Output:
# res is the text tensor. Size: batch × word_dim
def forward(self, x):
    # score by inner product. Size: batch × seq_len × 1
    scores = self.b(x)
    # softmax operation. Size: batch × seq_len × 1
    weights = F.softmax(scores, dim = 1)
    # The weighted sum is computed by matrix multiplication. Size:
      batch × word_dim × 1
    res = torch.bmm(x.transpose(1, 2), weights)
    # Delete the last dimension. Size: batch × word_dim
    res = res.squeeze(2)
    return res
```

The code above uses *nn.Linear* for inner product operation on vectors. The function *torch.bmm* is used to compute the multiplication between two batch matrices with dimension $batch \times a \times b$ and $batch \times b \times c$.

It is worth noting that the parametrized weighted sum is actually a self-attention mechanism, which will be covered in more detail in Section 3.4.

3.2 Answer multiple-choice questions: natural language understanding

Once a text vector is obtained using the methods in the previous section, we can carry out related text tasks. In NLP, there is a large category of text-classification tasks:

- Choose the correct answer from multiple choices in machine reading comprehension (MRC);
- Judge the news category (e.g., politics, finance, sports) given the news content;
- Judge whether a user's review is positive or negative;
- Classify the user's emotion (e.g., happy, depressed, angry) in a conversation system.

For a classification task, the model should choose from K categories given the input text. Thus the model is also known as the **discriminative**

model. These text classification tasks are called **Natural Language Understanding (NLU)**.

3.2.1 Network structure

In a deep learning network for classification, the text is first tokenized into words, which are presented by word vectors. These vectors go through various network layers such as fully connected layer, RNN and CNN. Finally, a text vector d of dimension d_dim is obtained. The network for the above process is called the **encoder**.

Next, the model computes a score for each of the K categories based on the text vector. The scores are usually from a fully connected layer of size $d\_dim \times K$. This fully connected layer is called the output layer. Thus the output of the NLU model consists of K scores: $\hat{y}_1, \hat{y}_2, \ldots, \hat{y}_K$, which are normalized by softmax into probabilities: $p_1, \ldots, p_K = \textit{softmax}(\hat{y}_1, \hat{y}_2, \ldots, \hat{y}_K)$. These probabilities are then compared with the correct answer to compute the loss function based on cross entropy (Appendix B.1.2.2). Here's the form of the loss function given the text vector d and the correct category $y^* \in \{1, 2, \ldots, K\}$:

$$f_{cross\_entropy}(\boldsymbol{\theta}) = -\log\left(p_{y^*}(\boldsymbol{d}; \boldsymbol{\theta})\right)$$

where $\boldsymbol{\theta}$ stands for the network parameters.

3.2.2 Implementing text classification

The following code implements a NLU model for text classification. It employs the *CNN_Maxpool* class defined in Section 3.1.2.

The code uses the PyTorch function *nn.CrossEntropyLoss* which conducts both the softmax operation and cross entropy computation. The input to *nn.CrossEntropyLoss* function is:
- a score FloatTensor of size *batch* $\times$ K; and
- a LongTensor of the ground-truth classification labels of size *batch*. Each element is between 0 and $K - 1$.

```
import torch
import torch.nn as nn
import torch.nn.functional as F
import torch.optim as optim
class NLUNet(nn.Module):
    # word_dim: dimension of word vectors
```

(Continued)

(Continued)

```
# window_size: window length of CNN
# out_channels: number of output channels
# K: number of categories
def __init__(self, word_dim, window_size, out_channels, K):
  super(NLUNet, self).__init__()
  # CNN and max-pooling
  self.cnn_maxpool = CNN_Maxpool(word_dim, window_size, out_channels)
  # fully connected output layer
  self.linear = nn.Linear(out_channels, K)

# Input:
# x: input tensor. Size: batch × seq_len × word_dim
# Output:
# class_score: predicted scores for each class. Size: batch × K
def forward(self, x):
  # text vector. Size: batch × out_channels
  doc_embed = self.cnn_maxpool(x)
  # classification scores. Size: batch × K
  class_score = self.linear(doc_embed)
  return class_score

K = 3  # 3 categories
net = NLUNet(10, 3, 15, K)
# 30 sequences, each with 5 words. Each word vector is 10D.
x = torch.randn(30, 5, 10, requires_grad = True)
# 30 ground-truth category labels, which are integers from 0 to K − 1
y = torch.LongTensor(30).random_(0, K)
optimizer = optim.SGD(net.parameters(), lr = 0.01)
# size of res: batch × K
res = net(x)
# cross entropy loss function in PyTorch, which includes softmax
  operation
loss_func = nn.CrossEntropyLoss()
loss = loss_func(res, y)
optimizer.zero_grad()
loss.backward()
optimizer.step()
```

During inference, the model computes the probability that the text belongs to each category, and then selects the category with the maximum probability. If the system is required to handle the case of "none of the cases," there are two possible solutions.

1. An optimal threshold can be determined on the validation data. When the K probability values are all below this threshold, the model produces "none of the cases."
2. "None of the cases" can be handled as an additional category.

Other than K-classification, the NLU tasks include the following types.

Multilabel classification assumes that the text can be simultaneously categorized into several classes, for example, a news article contains discussion on both politics and finance. One way is to establish K binary classifiers for all the K classes, each predicting whether the text belongs to a specific class. For example, one binary classifier judges whether a news article is in the sports category, and another classifier judges whether the news article is in the entertainment category. An appropriate threshold can be determined from the validation data, and multiple labels are allowed for one text sample.

Sequence labeling refers to the task of classifying each word in the text, which includes NER and POS tagging in Section 2.3. A single text vector is usually not required in a sequence labeling model. We can employ a RNN to get a hidden state for contextual representation of each word, which is then fed into an output layer to predict its category.

3.3 Write an article: natural language generation

An important topic in NLP is to produce natural text. Text generation is widely employed in machine translation, MRC (freestyle answers), text summarization, and text autocompletion. These tasks are usually referred to as **Natural Language Generation** (**NLG**), and the corresponding generation models are called **generative models**.

3.3.1 Network architecture

An NLG model generates text by analyzing the semantics of given text. For example, in an MRC task requiring freestyle answers, the model needs to first analyze the question and article. The NLU models introduced in the previous section can handle this text analysis task. Then, RNN is usually employed to produce text, since RNN can process text with varying lengths, which suits the text generation process of predicting new words given previous context.

To begin with, we prepend $<s>$ and append $</s>$ to all the text. The NLU module converts the input text into a vector d with dimension h_dim. The RNN module takes the first word $<s>$ and the initial hidden state $h_0 = d$ as the input. RNN then computes the new hidden state h_1, which is used to predict the next word to generate.

Suppose the vocabulary has $|V|$ words (including $<s>$ and $</s>$). The task of predicting the next word is equivalent to $|V|$-category classification. Therefore we feed h_1 into a fully connected layer of size $h\_dim \times |V|$, and obtain a vector with dimension $|V|$. This vector represents the scores given to each word by the model. Thus we select the word w_1 with the highest score as the predicted second word.

To continue, the word vector of w_1 and the hidden state h_1 are fed into RNN to predict the third word. This process goes on until $</s>$ is selected, indicating the end of generation.

Because the above text generation process converts hidden states into words, the corresponding network structure is called a **decoder** (Fig. 3.2). A decoder must use a one-way RNN **from left to right**. If a bidirectional RNN is used, the decoder will peek the words to generate, leading to a nearly 100% training accuracy. However, such a model has no generalization ability.

As the parameters in a neural network are randomly initialized, the decoder will produce text of poor quality in the early stage. Since a generated word is fed into the next RNN module, the generation error will propagate. Therefore a common technique for training the decoder is **teacher forcing**. Under teacher forcing, the word generated by the decoder does not enter the next RNN module during training. Instead, the ground-truth word is used as the next input. This can avoid error propagation and alleviate the cold-start problem, resulting in faster convergence. In practice, one can also intermingle teacher forcing and nonteacher forcing strategy during training. As shown in Table 3.1, in nonteacher forcing, the error starts to propagate from the second generated wrong word *often*, and the subsequent output is completely

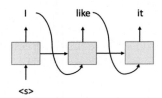

Figure 3.2 An RNN-based decoder for text generation. The first input word is the special symbol $<s>$.

Table 3.1 Teacher forcing strategy.

Ground-truth		<s>	I	like	the	weather	here	</s>
Teacher forcing	Input to RNN	<s>	I	like	the	weather	here	</s>
	Output	I	hate	there	weather	here	</s>	
Nonteacher forcing	Input to RNN	<s>	I	often	play	soccer	there	
	Output	I	often	play	soccer	there	</s>	

misguided. During inference, nonteacher forcing is used because the correct answer is unavailable.

3.3.2 Implementing text generation

Here is the implementation of an NLG model, *NLGNet*. It is trained with the teacher forcing strategy.

```python
import torch
import torch.nn as nn
import torch.nn.functional as F
import torch.optim as optim
class NLGNet(nn.Module):
    # word_dim: length of word vector
    # window_size: length of the CNN window
    # rnn_dim: dimension of RNN's hidden state
    # vocab_size: size of the vocabulary
    def __init__(self, word_dim, window_size, rnn_dim, vocab_size):
        super(NLGNet, self).__init__()
        # the word embedding matrix which returns word vector given
            word id
        self.embed = nn.Embedding(vocab_size, word_dim)
        # CNN and max-pooling
        self.cnn_maxpool = CNN_Maxpool(word_dim, window_size, rnn_dim)
        # single-layer one-way GRU
        self.rnn = nn.GRU(word_dim, rnn_dim, batch_first = True)
        # fully connected output layer, producing scores for each word
        self.linear = nn.Linear(rnn_dim, vocab_size)

# Input:
# x_id: word ids of input text. Size: batch × x_seq_len
# y_id: word ids of ground-truth output text. Size: batch × y_seq_len
```

(Continued)

(Continued)

```
# Output:
# word_scores: score for each word at each position. Size:
  batch × y_seq_len × vocab_size
    def forward(self, x_id, y_id):
        #  Obtain  word  vectors  for  input  text.  Size:  batch ×
           x_seq_len × word_dim
        x = self.embed(x_id)
        # Obtain word vectors for ground-truth output text. Size:
           batch × y_seq_len × word_dim
        y = self.embed(y_id)
        # text vector of size batch × cnn_channels
        doc_embed = self.cnn_maxpool(x)
        # use text vector as the initial RNN state. Size: 1 × batch ×
           y_seq_len × rnn_dim
        h0 = doc_embed.unsqueeze(0)
        # RNN hidden states at each position. Size: batch × y_seq_len ×
           rnn_dim
        rnn_output, _ = self.rnn(y, h0)
        # score for each word at each position. Size: batch × y_seq_len ×
           vocab_size
        word_scores = self.linear(rnn_output)
        return word_scores

vocab_size = 100   # 100 words
net = NLGNet(10, 3, 15, vocab_size) # set up the network
# 30 instances of input text, each containing 10 words
x_id = torch.LongTensor(30, 10).random_(0, vocab_size)
# 30 instances of ground-truth output text, each containing 8 words
y_id = torch.LongTensor(30, 8).random_(0, vocab_size)
optimizer = optim.SGD(net.parameters(), lr = 0.01)
# score for each vocabulary word at each position. Size: 30 × 8 ×
   vocab_size
word_scores = net(x_id, y_id)
# cross entropy loss function in PyTorch, which includes softmax
   operation
loss_func = nn.CrossEntropyLoss()
# convert word_scores into a 2D array and y_id into a 1D array to cal-
   culate the loss
loss = loss_func(word_scores[ :,: - 1,:].reshape( - 1, vocab_size), y_id
   [ :,1:].reshape( - 1))
optimizer.zero_grad()
loss.backward()
optimizer.step()
```

The input to *NLGNet* include word ids of the input text, *x_id*, and the word ids of the ground-truth output text, *y_id*. The class employs the word embedding module from PyTorch: *nn.Embedding*. This module turns word ids into corresponding word vectors. Then, the model uses CNN and max-pooling to obtain the text vector, which is fed into the RNN as the initial state. *NLGNet* employs the **Gated Recurrent Unit (GRU)** as the RNN module. As we use teacher forcing, the input to RNN at each timestep is the ground-truth output text from *y_id*.

Since the function *nn.CrossEntropyLoss* treats the second dimension as category by default, we need to squeeze the 3D tensor *word_scores* (size: *batch* × *y_seq_len* × *vocab_size*) to two dimensions. The code uses the *tensor.view* function in PyTorch for dimension transformation: *word_scores.view* (− 1, *vocab_size*) converts *word_scores* into a 2D tensor, where the size of the second dimension is *vocab_size*. As dimension transformation does not affect the total volume of the tensor, the size of the first dimension of the output tensor is *batch* × *y_seq_len*. Similarly, the ground-truth word id tensor *y_id* is converted into a 1D tensor. It's also worth noting that the predicted scores, *word_scores*, correspond to the second, third, fourth... produced word, since the first produced word is always <s>. Therefore we compare *word_scores* [:, : − 1, :] to *y_id* [:, 1:], that is, the second to the last words in the ground-truth output.

3.3.3 Beam search

During inference, the decoder produces words $\hat{y}_1, \hat{y}_2, \ldots, \hat{y}_n$ one at a time based on the input text $x_1, x_2, \ldots, x_m$. Since we use the one-way RNN, each generated word is based on the input text and previously produced words, that is, the ith generated word is characterized by the distribution $P(\hat{y}_i|\hat{y}_1 \ldots \hat{y}_{i-1}, x_1, x_2, \ldots, x_m)$. Note that this formula is very similar to the language model probability in Section 2.4, except that here the probability is also conditioned on the input text. Therefore the decoder needs to maximize the following conditional probability of the generated word sequence:

$$P(\hat{y}_1, \hat{y}_2, \ldots, \hat{y}_n|x_1, x_2, \ldots, x_m) = \prod_{i=1}^{n} P(\hat{y}_i|\hat{y}_1 \ldots \hat{y}_{i-1}, x_1, x_2, \ldots, x_m)$$

However, the number of possible word sequences is $|V|^n$, which is exponential. Thus an efficient solution to find the sequence with the highest probability is desired.

One idea is to reuse the Viterbi algorithm from Section 2.3. Recall that the Viterbi algorithm defines $f(i, j)$ to be the maximum HMM probability of the POS sequence of the first i generate words, given that the ith word is tagged with POS j, that is, $q_i = j$. However, in the generation model above, the hidden state of RNN is a real-valued vector, not one of the K parts of speech as in HMM. So, the Viterbi algorithm cannot be used here as we cannot define an array which takes a real vector as subscript.

One feasible approach is to use the greedy algorithm by always selecting the most likely word at each step:

$$\hat{y}_i = \underset{w \in V}{\mathrm{argmax}}\, P\big(w | \hat{y}_1 \ldots \hat{y}_{i-1}, x_1, x_2, \ldots, x_m\big)$$

Although this method can generate a reasonable word sequence, it is not always optimal. For example, the word $\hat{y}_1 = w$ that maximizes $P\big(\hat{y}_1 | x_1, x_2, \ldots, x_m\big)$ is not necessarily the first word of the globally optimal word sequence. For instance, suppose the input text is *What sports does he play* and the ground-truth response is *He plays soccer well*. If the greedy algorithm succeeds in generating the first word *he*, the next word is more likely to be *is* instead of *plays*, since in training text, *he is* appears much more often than *he plays*. So the trained decoder will assign a greater value to *P(is | he; what sports does he play)* than *P(plays | he; what sports does he play)*. As a result, the subsequent generated text may be irrelevant to the question, for example, *he is a boy*. However, the global probability *P(he plays soccer well | what sports does he play)* > *P(he is a boy | what sports does he play)*. Therefore, the biggest problem of greedy algorithm is short-sightedness since the local optimum may not correspond to the global optimum.

To alleviate this problem, we can use **beam search**. Beam search does not just select the single best candidate for the next word, instead it chooses B top candidates. The parameter B is called the beam width. As a result, after the first step, there are B candidates for the first word. In the second step, the algorithm looks for the most likely B candidates for the next word for each of the B words, ending with B^2 two-word sequences. Then, the top B sequences with the highest probability are chosen from these sequences and kept. The algorithm then goes on to generate the third word and so on. Therefore beam search always keeps B candidate sequences at each step.

In the process, if the sentence-ending symbol $</s>$ is among the top B candidates for the next word, the corresponding sequence S ends. S is saved into a buffer, removed from the list of candidate sequences, and replaced by the next best sequence. To prevent beam search from going on forever, we need to set a maximum length L. Once the candidate sequences reach the length of L words, the decoding process stops. Finally, the optimal word sequence with the highest probability is selected from all remaining candidate sequences and those in the buffer.

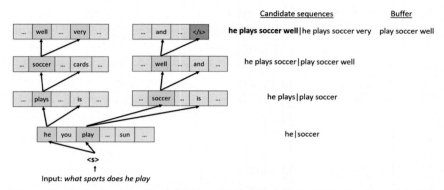

Figure 3.3 Example of beam search. The beam width is 2 and the maximum length of generated text is 4. The input text is *what sports does he play*. The solid arrow indicates the top 2 next-word candidates chosen for each candidate sequence. The green square contains the top 2 next-words among all candidate sequences.

Fig. 3.3 shows an example of beam search, where $B = 2$ and $L = 4$. The input text is *what sports does he play*. In the first step, beam search selects *he* and *play*. In the second step, the two remaining sequences are *he plays* and *play soccer*. In the last step, $</s>$ is among the top two candidates, so *play soccer well* is put into the buffer and *he plays soccer very* takes its spot. Finally, *he plays soccer well* is generated as it has the highest global probability among the candidate sequences and those in the buffer.

As the global probability $P(\hat{y}_1, \hat{y}_2, \ldots, \hat{y}_n | x_1, x_2, \ldots, x_m)$ is the product of all conditional probabilities of words, its value becomes smaller as the generated sequence is longer. This will bias the algorithm toward generating shorter sequences. Thus we usually employ length normalization to compensate for the length of sequence:

$$P_{norm}(\hat{y}_1, \hat{y}_2, \ldots, \hat{y}_n | x_1, x_2, \ldots, x_m) = \frac{P(\hat{y}_1, \hat{y}_2, \ldots, \hat{y}_n | x_1, x_2, \ldots, x_m)}{n}$$

In practice, a larger beam width may lead to a better solution, but will incur higher computational complexity. Thus one needs to strike a balance between the model's quality and efficiency.

3.4 Keep focused: attention mechanism

Attention mechanism was original proposed in computer vision. It is based on the intuitive idea that humans do not need to look at each pixel in detail when recognizing an object in an image. Instead, they concentrate on certain parts of the image, and this focus may move to another area when recognizing another object. The same idea holds in the case of language understanding: we focus on different parts of the text looking for different information. Likewise, deep learning models can put more weights on certain words according to the current comprehension task, and these weights may be automatically adjusted for other tasks. This is the attention mechanism for NLP.

3.4.1 Attention mechanism

The input to the attention mechanism includes:
1. The attended items, which are represented by a group of vectors (e.g., word vectors, sentence vectors): $\{a_1, a_2, \ldots, a_n\}$;
2. The item paying attention to the above items, which is a single vector x.

Firstly, we compute the strength of relationship between x and $\{a_1, a_2, \ldots, a_n\}$. This is characterized by n scores, and a higher score indicates that the corresponding item is more focused on by x. This is implemented through the attention function, which produces a similarity score between two vectors. For instance, we can use the inner product function when x and a have the same dimension: $s_i = f(x, a_i) = x^T a_i, 1 \leq i \leq n$. Then, the softmax function normalizes the scores to get attention weights: $\beta_i = \frac{e^{s_i}}{\sum_j e^{s_j}}, 1 \leq i \leq n$. Finally, the weights are employed to compute a weighted sum of the attended items, resulting in the attention vector $c = \beta_1 a_1 + \beta_2 a_2 + \cdots + \beta_n a_n$. Here, the attention vector c is a linear combination of $\{a_1, a_2, \ldots, a_n\}$, and the weights come from the interaction between x and each a_i.

The attention mechanism can also be computed for multiple vectors like x. We define the following *Attention* function over $\{a_1, a_2, \ldots, a_n\}$ and $\{x_1, x_2, \ldots, x_m\}$. The output $\{c_1, c_2, \ldots, c_m\}$ has the same number of vectors as $\{x_1, x_2, \ldots, x_m\}$ and each vector has the same dimension as a_i.

$$Attention(\{a_1, a_2, \ldots, a_n\}; \{x_1, x_2, \ldots, x_m\}) = \{c_1, c_2, \ldots, c_m\},$$

$$c_j = \beta_{j,1} a_1 + \beta_{j,2} a_2 + \cdots + \beta_{j,n} a_n, 1 \leq j \leq m,$$

$$\beta_{j,i} = \frac{e^{f(x_j, a_i)}}{\sum_{k=1}^{n} e^{f(x_j, a_k)}}, 1 \leq i \leq n$$

3.4.2 Implementing attention function

Here is the PyTorch implementation of attention function based on the inner product.

```
'''
    a: the attended items/vectors. Size: batch × m × dim
    x: the items/vectors attending to a. Size: batch × n × dim
'''
def attention(a, x):
    # use inner product to compute attention scores. Size: batch × n × m
    scores = x.bmm(a.transpose(1, 2))
    # softmax over the last dimension
    alpha = F.softmax(scores, dim = - 1)
    # attention vector. Size: batch × n × dim
    attended = alpha.bmm(a)
    return attended
```

The code computes the inner product values via the *torch.bmm* function, then uses *F.softmax* to normalize the scores, and finally calculates the weighted sum of the input vectors *a*. As a result, each vector in *x* receives a corresponding attention vector with a dimension of *dim*.

3.4.3 Sequence-to-sequence model

An important application of the attention mechanism is in the decoder. Section 3.3 mentions that the input text vector is used as the initial hidden state of the decoder RNN. But is hard for this single vector to contain all relevant information in the text, especially when the text is long. On the other hand, the decoder needs to focus on certain parts of the input text when generating words. For example, the decoder in an MRC model may only need to attend to a small portion of the article when generating the fifth answer word. Therefore, we can use the **sequence–to–sequence (seq2seq) model** with attention mechanism.

The two sequences in seq2seq refer to the input and output text. The encoder uses an RNN to process the input text and the last hidden state is used as the initial hidden state to the decoder. The hidden states for all the input words, $a_1, a_2, \ldots, a_m$, are also preserved. When the decoder tries

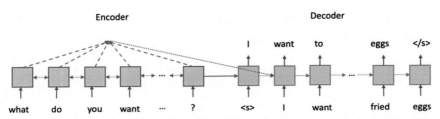

Figure 3.4 Sequence-to-sequence (seq2seq) model with attention mechanism. The decoder RNN uses attention mechanism (blue dashed arrows) to get the context vector at each step, which is fed into the RNN together with the hidden state.

to use the hidden state h_{t-1} to generate the tth word, it attends to the hidden states of input text and computes an attention vector c_t:

$$Attention(\{a_1, a_2, \ldots, a_n\}; h_{t-1}) = c_t$$

Since c_t represents the related information from the input, it is also called *context vector*. This context vector is merged with h_{t-1} and fed into the decoder RNN. In this way, the decoder can focus on different parts of the input text at different decoding steps. This technique can significantly improve the quality of generated text in many applications.

Fig. 3.4 illustrates a seq2seq model with attention. The encoder RNN firstly computes hidden states for each input word. Then, the decoder generates a word by leveraging the context vector c_t at each step. The implementation is given in Section 4.4.4 with more details.

3.5 Summary

- Many NLP models need to convert multiple word vectors into a single text vector to handle text with varying lengths. This can be achieved by using the final state of RNN, CNN + Pooling, and a parametrized weighted sum of word vectors.
- **Natural Language Understanding** (NLU) refers to text classification tasks such as answering multiple choice questions in MRC, which are solved by discriminative models. The model needs to produce a score for each category.
- **Natural Language Generation** (NLG) refers to text generation tasks such as producing freestyle answers in MRC, which are solved by generative models. The model is usually trained with teacher forcing and produces text via beam search.

- Most text generation models in deep learning use the encoder—decoder architecture. The encoder processes input text (e.g., article and question), and the decoder produces the text (e.g., answer).
- **Attention mechanism** dynamically assigns weights to different parts of the text, enabling the models to focus on specific parts of the input text. Attention mechanisms can be applied in sequence-to-sequence (seq2seq) models.

PART II

Architecture

CHAPTER 4

Architecture of machine reading comprehension models

4.1 General architecture of machine reading comprehension models

Although machine reading comprehension (MRC) models based on deep learning have various structures, a general framework has been widely adopted after years of exploration and practice.

As an MRC model takes the article and question as input, it firstly represents text in numerical format, also known as encoding. The encoding should preserve the semantics of the original text, so it must carry contextual information for each word, phrase, and sentence. We refer to this encoding module as the **encoding layer**.

Next, to give correct answers, the model needs to understand the relationship between the article and the question. For example, if the word *Washington* appears in the question and *D.C.* appears in the article, although the two words are not exactly the same, they have similar meanings. Therefore, *D.C.* and its neighboring text in the article should become the focus of the model. This can be addressed by the attention mechanism in Section 3.4. In this process, the MRC model jointly analyzes the semantics of the article and question in depth. We refer to this module as the **interaction layer**.

After the model establishes the relationship between the article and question in the interaction layer, it already captures clues to the answer. The final module that gives the answer prediction is called the **output layer**. According to Section 1.4.1, there are several answer types in MRC tasks, such as multiple choice, extractive, and freestyle. Therefore the design of the output layer should match the required answer type. In addition, this layer determines the evaluation process and loss function for optimization.

Fig. 4.1 shows the general architecture of MRC models. As shown, the encoding layer converts text into numerical embeddings. The interaction layer focuses on the semantic relation between the article and the question, and deepens its understanding of both parts via mutual information. Based on the result from this semantic analysis, the output layer generates the answer in the required format.

Machine Reading Comprehension. DOI: https://doi.org/10.1016/B978-0-323-90118-5.00004-7
© 2021 Beijing Huazhang Graphics & Information Co., Ltd/China Machine Press.
Published by Elsevier Inc. All rights reserved.

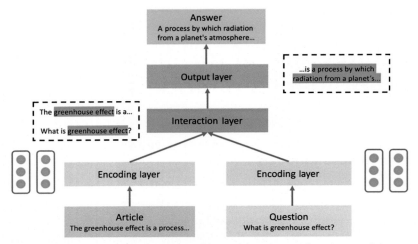

Figure 4.1 General architecture of a machine reading comprehension model.

Within this general architecture, different MRC models design various submodules in all layers to improve the efficiency and accuracy. It is worth noting that a majority of the innovations happen in the interaction layer, where numerous ways to process the article and question can be carried out.

4.2 Encoding layer

Similar to other deep learning models for natural language processing, the first step in an MRC model is to convert article and question text into word vectors. Here, we can use the tokenization and embedding methods introduced in Sections 2.1 and 2.2, as well as incorporating richer information such as character embedding and contextual embedding.

4.2.1 Establishing the dictionary

Suppose the encoding layer employs dictionary-based tokenization, it needs to first establish the dictionary. After tokenizing the text in the training set, the model selects words that appear more than a certain number of times to build a dictionary V. Words not in the dictionary are considered as **Out-Of-Vocabulary (OOV)** words and represented by the special token <UNK>. There are two ways to get the word vectors:

- use pretrained word embeddings (e.g., 300D vectors in word2vec) and keep them unchanged during training; and

- treat word embeddings as parameters, which are optimized together with other network parameters. The word vectors can be initialized randomly or with pretrained embeddings.

The advantage of the first choice is that there will be fewer parameters and the initial performance of the model is better. The advantage of the second option is that the word vectors can be adjusted during training to obtain better results. Usually, initialization with pretrained embeddings achieves much better results in the early rounds of optimization compared with random initialization.

In addition to word vectors, named entity recognition (NER) and part-of-speech (POS) information can also improve the representation of words. Suppose there are N named entities, we can set up a dictionary with N entries, each represented by a vector of length d_N. Similarly, suppose there are P parts of speech, we can set up another dictionary with P entries, each represented by a vector of length d_P. Vectors in both dictionaries are trainable parameters. For any word, its NER and POS embeddings are appended to the word vector. As the NER and POS of a word is dependent on its context, this joint embedding can better represent the semantics, leading to notable improvement in performance.

Another type of encoding particularly useful in MRC is *exact match*. Exact match encoding is a single bit for each article word: it is set to 1 if the word appears in the question, and 0 otherwise. Apart from the strict matching, an additional bit can indicate whether the stem of the article word is the same as the stem of any question word, since a word may have various forms (e.g., plural forms, past tense). For example, in Fig. 4.2, the word *ate* does not appear in the question, but its stem *eat* does, so its stem matching embedding is 1. Exact match embedding allows

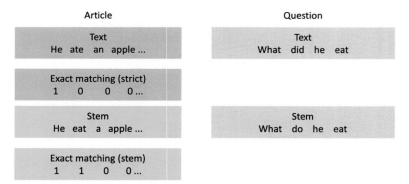

Figure 4.2 Exact match embeddings, including strict matching and stem matching.

the model to quickly find the part of article that contains question words, which is often near the answer's location.

4.2.2 Character embeddings

Spelling errors are common in text and it is often the case that all but a few characters are correct. Therefore many misspelled words can be recognized by their combination of characters. In addition, some character groups known as roots commonly appear with certain meanings, for example, in English *inter-* means between and among, and *-ward* means direction. Thus characters and their combination play an important role in a word's meaning.

To make better use of the character information, the encoding layer can use character embedding, that is, each character is represented by a vector. Since word length varies, each word may have a different number of character vectors. To produce a fixed-length vector, we reuse the methods in Section 3.1 to merge multiple character vectors into a single embedding. The most commonly used model is the **Character Convolution Neural Network (Char-CNN)**.

Suppose a word has K characters, each with a c-dim embedding: $c_1, c_2, \ldots, c_K$. A char-CNN employs a convolutional neural network (CNN) with a window of length W and f output channels to obtain $(K - W + 1)$ vectors with f dimensions. Next, it uses max-pooling to compute the maximum value for each dimension among these vectors, resulting in a character embedding with f dimensions. Fig. 4.3 shows a char-CNN with a window of size 3 and three output channels. Each word is encoded by a 3D character embedding.

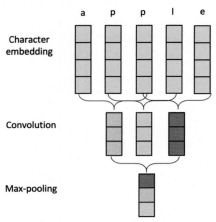

Figure 4.3 Character convolutional neural network (char-CNN) with a window size of 3 and three output channels.

Code 4-1 shows the PyTorch implementation of char-CNN. The input is a 3D tensor *char_ids*. After character embeddings are obtained from the dictionary *self.char_embed*, the resulting tensor *x* has four dimensions. To feed *x* into the char-CNN, its first two dimensions are merged. And the result from char-CNN is expanded back into three dimensions, representing one character embedding of size *out_channels* per word.

Code 4-1 Character convolutional neural network

```
import torch
import torch.nn as nn
import torch.nn.functional as F
class Char_CNN_Maxpool(nn.Module):
    # char_num: size of character dictionary
    # char_dim: length of character vector
    # window_size: window size of CNN
    # out_channels: number of output channels in CNN
    def __init__(self, char_num, char_dim, window_size, out_channels):
        super(Char_CNN_Maxpool, self).__init__()
        # character embedding matrix, with char_num vectors of a
          dimension of char_dim
        self.char_embed = nn.Embedding(char_num, char_dim)
        # 1 input channel, out_channels output channels, the filter
          size is window_size × char_dim
        self.cnn = nn.Conv2d(1, out_channels, (window_size, char_dim))

    # Input:
    # char_ids: character ids (0~char_num-1). Size: batch × seq_len
      × word_len. batch is the number of input text samples, seq_len
      is the maximum number of words in one sample, and word_len is the
      maximum length of word.
    # Output:
    # res: character embedding of all words. Size: batch × seq_len ×
      out_channels
    def forward(self, char_ids):
        # obtain character vectors from character ids. Size: batch ×
          seq_len × word_len × char_dim
        x = self.char_embed(char_ids)
        # merge the first two dimensions to make a single input channel
          Size: (batch × seq_len) × 1 × word_len × char_dim
        x_unsqueeze = x.view(-1, x.shape[2], x.shape[3]).unsqueeze(1)
```

(Continued)

(Continued)

```
        # go through the CNN layer. Size: (batch × seq_len) ×
          out_channels × new_seq_len × 1
        x_cnn = self.cnn(x_unsqueeze)
        # remove the last dimension. Size: (batch × seq_len) ×
          out_channels × new_seq_len
        x_cnn_result = x_cnn.squeeze(3)
        # max-pooling takes the maximum value over the last dimension.
          Size: (batch × seq_len) × out_channels
        res, _ = x_cnn_result.max(2)
        return res.view(x.shape[0] , x.shape[1] , -1)
```

4.2.3 Contextual embeddings

The English linguist J. R. Firth stated in 1957 that "*You shall know a word by the company it keeps.*" Indeed, many words need to be disambiguated by the words and phrases around them. However, the word vectors for a dictionary are fixed and cannot vary with the context. This leads to situations where the same word has different semantics in different text but is represented by the same embedding. Therefore the encoding layer should produce **contextual embedding** for each word, which varies based on the word's context to reflect its actual meaning.

In deep learning, contextual understanding is usually achieved via transferring information among words. The most commonly used module is the recurrent neural network (RNN), since RNN can transfer semantic information via hidden states. A bidirectional RNN can better facilitate this process by leveraging both directions of context. In practice, many models adopt multiple RNN layers to extract various levels of contextual semantics.

Code 4-2 implements a multilayer bidirectional RNN to obtain contextual embeddings. The input to RNN is word vectors of dimension *word_dim*. The produced contextual embeddings have a dimension of $2 \times state\_dim$, since there are two directions in the RNN.

Code 4-2 Generating contextual embeddings with a multilayer bidirectional RNN

```
class Contextual_Embedding(nn.Module):
    # word_dim: dimension of word vectors
```

(Continued)

```
(Continued)
    # state_dim: dimension of hidden states in RNN
    # rnn_layer: number of RNN layers
     def __init__(self, word_dim, state_dim, rnn_layer):
        super(Contextual_Embedding, self).__init__()
        # multi-layer bidirectional GRU with input dimension
          word_dim and hidden state dimension state_dim
        self.rnn = nn.GRU(word_dim, state_dim, num_layers =
            rnn_layer, bidirectional = True, batch_first = True)

    # Input:
    # x: the input word vectors. Size: batch × seq_len × word_dim.
      batch is number of text samples, seq_len is the maximum number
      of words in one text sample, and word_dim is the dimension of
      word vectors.
    # Output:
    # res: contextual embeddings for all words. Size: batch ×
      seq_len × out_dim
    def forward(self, x):
        # contextual embedding. Size: batch × seq_len × out_dim,
          where out_dim = 2 × state_dim.
        res, _ = self.rnn(x)
        return res
```

Moreover, researchers find that if the model is first pretrained on large-scale text corpora and then fine-tuned for MRC tasks, there will be a significant improvement of performance. For example, the CoVe model [1] trains a sequence-to-sequence (seq2seq) model on large-scale machine translation data, and then uses the RNN in the encoder for the SQuAD dataset, which improves the $F1$ score of answer by nearly 4%. In Chapter 6, Pretrained Language Model, we will introduce the application of pretrained models in MRC.

In summary, for each question word, the encoding layer produces word embeddings, NER embeddings, POS embeddings, character embeddings, and contextual embeddings. Each article word has an additional exact match embedding.

4.3 Interaction layer

The encoding layer of an MRC model obtains semantic representations of each word in the article and question. However, it does not contain any mutual information. In order to get the correct answer, the model needs to grasp the relationship between the article and the question. Therefore the interaction layer fuses the semantic information from the article and question to obtain a deeper understanding of both parts.

4.3.1 Cross-attention

The input to the interaction layer includes the article word vectors $(p_1, p_2, \ldots, p_m)$ and the question word vectors $(q_1, q_2, \ldots, q_n)$. Most interaction layers employ the attention mechanism introduced in Section 3.4 to process the semantic relationship between the article and the question. Recall that the input to attention mechanism includes a vector x and a group of vectors $A = (a_1, a_2, \ldots, a_n)$. The attention mechanism then summarizes A from the perspective of x, and obtains the part of information within A that is related to x. The result of this summarization is an attention vector x^A, which is a linear combination of vectors in A. Vectors in A that are more similar to x are assigned a larger weight.

For example, suppose x is the word vector of *like*, and $A = (a_1, a_2, a_3)$ contains the word vectors of *I*, *love*, and *soccer*. The attention vector can be $x^A = 0.1 \times a_1 + 0.85 \times a_2 + 0.05 \times a_3$.

In MRC, we can use the attention mechanism to obtain the attention vectors for each article word. In other words, each time the model sets $x = p_i$ and $A = (q_1, q_2, \ldots, q_n)$.

Section 3.4 introduces the attention function which assigns scores. The attention function should reflect the similarity between vectors p_i and q_j. Common forms of attention functions include:

- inner product function: $s_{i,j} = f(p_i, a_j) = p_i^T q_j$, which can be employed when p_i and q_j have the same dimensions;
- quadratic function: $s_{i,j} = f(p_i, q_j) = p_i^T W q_j$, where W is a learnable parameter matrix;
- additive function: $s_{i,j} = f(p_i, q_j) = v^T tanh(W_1 p_i + W_2 q_j)$, where W_1 and W_2 are parameter matrices and v is a parameter vector; and
- bitransformational function: $s_{i,j} = f(p_i, q_j) = p_i^T U^T V q_j$, where $p_i \in R^{a \times 1}$, $U \in R^{d \times a}$, $V \in R^{d \times b}$, $q_j \in R^{b \times 1}$ and $d < a, d < b$. This function converts both article and question word vectors into a lower dimension for multiplication, which saves many parameters.

After the attention function computes the attention scores $s_{i,j}$ for each q_j, the softmax function normalizes the scores into attention weights:

$$\beta_{i,j} = \frac{e^{s_{i,j}}}{\sum_{k=1}^{n} e^{s_{i,k}}}$$

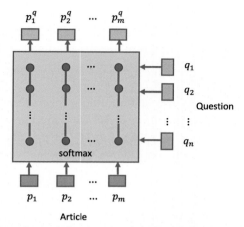

Figure 4.4 The attention mechanism in the interaction layer. Each article word vector p_i obtains a linear combination, p_i^q, of the question word vectors via the attention function.

Finally, the attention vector p_i^q is the weighted sum of $(q_1, q_2, \ldots, q_n)$:

$$p_i^q = \beta_{i,1} q_1 + \beta_{i,2} q_2 + \ldots + \beta_{i,n} q_n$$

We denote the whole process by the *Attention* function:

$$Attention((p_1, p_2, \ldots, p_m), (q_1, q_2, \ldots, q_n)) = (p_1^q, p_2^q, \ldots, p_m^q)$$

Fig. 4.4 illustrates the attention mechanism above. Note that the number of attention vectors is m, the same as the number of article words. Each attention vector p_i^q is a linear combination of all question word vectors, but the weights come from the semantic similarity between the article and the question. Thus each article word w focuses on the part of the question which is more related to w.

Similarly, we can also compute the attention vectors from the question to the article, that is, q_i^p, $1 \le i \le n$. In this way, the model will comprehend the semantics of each question word based on its relationship to the article. The two attention mechanisms above are referred to as **cross–attention**.

4.3.2 Self-attention

RNN transfers information in a linear way: from left to right or from right to left. In this process, the information of a word decays when the distance increases. As a result, there is very little information transmitted between words at the beginning of a long article and those at the end. However, some answers require a mutual understanding of distant parts in the article.

To solve this problem, we can use the **self–attention** mechanism. Self-attention is very similar to cross–attention. The only difference is that self-attention computes the attention vectors from a vector group to itself:

$$Self - Attention((p_1, p_2, \ldots, p_m), (p_1, p_2, \ldots, p_m)) = (p_1^{self}, p_2^{self}, \ldots, p_m^{self})$$

Code 4-3 implements the self-attention mechanism. The attention function employs a parameter matrix W to project a vector to a lower dimensional space, that is, $f(p_i, p_j) = p_i^T W^T W p_j$. This can effectively reduce time and space complexity when the original vectors have a high dimension.

Code 4-3 Computing self-attention

```
class SelfAttention(nn.Module):
    # dim: dimension of input vectors
    # hidden_dim: the (lower) projection dimension in attention
    def __init__(self, dim, hidden_dim):
        super(SelfAttention, self).__init__()
        # parameter matrix W
        self.W = nn.Linear(dim, hidden_dim)

# Input:
# x: the group of vectors for self-attention. Size: batch × n × dim
# Output:
# attended: attention vectors. Size: batch × n × dim
def forward(self, x):
    # project x to a lower dimensional space. Size: batch × n ×
        hidden_dim
    hidden = self.W(x)
    # compute attention scores. Size: batch × n × n
    scores = hidden.bmm(hidden.transpose(1, 2))
    # softmax over the last dimension
    alpha = F.softmax(scores, dim=-1)
    # attention vectors. Size: batch × n × dim
    attended = alpha.bmm(x)
    return attended
```

In self-attention, the attention scores of all word pairs are computed regardless of their locations in the text. This allows information between words at any distance to directly interact, greatly improving the efficiency. Furthermore, since the attention score for each word is independent, parallel computing can be used to expedite the process. In comparison, RNN cannot be parallelized at different text locations due to its dependency on previous hidden states.

However, the self-attention mechanism discards the positional information of words, which is important in understanding language. Therefore self-attention is usually used in conjunction with RNN. In addition, Section 6.4 will introduce positional encoding to add positional information into self-attention.

4.3.3 Contextual embeddings

The interaction layer in MRC also leverages contextual embeddings. RNN is typically used as in the encoding layer. As a result, the interaction layer usually incorporates multiple modules for cross-attention, self-attention, and contextual encoding. Take the module processing the article as an example: cross-attention obtains information from the question, self-attention gets the semantic relationship among article words, and contextual embedding transfers word meanings. A repeated usage of these modules enables the model to better comprehend the words, sentences, and article, as well as integrating the question meaning to improve the accuracy of answer prediction.

As the interaction layer has a very flexible usage of various modules, it becomes the most diverse and important part of any MRC models. For instance, the BiDAF model uses RNN → cross-attention → RNN in the interaction layer, the r-net model uses RNN → cross-attention → RNN → self-attention → RNN, and the FusionNet model uses cross-attention → RNN → self-attention → RNN.

However, it is worth noting that as the structure of the interaction layer becomes more and more complex, the huge parameter space and very deep network structure may cause problems for optimization such as gradient explosion/vanishing and slow convergence. Therefore it is better to start with fewer layers and gradually add modules for attention and contextual encoding, while closely monitoring the effect on the validation data. Various techniques can be applied to improve the optimization performance, for example, dropout, gradient clipping, learning rate schedules.

4.4 Output layer

After the encoding and interaction layers, the model has already obtained necessary semantic information from the article and question, which contains clues to the answer. Thus the output layer needs to collect these analyzed information and generate the answer in the required format. The output layer should also construct an effective loss function for optimization.

4.4.1 Construct the question vector

The interaction layer produces vector representation for all n question words: $(q_1, q_2, \ldots, q_n)$. In order to facilitate answer generation from the article, the question information needs to be condensed into one single vector q.

Section 3.1 describes three ways to produce a text vector from multiple word vectors. All these methods can generate the question vector q from $(q_1, q_2, \ldots, q_n)$. Take the parameterized weighted sum as an example, we first set up a parameter vector b which has the same dimension as each q_i. We then use the inner product function to calculate a score for each word: $s_i = b^T q_i$. These scores are then normalized by the softmax function: $(w_1, w_2, \ldots, w_n) = softmax\,(s_1, s_2, \ldots, s_n)$. Finally, we compute a weighted sum of all question word vectors and obtain a single vector representing the question: $q = \sum_{i=1}^{n} w_i q_i$.

4.4.2 Generate multiple-choice answers

In an MRC dataset with multiple-choice answers, several choices are given together with the article and question. A common approach is to let the output layer produce a score for each choice and selects the choice with the highest score.

Suppose there are a total of K choices. The model can encode the semantics of each choice in a similar way as the question: embed each choice word into a vector, compute attention vector with the question and article, and obtain a choice vector c_k representing the semantics of the kth choice. Suppose in the output layer, the article is represented by vectors $(p_1, p_2, \ldots, p_m)$ and the question vector is q. Here are two possible ways to compute scores for choices:

- Use methods in Section 4.4.1 to get a single article vector p. The choice score can then be computed as: $s_k = p^T W_c c_k + p^T W_q q$, where W_c and W_q are parameter matrices.
- Concatenate the question vector q and the choice vector c_k: $t_k = [q; c_k]$. Use t_k as the initial hidden state of an RNN, and take $(p_1, p_2, \ldots, p_m)$ as the input. The RNN outputs the hidden states $(h_1, h_2, \ldots, h_m)$. The score for the choice is then the inner product of the last hidden state h_m and a parameter vector b: $s_k = h_m^T b$.

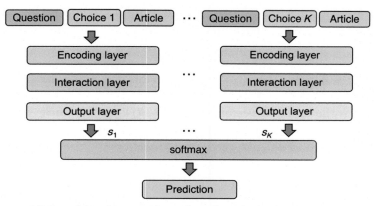

Figure 4.5 MRC model architecture for tasks with multiple-choice answers.

As the selection of the correct choice is a classification problem, it belongs to the category of natural language understanding. Thus, the output layer can employ the cross entropy loss function. In detail, the softmax operation normalizes the scores $\{s_k\}_{k=1}^{K}$ into probabilities $\{p_k\}_{k=1}^{K}$ and the loss function is $f_{cross\_entropy} = -\log(p_{k^*})$, if the correct choice is the k^*th one. The process is shown in Fig. 4.5.

It's worth noting that the model uses the same network to calculate scores for each choice, so the number of parameters does not change with the number of choices.

4.4.3 Generate extractive answers

An extractive answer is a continuous segment in the article. If an article has m words, there are $m(m+1)/2$ possible extractive answers. In practice, the answer length is usually bounded. For example, for the SQuAD dataset, most models limit the maximum length of generated answer to be 15 words, based on statistics from the training data. However, even if the answer contains at most L words, there are still approximately $L \times m$ possible answers. Thus the answer selection cannot be framed as a classification problem since there will be too many categories.

To solve this problem, most MRC models predict the start and end position of the extractive answer within the article. The output layer calculates two scores for each word, that is, g_i^S and g_i^F, which correspond to the probability that the ith article word is the first word in the answer and the probability that the ith article word is the last word in the answer. One way to compute these scores is as follows:

$$g_i^S = q^T W_S p_i$$

$$g_i^E = q^T W_E p_i$$

where q is the question vector, $(p_1, p_2, \ldots, p_m)$ are the article word vectors, and W_S and W_E are parameter matrices. Next, the scores are normalized into probabilities by the softmax function:

$$P_1^S, P_2^S \ldots, P_m^S = softmax\left(g_1^S, g_2^S, \ldots g_m^S\right)$$

$$P_1^E, P_2^E \ldots, P_m^E = softmax(g_1^E, g_2^E, \ldots g_m^E)$$

In the above process, the probabilities for the answer's start position and end position are independent of each other. Alternatively, the model can transfer information between the two components. For instance, FusionNet [2] uses a GRU to conduct a single-step RNN computation before calculating probability for the end position:

$$v = GRU\left(q, \sum_i P_i^S p_i\right)$$

The output hidden state v is used to calculate the score for the end position: $g_i^E = v^T W_E p_i$. In this way, it establishes an association between the prediction of the answer's start position and end position.

Since the prediction above is a multiclass classification task, we can use the cross entropy loss function. Suppose the correct answer starts from the $i*$th word and ends at the $j*$th word in the article, the loss function value is:

$$f_{cross\,entropy} = -\log\left(P_{i*}^S\right) - \log\left(P_{j*}^E\right)$$

To find the most likely answer position, the model selects the start position i^R and end position j^R corresponding to the maximum prediction probability. All the words in-between form the answer.

$$i^R, j^R = \underset{1 \le i \le j \le m, j - i + 1 \le L}{argmax} P_i^S P_j^E$$

Here, L is the maximum number of words in an answer. Fig. 4.6 shows an example of extractive answer selection where $L = 4$. The answer with the highest probability is selected: *the capital of USA*.

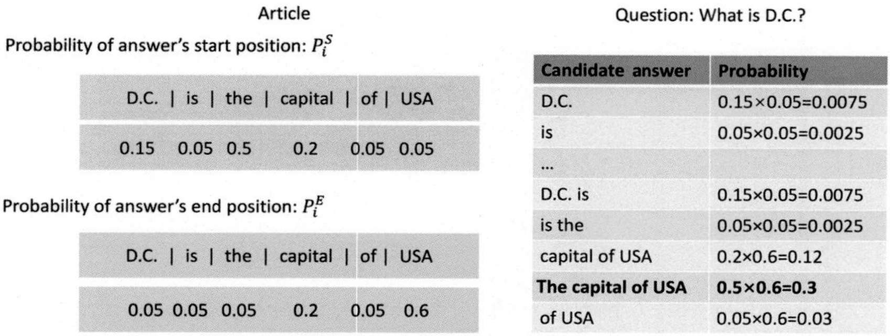

Article   Question: What is D.C.?

Probability of answer's start position: P_i^S

D.C.	is	the	capital	of	USA
0.15	0.05	0.5	0.2	0.05	0.05

Probability of answer's end position: P_i^E

D.C.	is	the	capital	of	USA
0.05	0.05	0.05	0.2	0.05	0.6

Candidate answer	Probability
D.C.	0.15×0.05=0.0075
is	0.05×0.05=0.0025
...	
D.C. is	0.15×0.05=0.0075
is the	0.05×0.05=0.0025
capital of USA	0.2×0.6=0.12
The capital of USA	**0.5×0.6=0.3**
of USA	0.05×0.6=0.03

Figure 4.6 Predict extractive answers. The maximum answer length is set at $L = 4$ words.

Code 4-4 implements how to select the optimal start and end positions for the answer given the prediction probabilities. The tensor *prob_s* of length m contains the probability that the answer starts from each article word; the tensor *prob_e* of length m contains the probability that the answer ends at each article word. L is the maximum number of words in the predicted answer.

Code 4-4 Generating extractive answer

```
import torch
import numpy as np
# Input:
# the article has m words
# prob_s of size m is the probability that the answer starts from
  each article word
# prob_e of size m is the probability that the answer ends at each
  article word
# L is the maximum number of words in the predicted answer
# Output:
# best_start, best_end indicate the start and end positions with the
  highest probability
def get_best_interval (prob_s, prob_e, L):
    # obtain an m x m matrix prob, where prob[ i, j] = prob_s[ i] x
      prob_e[ j]
    prob = torch.ger (prob_s, prob_e)
    # limit prob to contain only valid start-end position pairs, i.e.
      prob[ I, j] ←0 if i>j or j-i+1>L
    prob.triu_().tril_(L - 1)
    # convert prob into a numpy array
    prob = prob.numpy()
```

(Continued)

(Continued)

```
    # the predicted answer starts from the best_start-th word and
      ends at the best_end-th word, with the highest probability
    best_start, best_end = np.unravel_index(np.argmax(prob), prob.
      shape)
    return best_start, best_end
```

The code above uses the *torch.ger* function, which generates a matrix S from two 1D vectors x and y, where $S[i, j] = x[i] \times y[j]$. Then, it uses the *triu_* function to obtain an upper-triangular matrix, ensuring that the start position is no later than the end position. And the *tril_* function ensures that the end position is less than the start position plus L.

4.4.4 Generate freestyle answers

A freestyle answer consists of words and phrases not necessarily from the article. The generation of freestyle answers is an natural language generation process. Therefore the output layer usually takes the form of the seq2seq architecture, also known as the encoder—decoder model.

The encoder gets the article word vectors from the interactive layer, $(p_1, p_2, \ldots, p_m)$, and then uses a bidirectional RNN to process these embeddings. As a result, each word has a hidden state h_i^{enc}. Here, we can use the question vector q as the initial hidden state of RNN.

The decoder uses a unidirectional RNN to produce answer words one at a time. The initial hidden state h_0^{dec} is set to be the last encoder state h_m^{enc}. As introduced in Section 3.3.1, the first answer word is generally set to be the special symbol $<s>$. The output hidden state from the RNN cell, h_1^{dec}, is used to produce the next answer word.

Suppose the vocabulary has $|V|$ words, and each word vector has a dimension of d. The model creates a fully connected layer of size $d \times |V|$ to convert h_1^{dec} into a $|V|$-dim vector (if the dimension of h_1^{dec} is not d, we can first use another fully connected layer to convert it into d-dim), representing the scores assigned to each word in the vocabulary. These scores are normalized by softmax into probabilities: $P_1, P_2, \ldots, P_{|V|}$. During training, if the first word in the correct answer is the ith word in the vocabulary, the cross entropy loss function for this position has a value of:

$$f_{cross_{entropy}}(\boldsymbol{\theta}) = -\log(P_i)$$

where $\boldsymbol{\theta}$ stands for the network parameters.

Next, h_1^{dec} is passed to the second RNN cell. If teacher forcing is used, this cell uses the embedding of the first word in the ground-truth answer; otherwise it uses the embedding of the first generated word with the highest probability. This RNN cell generates the probability distribution for the second word and the process goes on until a maximum answer length is reached or the end symbol $</s>$ is generated.

In practice, the encoder's word embeddings, decoder's word embeddings, and the final fully connected layer share the parameters, which are of size $d \times |V|$ or $|V| \times d$. This will not only save the number of parameters but also improve the efficiency and quality of training.

In addition, the vocabulary takes a special symbol $<UNK>$ to represent words not in it. Therefore the decoder may produce $<UNK>$ at certain locations in the answer. One trick to improve accuracy is to replace all the produced $<UNK>$ tokens with randomly selected article words, since this will not reduce the accuracy while removing these special symbols.

4.4.4.1 Application of attention mechanism

The words at different locations in the answer may be related to different sections in the article. However, the only article information transferred to the decoder is the final hidden state vector of the encoder RNN, h_m^{enc}. Thus it is difficult for a single state vector to accurately retain information from the whole article. Therefore, the attention mechanism is often applied in the decoder to provide information about the article in more detail.

As introduced in Section 3.4.3, when the decoder generates the ith answer word, it computes the attention vector between h_{i-1}^{dec} and all encoder states $h_1^{enc}, h_2^{enc}, \ldots, h_m^{enc}$, also known as the context vector:

$$Attention\left(h_{i-1}^{dec}, \left(h_1^{enc}, h_2^{enc}, \ldots, h_m^{enc}\right)\right) = c_{i-1}$$

The context vector c_{i-1} is a linear combination of the encoder's hidden vectors, and it carries the relevant article information for the current decoding step. c_{i-1} is then fed into the decoder RNN. As the context vector varies with each decoding step, it enables the decoder to focus on different parts of the article as each answer word is produced.

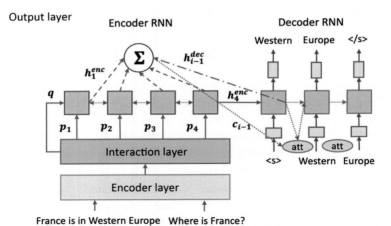

Figure 4.7 The output layer uses the encoder−decoder architecture with attention mechanism. The yellow block below the decoder represents the word vector, and the yellow block above represents the fully connected layer for word generation. The circle around *att* stands for the attention mechanism.

Fig. 4.7 illustrates an output layer based on the encoder−decoder architecture with attention mechanism. The decoder computes the context vector at each step and feeds it into the RNN to generate the next word.

Code 4-5 implements an output layer to generate freestyle answers, which includes an encoder, a decoder, and attention mechanism. The code assumes that the dimension of RNN's hidden state is the same as that of the word vector, that is, *word_dim*, and the encoder employs a one-way RNN. In practice, we can use *nn.Linear* to convert between any two dimensions.

Code 4-5 Output layer for freestyle answer generation

```
import torch.optim as optim
class Seq2SeqOutputLayer(nn.Module):
    # word_dim: dimension of question vector and article word vectors
      from the interaction layer
    # embed: the word embedder module from the encoding layer, i.e.
      nn.Embedding(vocab_size, word_dim)
    # vocab_size: size of the vocabulary
    def __init__(self, embed, word_dim, vocab_size):
        super(Seq2SeqOutputLayer, self).__init__()
        # reuse the word embedder from the encoding layer
        self.embed = embed
```

(Continued)

(Continued)

```
    self.vocab_size = vocab_size
    # encoder RNN is a single-layer one-way GRU
    self.encoder_rnn = nn.GRU(word_dim, word_dim, batch_first
       = True)
    # decoder RNN cell (GRU)
    self.decoder_rnncell = nn.GRUCell(word_dim, word_dim)
    # convert the concatenation of hidden state and attention
       vector into a vector of dimension word_dim
    self.combine_state_attn = nn.Linear(word_dim + word_dim,
       word_dim)
    # fully connected layer for generating word scores
    self.linear = nn.Linear(word_dim, vocab_size, bias = False)
    # share parameters between the fully connected layer and
       word embedder
    self.linear.weight = embed.weight

# Input:
# x: article word vectors from the interaction layer. Size: batch
    × x_seq_len × word_dim
# q: question vector from the interaction layer. Size: batch ×
    word_dim
#  y_id: word ids of ground-truth answers. Size: batch ×
    y_seq_len
# Output:
# scores: predicted scores of each answer word. Size: batch ×
    y_seq_len × vocab_size
 def forward(self, x, q, y_id):
    # embed the words in ground-truth answers. Size: batch ×
       y_seq_len × word_dim
    y = self.embed(y_id)
    # the encoder RNN takes question vector q as the initial
       state
    # enc_states are the hidden states of each article word.
       Size: batch × x_seq_len × word_dim
    # enc_last_state is the last hidden state. Size: 1 × batch
       × word_dim
    enc_states, enc_last_state = self.encoder_rnn(x,
       q.unsqueeze(0))
    # enc_last_state is used as the initial state of the decoder
       RNN. Size: batch × word_dim
```

(Continued)

(Continued)

```
        prev_dec_state = enc_last_state.squeeze(0)
        # scores contains the scores assigned to answer words at
          each position
        scores = torch.zeros(y_id.shape[0], y_id.shape[1], self.
          vocab_size)
        for t in range(0, y_id.shape[1]):
            # feed the previous hidden state and the word vector of
              the t-th word in the ground-truth answer into the
              decoder RNN. Size: batch × word_dim
            new_state = self.decoder_rnncell(y[:,t,:].squeeze(1),
              prev_dec_state)
            # use the attention function in Section 3.4 to obtain the
              attention vector. Size: batch × word_dim
            context = attention(enc_states, new_state.unsqueeze(1)).
              squeeze(1)
            # convert the concatenation of hidden state and attention
              vector into word_dim-dimension. Size: batch ×
              word_dim
            new_state = self.combine_state_attn(torch.cat
              ((new_state, context), dim=1))
            # predict the scores for all dictionary words
            scores[:, t, :] = self.linear(new_state)
            # pass the new hidden state to the next GRU cell
            prev_dec_state = new_state
        return scores

# 100 words
vocab_size = 100
# word vectors are 20D
word_dim = 20
embed = nn.Embedding(vocab_size, word_dim)
# word ids of 30 ground-truth answers, each with 8 words
y_id = torch.LongTensor(30, 8).random_(0, vocab_size)
# the encoding and interaction layers are omitted here, replaced by
  randomized tensors
# the interaction layer outputs:
# 1) article word vectors x. Size: 30 × x_seq_len × word_dim
# 2) question vector q. Size: 30 × word_dim
x = torch.randn(30, 10, word_dim)
q = torch.randn(30, word_dim)
```

(Continued)

```
(Continued)
# set up the network
net = Seq2SeqOutputLayer(embed, word_dim, vocab_size)
optimizer = optim.SGD(net.parameters(), lr=0.1)
# get the scores for words at each position. Size: 30 × y_seq_len ×
    vocab_size
word_scores = net(x, q, y_id)
# nn.CrossEntropyLoss contains both softmax and cross entropy
    computation
loss_func = nn.CrossEntropyLoss()
# convert word_scores into a 2D tensor and y_id into a 1D tensor to
    calculate the loss
# word_scores contain scores for the 2nd, 3rd, 4th... word, so it is
    offset by 1 position before comparing with y_id
loss = loss_func(word_scores[ :,:-1,:].contiguous().view
    (-1, vocab_size), y_id[ :,1:].contiguous().view(-1))
optimizer.zero_grad()
loss.backward()
optimizer.step()
```

The code above reuses the encoder's word embedding matrix *embed* as the decoder's embedding matrix and the final fully connected layer. In each decoding step, the decoder uses the *attention* function from Section 3.4 to calculate the context vector which is concatenated with the hidden state of RNN. The resulting vector is passed to the next RNN and used to compute the scores of each word in the dictionary. Note that the decoder uses a GRU cell instead of a full GRU module since at each step it only needs to predict the next word. Furthermore, the decoding uses teacher-forcing, that is, the ground-truth answer word is used as input to predict the next word.

4.4.4.2 Copy-generate mechanism

The encoder—decoder architecture has been widely used in various text generation tasks such as MRC, machine translation, and conversation generation. However, the MRC task has a unique feature, which is that the answer must be related to the article, and it often directly quotes text within the article. On the other hand, the predefined dictionary may not contain all article words, especially keywords like proper nouns. As a result, the model may produce <UNK> symbols, which affects the performance. To solve this problem, we can use the **copy-generate mechanism** [3] which allows the model to directly copy a word from the article, regardless of whether it is in the dictionary.

In the copy-generate mechanism, the next word can be generated from the dictionary or copied from the article. Therefore the decoder needs to produce three probabilities:

1. the probability to generate each dictionary word w: $P_g(w)$;
2. the probability to copy the ith word w_i from the article: $P_c(i)$; and
3. the probability to generate instead of copying in this step: P_{gen}.

Then, the decoder combines the distributions to obtain the final distribution over words:

$$P(w) = (1 - P_{gen}) \sum_{w_i = w} P_c(i) + P_{gen} P_g(w)$$

To obtain $P_c(i)$, we can reuse the normalized attention weights in the attention mechanism at this step.

To generate $P_{gen} \in [0, 1]$, we can utilize the context vector c_{i-1}, the previous hidden state h_{i-1}^{dec}, and the current input word vector t_{i-1}:

$$P_{gen} = \sigma\left(w_c^T c_{i-1} + w_h^T h_{i-1}^{dec} + w_t^T t_{i-1} + b\right) \in R$$

where w_c^T, w_h^T, w_t^T, b are parameters and σ is the sigmoid function.

As the copy-generate mechanism enlarges the source of generated words, it can effectively improve the richness and accuracy of generated answers. Fig. 4.8 illustrates the copy-generate mechanism. As shown, the final prediction of word distribution comes from both the decoder's generation probabilities and the encoder's copying probabilities, that is, attention weights.

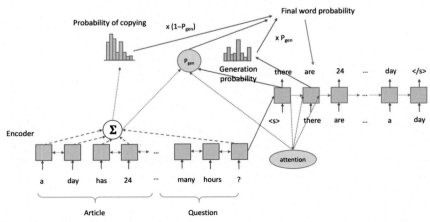

Figure 4.8 Copy-generate mechanism.

4.5 Summary

- The general architecture of an MRC model consists of the **encoding layer**, the **interaction layer**, and the **output layer**.
- The encoding layer generates word embeddings, NER embeddings, POS embeddings, character embeddings, exact match embeddings, and contextual embeddings.
- The interaction layer fuses the information from the article and the question, and usually employs the cross-attention mechanism.
- The output layer generates answers in the required format. A classification model is used for producing multiple-choice and extractive answers, and an encoder—decoder model is used for producing free-style answers.
- The **copy-generate mechanism** allows the model to directly copy article words, including those not from the predefined dictionary.

References

[1] McCann B, Bradbury J, Xiong C, Socher R. Learned in translation: contextualized word vectors. Advances in neural information processing systems. 2017. p. 6294—305.
[2] Huang HY, Zhu C, Shen Y, Chen W. Fusionnet: fusing via fully-aware attention with application to machine comprehension. arXiv preprint arXiv 2017; 1711.07341.
[3] Gu J, Lu Z, Li H, Li VO. Incorporating copying mechanism in sequence-to-sequence learning. arXiv preprint arXiv 2016; 1603.06393.

CHAPTER 5

Common machine reading comprehension models

5.1 Bidirectional attention flow model

The **Bidirectional Attention Flow (BiDAF)** model [1] was proposed in 2016. It is based on the attention mechanism between article and questions. BiDAF is one of the pioneering works in machine reading comprehension (MRC), which formally establishes the structure of an MRC model: encoding, interaction, and output layers. Also, the implementation of the attention mechanism in BiDAF has become the standard for many subsequent approaches.

5.1.1 Encoding layer

BiDAF leverages three types of encoding introduced in Section 4.2 for both article and question words: word embeddings, character embeddings, and contextual embeddings. The word vectors come from the GloVe embeddings and they are locked during training, that is, the embeddings are not updated. This reduces the number of parameters in the optimization. The character embeddings are obtained by convolutional neural network (CNN) and max-pooling.

BiDAF concatenates the word embedding and character embedding of each word into a vector of dimension d, which is fed into a **highway network** [2]. The input to a highway network is a vector x. The network computes a weighted sum of x and the $H(x)$, where H is a network layer. The weights depend on the gate function $T(x)$:

$$y = H(x) \odot T(x) + x \odot (1 - T(x))$$

Here, the $\odot$ function refers to the elementwise multiplication of two vectors. For example:

$$[1, 2, 3] \odot [4, 5, 6] = [4, 10, 18]$$

Therefore the highway network selectively uses the original input x and the layer output $H(x)$ in each dimension, which makes part of the

Machine Reading Comprehension. DOI: https://doi.org/10.1016/B978-0-323-90118-5.00005-9
© 2021 Beijing Huazhang Graphics & Information Co., Ltd/China Machine Press.
Published by Elsevier Inc. All rights reserved.

final derivative directly dependent on the input x. This reduces the average chain length when applying the chain rule to compute the gradients, alleviating the problem of gradient explosion and vanishing.

In a typical highway network, $H(x) = tanh(W_H x + b_H)$ and $T(x) = \sigma(W_T x + b_T)$, where W_H, b_H, W_T, b_T are parameters. It is worth noting that the output vector y has the same dimension as the input vector x.

BiDAF feeds the output of the highway network into a bidirectional long short-term memory (LSTM) and obtains the contextual embedding for each word. Because the recurrent neural network (RNN) has two directions, the output of the encoding layer is a $2d$-dimensional vector for each article and question word.

5.1.2 Interaction layer

BiDAF employs the attention mechanism in the interaction layer to obtain mutual semantic information between the article and the question. Prior to the BiDAF model, there were three common types of attention mechanism in MRC:

- Representing the article with a vector and then conduct attention. However, it is very hard to embed the semantics of a long article into a single vector.
- Using multihop attention, which is time-consuming and cannot be parallelized.
- One-way attention, that is, only attend from the article to the question.

BiDAF proposes to apply a bidirectional attention mechanism: from the article to the question and vice versa. Furthermore, BiDAF retains each word vector in the process. Finally, BiDAF uses a memory-less mode: all attention modules are computed independently to avoid error accumulation. These innovations make BiDAF better understand the semantic relationship between the article and the question.

5.1.2.1 Attend from article to question

BiDAF uses cross-attention, as described in Section 4.3, from the article to the question (**Context-to-Query Attention, C2Q**). First, the encoding layer obtains m article word vectors with a dimension of $2d$: $H = (h_1, h_2, \ldots, h_m)$, and n question word vectors with a dimension of $2d$: $U = (u_1, u_2, \ldots, u_n)$. Next, the model computes the attention scores between each pair of article and question words. The ith article word and the jth question word receive a score of:

$$s_{i,j} = w_S^T[h_i; q_j; h_i \odot q_j]$$

where $h_i \odot q_j$ represents the elementwise multiplication of the two vectors. Note that if $w_S = [0, \ldots 0; 0, \ldots 0; 1, \ldots, 1]$, $s_{i,j}$ is essentially the inner product h_i and q_j. Therefore this attention function is an extension of the inner product.

The model then normalizes $s_{i,j}$ by softmax to get the attention weights $\beta_{i,j}$, based on which the attention vector $\tilde{u}_i$ is computed:

$$\beta_{i,j} = \frac{e^{s_{i,j}}}{\sum_{k=1}^n e^{s_{i,k}}}$$

$$\tilde{u}_i = \beta_{i,1}u_1 + \beta_{i,2}u_2 + \cdots + \beta_{i,n}u_n, \ 1 \le i \le m$$

$$\tilde{U} = [\tilde{u}_1; \tilde{u}_2; \ldots; \tilde{u}_m]$$

5.1.2.2 Attend from question to article

The attention from question to article (**Query-to-Context Attention, Q2C**) in BiDAF is not simply symmetric to the article-to-question attention. BiDAF reuses the attention scores in C2Q, that is, $s_{i,j}$. For each article word w_i, the model computes the maximum similarity score: $t_i = \max_{1 \le j \le n} s_{i,j}$. Then, these scores are normalized by softmax to compute a weighted sum of article word vectors, $\tilde{h}$:

$$b_i = \frac{e^{t_i}}{\sum_{j=1}^m e^{t_j}}$$

$$\tilde{h} = b_1 h_1 + b_2 h_2 + \cdots + b_n h_n$$

Finally, the column vector $\tilde{h}$ is repeated m times to obtain the matrix $\tilde{H} = [\tilde{h}; \tilde{h}; \ldots; \tilde{h}]$. Fig. 5.1 illustrates an example of $m = 4$ article words and $n = 3$ question words. The 4D vector t is obtained by taking maximum over each row of $\{s_{i,j}\}$, which is normalized into b. The vector b is employed to compute a weighted sum of all article word vectors, $\tilde{h}$, which is repeated four times to get the matrix $\tilde{H}$.

Note that both the result of C2Q attention, $\tilde{U}$, and the result of Q2C attention, $\tilde{H}$, have a dimension of $2d \times m$. Therefore, like the article word vectors H, they all represent semantics of the articles, but $\tilde{U}$ and $\tilde{H}$ also contain a mutual understanding of question.

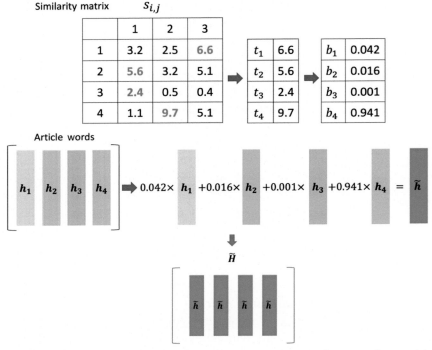

Figure 5.1 The query-to-context (Q2C) attention in BiDAF. There are four article words and three question words.

The final step is to combine the three matrices H, $\tilde{U}$, and $\tilde{H}$:

$$G = \left[H; \tilde{U}; \tilde{H}\right] = \left[g_1; g_2; \ldots, g_m\right]$$

$$g_i = \left[h_i; \tilde{h}; h_i \odot \tilde{h}; h_i \odot \tilde{u}_i\right] \in R^{8d}$$

Now, each article word is represented by a vector g_i with a dimension of $2d + 2d + 2d + 2d = 8d$, which contains the meaning of the word, its context in the article, and the question's meaning.

Finally, these article word vectors pass through a bidirectional RNN to obtain the final vector representations $M = \{m_i\}_{i=1}^m$, each with a dimension of $2d$. These word vectors contain information from both the article's context and the question's meanings.

$$M = LSTM(G) = [m_1; m_2; \ldots, m_m]$$

$$m_i \in R^{2d}$$

5.1.3 Output layer

BiDAF is designed to produce extractive answers. Therefore the output layer predicts the start and end position of the answer based on the article word vectors from the interaction layer. The probability that the answer starts from each position in the article is:

$$\boldsymbol{p}_{begin} = \text{softmax}(\boldsymbol{w}^T_{begin}[\boldsymbol{G}; \boldsymbol{M}])$$

Here, the model concatenates each $\boldsymbol{g}_i$ and $\boldsymbol{m}_i$ into a $10d$-D vector and calculates its inner product with the parameter vector $\boldsymbol{w}_{begin}$, before normalizing by softmax.

Next, BiDAF feeds $\boldsymbol{M}$ into an LSTM to get the hidden states $\boldsymbol{M}_2$, which is used to compute the probability of end positions in a similar way:

$$\boldsymbol{p}_{end} = \text{softmax}(\boldsymbol{w}^T_{end}[\boldsymbol{G}; \boldsymbol{M}_2])$$

BiDAF leverages the cross entropy loss function during training:

$$L(\theta) = -\frac{1}{N} \sum_{i=1}^{N} \left[\log\left(p^i_{begin}\left(y^i_{begin}\right)\right) + \log\left(p^i_{end}\left(y^i_{end}\right)\right) \right]$$

where y^i_{begin} and y^i_{end} refer to the ith ground-truth answer's start and end positions in the article.

The main contribution of the BiDAF model is twofold:
1. BiDAF establishes the MRC model's architecture as an encoding layer, an interaction layer, and a output layer; and
2. BiDAF proposes the standard cross–attention mechanism between the article and the question.

The BiDAF model achieved first place in the SQuAD competition. More importantly, its pioneering architecture and attention mechanism have significantly impacted later MRC models.

5.2 R-NET

After the BiDAF model, the majority of research in MRC has focused on the interaction layer, especially the contextual embedding and attention mechanism. As a typical example, R-NET [3] proposes a gating mechanism in attention, which dynamically controls the model to utilize information from various sources and achieves impressive results.

5.2.1 Gated attention-based recurrent network

Section 3.4 describes the sequence-to-sequence model based on the attention mechanism, which dynamically assigns weights to different parts of the input sequence. Actually the attention can also be applied in an RNN.

Suppose the article word vectors are $u_1^P, \ldots, u_m^P$ and the question word vectors are $u_1^Q, \ldots, u_n^Q$. If we apply an gated recurrent unit (GRU) on the article words, the GRU unit has two inputs at the tth step: the current word vector u_t^P and the previous hidden state v_{t-1}^P. The attention mechanism can be employed here to incorporate the question information and obtain a context vector c_t:

$$s_j^t = v^T tanh\left(W_u^Q u_j^Q + W_u^P u_t^P + W_v^Q v_{t-1}^P\right)$$

$$\alpha_i^t = \frac{\exp\left(s_i^t\right)}{\sum_j \exp\left(s_j^t\right)}$$

$$c_t = \sum_{i=1}^{n} \alpha_i^t u_i^Q$$

Then, the vector c_t and v_{t-1}^P are fed into the GRU unit to get the next hidden v_t^P:

$$v_t^P = GRU\left(v_{t-1}^P, c_t\right)$$

This attention-based RNN contains both contextual information from the article and related question information. R-NET further makes two improvements to this RNN. First, it concatenates the word vector with the context vector as the RNN input, which emphasizes the impact of the current word on contextual information:

$$v_t^P = GRU\left(v_{t-1}^P, \left[u_t^P; c_t\right]\right)$$

Secondly, R-NET proposes the **gating mechanism**. The gating mechanism is similar to the concept of the highway network in Section 5.1.1: its input is a vector x, and the output controls the portion of each component of x passing through the gate:

$$gate(x) = g \odot x$$

$$g = \sigma(W_g x)$$

where W_g is a square parameter matrix to compute the gate vector g. Since the sigmoid function is used, each component of g is between 0 and 1, equivalent to many "gates" to control the portion of x to pass through. For example, if $g = [0, 0.5, 1], x = [0.7, -0.5, 1.2]$, then $gate(x) = g \odot x = [0, -0.25, 1.2]$, that is, the first component of x is completely discarded, the second component is reduced in half and the third component is completely preserved. R-NET applies the gating mechanism in RNN as follows:

$$v_t^P = \text{GRU}\big(v_{t-1}^P, \text{gate}\big(\big[u_t^P; c_t\big]\big)\big)$$

With the gating mechanism, R-NET can freely control the portion in RNN's input that comes from the current word, that is, u_t^P, and the portion that comes from the question, that is, c_t. This greatly increases the flexibility and expressibility of the network.

5.2.2 Encoding layer

R-NET represents each word in the article and question with a 300D vector from GloVe, obtaining $\{e_t^P\}$ and $\{e_t^Q\}$. Then, R-NET employs a bidirectional character RNN to get the character embeddings c_t^P and c_t^Q as the following. The character RNN converts a word to a character sequence, embeds each character into a vector and feeds them to an RNN. The last hidden state is used as the word's character embedding. Like the character CNN, the character RNN makes the model robust to spelling errors and interprets word semantics by its morphology. Finally, R-NET employs a bidirectional GRU to get the contextual word embeddings:

$$u_t^P = \text{BiGRU}_\text{P}\big(u_{t-1}^P, \big[e_t^P, c_t^P\big]\big)$$

$$u_t^Q = \text{BiGRU}_\text{Q}\big(u_{t-1}^Q, \big[e_t^Q, c_t^Q\big]\big)$$

5.2.3 Interaction layer

R-NET applies the gated attention–based RNN again in the interaction layer, obtaining representations for each article word, h_t^P:

$$h_t^P = \text{GRU}\big(h_{t-1}^P, \text{gate}\big(\big[v_t^P; c_t\big]\big)\big)$$

$$s_j^t = v^T tanh\big(W_v^P v_j^P + W_v^{\tilde{P}} v_t^P\big)$$

$$\alpha_i^t = \frac{\exp\left(s_i^t\right)}{\sum_j \exp\left(s_j^t\right)}$$

$$c_t = \sum_{i=1}^{m} \alpha_i^t v_i^P$$

As shown, the attention is from the article to itself. This self-attention alleviates the problem of information decaying in RNN for far-apart words in the article.

5.2.4 Output layer

R–NET produces extractive answers. First, the model calculates the question vector r^Q by the weighted sum:

$$s_j = v^T \tanh\left(W_u^Q u_j^Q + W_v^Q V_r^Q\right)$$

$$\alpha_i = \frac{\exp(s_i)}{\sum_j \exp(s_j)}$$

$$r^Q = \sum_{i=1}^{n} \alpha_i u_i^Q$$

where V_r^Q is a parameter vector. Then, R–NET calculates the probability that the answer starts from the ith word in the article, α_i^1, and ends at the ith word in the article, α_i^2:

$$s_j^M = v^T \tanh\left(W_h^P h_j^P + W_v^a h_{M-1}^a\right), M = 1, 2$$

$$\alpha_i^M = \frac{\exp\left(s_i^M\right)}{\sum_j \exp\left(s_j^M\right)}$$

$$c_M = \sum_{i=1}^{m} \alpha_i^M h_i^P$$

$$h_M^a = \text{RNN}\left(h_{M-1}^a, c_M\right), \quad h_0^a = r^Q$$

Here, R–NET uses the question vector r^Q as the initial hidden state h_0^a of an RNN cell to compute h_1^a. h_0^a and h_1^a are used to compute the probabilities α_i^1 and α_i^2.

R–NET uses cross entropy as the loss function during optimization:

$$L(\theta) = -\frac{1}{N} \sum_{i=1}^{N} \log\left(\alpha_{y_{begin}^i}^1\right) + \log\left(\alpha_{y_{end}^i}^2\right)$$

where y_{begin}^i and y_{end}^i indicate the ith ground-truth answer's start and end positions in the article.

To summarize, the main contribution of R–NET is its innovation on RNN in MRC. R–NET applies attention in RNN and uses the gating mechanism to achieve a fine-grained control of information transfer. This is very similar to the way humans solve reading comprehension by alternatingly focusing on the article and question.

In March 2017 R–NET took the first place in the SQuAD competition both in single-model and ensemble-model categories, and it stayed at the top for 6 months. In May 2017 R–NET also won the first place in the MS-MARCO competition.

5.3 FusionNet

FusionNet [4] is an MRC model that improves contextual embedding and attention in the multilayer scenario, in terms of both computational efficiency and model accuracy. We first introduce two central concepts of FusionNet: history of word and fully-aware attention.

5.3.1 History of word

In order to extract deeper semantic information, neural networks for MRC often contain multiple layers for attention, contextual embedding, and other types of neural computation. It is generally believed that a lower network layer can process basic text semantics in each word and its surrounding phrases, while a higher network layer is capable of analyzing advanced semantics in a broader scope.

To preserve multiple levels of information, the FusionNet model concatenates the output word vectors from the first layer to the $(i-1)$th network layer as input to the ith layer. This concatenated word vector is called **History of Word (HoW)**, as it contains all levels of encodings applied to the word.

On one hand, history of word enables a deep network to better represent various levels of text meanings. But on the other hand, as the network deepens, the total length of the word vector becomes larger. As a result, the time and space complexity of computation rises, which significantly reduces the efficiency of processing.

For example, suppose an MRC model has a cross-attention layer, a bidirectional RNN layer, and a self-attention layer. If the raw word vector is 300D, each article word vector will be concatenated with a 300D context vector after the cross-attention layer. Suppose the RNN layer has a 400D output, each article word will in total have a vector representation with a dimension of 1000. As the output of the self-attention layer has the same dimension as the input, the final length of each article word vector will be 2000. This dimension will further increase if more network layers are employed, which reduces computational efficiency and affects the quality of optimization.

However, if the model does not keep previous layers' outputs due to efficiency concerns, lower levels of information will be inevitably lost. As shown in Fig. 5.2, each vertical bar refers to a vector representation of a word with corresponding semantics. A darker bar indicates the output from higher network layers. For instance, the article word *David* is interpreted as a person's name by the first layer, a player by the second layer, and a numbered player by the third layer. While the level of semantic understanding gets higher, some low-level details get lost, for example, the number 10 in the question is different from the number 12 in the article, but the highest network

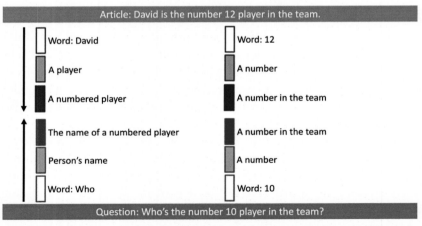

Figure 5.2 Multilayer understanding of article and question. Each vertical bar refers to a vector representation of a word with corresponding semantics. A darker bar indicates the output from higher network layers.

layer considers both of them as *numbers in the team* which well match with each other. As a result, the model incorrectly predicts the answer as *David*. In order to retain multiple levels of information without compromising computational efficiency, FusionNet proposes a fully-aware attention mechanism.

5.3.2 Fully-aware attention

The fully-aware attention takes the history of word as input, that is, $X = (x_1, x_2, \ldots, x_n)$, where $x_i = [x_i^{(1)}, x_i^{(2)}, \ldots, x_i^{(K)}]$ represents the concatenated vector for the ith word from the output of K previous layers. Suppose the model computes the attention from vector y to X. The attention scores and weights are respectively $s_i = x_i^T y$ and $\beta_i = \frac{e^{s_i}}{\sum_j e^{s_j}}$. Next, FusionNet uses the attention weights to calculate the weighted sum of *a certain layer* in history of word to obtain the attention vector, $\tilde{y}$:

$$\tilde{y} = \sum_{i=1}^{n} \beta_i x_i^{(K)}$$

In this way, the output dimension reduces to that of one previous layer, and all historical information is still used in the weights $\{\beta_i\}$. In practice, the fully-aware attention can be applied multiple times to capture richer semantic information, for example, $\tilde{y}_1 = \sum_{i=1}^{n} \beta_i x_i^{(K)}$, $\tilde{y}_2 = \sum_{i=1}^{n} \gamma_i x_i^{(K-1)}$.

Moreover, FusionNet proposes a parametrized attention function:

$$s_i = \text{ReLU}(\mathbf{U}x_i)^T \mathbf{D} \text{ReLU}(\mathbf{U}y)$$

where $x_i \in R^d$, $y \in R^d$, $\mathbf{U} \in R^{c \times d}$, $\mathbf{D} \in R^{c \times c}$, $c < d$. This attention function reduces the dimension via the parameter matrix $\mathbf{U}$ to improve computational efficiency.

5.3.3 Encoding layer

In FusionNet, each word in the article and question is represented by a 300D GloVe vector g and a 600D CoVe vector c (more detail in Section 6.2). In addition, each article word is assigned a 12D part-of-speech (POS) embedding, an 8D named entity recognition (NER) embedding, a 1D word frequency embedding and a 1D exact match embedding (1 if the word appears in the question and 0 otherwise). Therefore each article word is represented by a vector $w_i^C \in R^{922}$, and each question word is represented by $w_i^Q \in R^{900}$.

5.3.4 Interaction layer
5.3.4.1 Word-level attention layer
This layer computes the article-to-question attention, using the 300D GloVe word vectors. Therefore each article word is assigned a 300D attention vector, which is a weighted sum of the question word vectors. As a result, each article word is now represented by a vector $\tilde{w}_i^C$ of dimension $922 + 300 = 1222$.

5.3.4.2 Reading layer
Each article word vector $\tilde{w}_i^C$ and question word vector w_i^Q pass through a two-layer bidirectional LSTM. The lower layer produces $h^l \in R^{250}$ and the higher layer produces $h^h \in R^{250}$:

$$h_1^{Cl}, \ldots h_m^{Cl} = \text{BiLSTM}\left(\tilde{w}_1^C, \ldots, \tilde{w}_m^C\right), \quad h_1^{Ql}, \ldots h_n^{Ql} = \text{BiLSTM}\left(w_1^Q, \ldots, w_n^Q\right),$$

$$h_1^{Ch}, \ldots h_m^{Ch} = \text{BiLSTM}\left(h_1^{Cl}, \ldots h_m^{Cl}\right), \quad h_1^{Qh}, \ldots h_n^{Qh} = \text{BiLSTM}\left(h_1^{Ql}, \ldots h_n^{Ql}\right),$$

5.3.4.3 Question understanding layer
This layer concatenates h^{Ql} and h^{Qh} and feeds it into another bidirectional LSTM to obtain the *final question representation* $u^Q \in R^{250}$:

$$u_1^Q, \ldots u_n^Q = \text{BiLSTM}\left(\left[h_1^{Ql}; h_1^{Qh}\right], \ldots \left[h_n^{Ql}; h_n^{Qh}\right]\right)$$

5.3.4.4 Fully-aware multilevel fusion layer
FusionNet applies the previously introduced fully-aware attention mechanism to the history of word, which is a $300 + 600 + 250 + 250 = 1400$D vector:

$$\mathbf{HoW}_i^C = \left[g_i^C; c_i^C; h_i^{Cl}; h_i^{Ch}\right], \quad \mathbf{HoW}_i^Q = \left[g_i^Q; c_i^Q; h_i^{Ql}; h_i^{Qh}\right]$$

As the resulting attention vector is very long, FusionNet compresses its dimension. Specifically, it computes three levels of fusions, that is, attention:
1. low-level fusion: $\hat{h}_i^{Cl} = \sum_j \alpha_{ij}^l h_j^{Ql}, \alpha_{ij}^l \propto \exp(S^l(\mathbf{HoW}_i^C, \mathbf{HoW}_j^Q));$
2. high-level fusion: $\hat{h}_i^{Ch} = \sum_j \alpha_{ij}^h h_j^{Qh}, \alpha_{ij}^h \propto \exp(S^h(\mathbf{HoW}_i^C, \mathbf{HoW}_j^Q));$ and
3. understanding layer fusion: $\hat{u}_i^C = \sum_j \alpha_{ij}^u u_j^Q, \alpha_{ij}^u \propto \exp(S^u(\mathbf{HoW}_i^C, \mathbf{HoW}_j^Q)).$

where S^l, S^h, and S^u are attention functions in the form $s(x, y) = \text{ReLU}(\mathbf{U}x)^T \mathbf{D}\text{ReLU}(\mathbf{U}y)^T$ with separate parameters. Each fusion results in a 250D vector, far less than the dimension of the history of word.

Afterwards, the representation of article words is processed by a bidirectional LSTM to obtain a 250D vector for each word, $\{v_i^C\}_{i=1}^m$:

$$v_1^C, \ldots v_m^C = \text{BiLSTM}\left(\left[h_1^{Cl}; h_1^{Ch}; \hat{h}_1^{Cl}; \hat{h}_1^{Ch}, \hat{u}_1^C\right], \ldots, \left[h_m^{Cl}; h_m^{Ch}; \hat{h}_m^{Cl}; \hat{h}_m^{Ch}, \hat{u}_m^C\right]\right)$$

5.3.4.5 Fully-aware self-boosted fusion layer

At this stage, the full history of article word has a dimension of $300 + 600 + 250 \times 6 = 2400$:

$$\mathbf{HoW}_i^C = \left[g_i^C; c_i^C; h_i^{Cl}; h_i^{Ch}; \hat{h}_i^{Cl}; \hat{h}_i^{Ch}, \hat{u}_i^C; v_i^C\right] \in R^{2400}$$

The model reuses fully-aware attention and dimension reduction to compute self-attention, obtaining a 250D vector $\hat{v}_i^C$ for each word:

$$\hat{v}_i^C = \sum_j \alpha_{ij}^s v_j^C, \alpha_{ij}^s \propto \exp\left(S^s\left(\mathbf{HoW}_i^C, \mathbf{HoW}_j^C\right)\right)$$

Finally, v_i^C and $\hat{v}_i^C$ are concatenated and fed into a bidirectional LSTM to obtain *the final representation of article words*, $u^C \in R^{250}$:

$$u_1^C, \ldots u_n^C = \text{BiLSTM}\left(\left[v_1^C; \hat{v}_1^C\right], \ldots \left[v_m^C; \hat{v}_m^C\right]\right)$$

5.3.5 Output layer

FusionNet produces extractive answers. Firstly, the output layer uses parametrized weighted sum to get the question vector u^Q:

$$u^Q = \sum_i \beta_i u_i^Q, \beta_i \propto \exp\left(w^T u_i^Q\right)$$

Next, it calculates the probability that the answer starts from each position in the article:

$$P_i^S \propto \exp\left(\left(u^Q\right)^T W_S u_i^C\right)$$

The output layer then employs a GRU unit to compute a new question vector based on P_i^S and u^Q:

$$v^Q = \text{GRU}\left(u^Q, \sum_i P_i^S u_i^C\right)$$

Finally, it calculates the probability that the answer ends at each position in the article:

$$P_i^E \propto \exp\left(\left(v^Q\right)^T W_E u_i^C\right)$$

Here, w, W_S, W_E are parameters. FusionNet uses the cross entropy loss function $L(\theta)$:

$$L(\theta) = -\frac{1}{N}\sum_{i=1}^{N}\left(\log\left(P_{y_{begin}^i}^S\right) + \log\left(P_{y_{end}^i}^E\right)\right)$$

where y_{begin}^i and y_{end}^i refer to the ith ground-truth answer's start and end positions in the article.

The main contribution of FusionNet is its optimization to the computational efficiency for deep MRC networks. The fully-aware attention mechanism is applied to the history of word, which may be a very high-dimensional vector. Thus, FusionNet proposes an effective dimension compression technique. This approach is more and more important as MRC models become deeper and more complex. In October 2017 FusionNet took the first place in the SQuAD competition in both the single-model and ensemble-model categories.

5.4 Essential-term-aware retriever–reader

In corpus-based MRC tasks, there is no given article for a question. Instead, the MRC model needs to retrieve related text from the corpus and find the answer within it. Thus the model must include an efficient and effective retrieval module.

The Essential-Term-Aware Retriever–Reader model (ET-RR) [5] is such a model proposed in 2019 for large-scale corpus-based MRC tasks. The ET-RR model contains a retriever and a reader. The retriever leverages an essential-term selector to greatly improve the quality of retrieved text, and the reader is a network taking the retrieved results, questions, and answer options as input.

5.4.1 Retriever

The retriever aims to return most relevant parts in a massive corpus given a question Q. Typically, the retrieved result is the concatenation of the top S related sentences to Q, which is used as the article in subsequent steps.

The ET-RR model is targeted for multichoice answers. Therefore in addition to the question, there are N choices $C_1, \ldots, C_N$. ET-RR concatenates the question Q with each choice C_i as a query and feeds it into the retriever to obtain an article P_i. Then the reader model computes the probability that C_i is the correct answer given Q and P_i. Finally, the model selects the choice with the highest probability.

Because the reader is only exposed to P_i from the whole corpus, the accuracy of retrieved results, that is, the relevance between P_i and $Q + C_i$, has a large impact on the answer's correctness. In many cases, the question Q contains a lot of background information, resulting in a long description, which severely reduces the quality of retrieved results. Therefore the top priority of a corpus-based MRC model is to improve the quality of retrieval.

In ET-RR, the retriever first selects a number of essential terms in the question and uses the concatenation in the replacement of the question description. These essential terms retain the key information while shortening the query length. In many cases, this can improve the quality of retrieval.

Now the problem becomes how to select essential terms. ET-RR frames this problem as a classification task, that is, to predict whether each word is an essential term of not. ET-RR leverages a neural network ET-Net to solve the task.

In the encoding layer, ET-Net uses GloVe, NER, and POS embeddings for each word in the question and choice. Suppose all the question word vectors are $\boldsymbol{Q} \in R^{q \times d_Q}$ and all the choice word vectors are $\boldsymbol{C} \in R^{c \times d_C}$. Next, ET-Net calculates the attention from the question to the choice:

$$\boldsymbol{M'}_{QC} = \boldsymbol{Q}\boldsymbol{W}_Q(\boldsymbol{C}\boldsymbol{W}_C)^T \in R^{q \times c}$$

$$\boldsymbol{M}_{QC} = \mathrm{softmax}\left(\boldsymbol{M'}_{QC}\right) \in R^{q \times c}$$

$$\boldsymbol{W}_Q^C = \boldsymbol{M}_{QC}(\boldsymbol{C}\boldsymbol{W}_C) \in R^{q \times d}$$

where $\boldsymbol{W}_Q \in R^{d_Q \times d}$ and $\boldsymbol{W}_C \in R^{d_C \times d}$ are parameter matrices to reduce the dimension to d. ET-Net then uses a bidirectional LSTM to get the contextual embeddings $\boldsymbol{H}^Q$:

$$\boldsymbol{H}^Q = \mathrm{BiLSTM}\left(\left[\boldsymbol{Q}; \boldsymbol{W}_Q^C\right]\right)$$

Finally, a fully connected layer computes probability that each question word is an essential term:

$$\boldsymbol{P} = \mathrm{softmax}\left(\left[\boldsymbol{H}^Q; \boldsymbol{Q}\right]\boldsymbol{w}^s\right) \in R^{q \times 1}$$

ET–Net is trained on the public Essentiality Dataset and uses the binary cross entropy loss function. If the predicted probability for a word is greater than 0.5, this word is considered to be an essential keyword.

These essential terms in Q are then concatenated with each choice C_i as a query into the search engine Elastic Search. The top K retrieved sentences are concatenated as the article P_i to the reader module.

5.4.2 Reader

The reader's input includes the question Q, choice C_i, and article P_i. The reader's goal is to generate the possibility that C_i is the correct answer to Q. To simplify notations, we will omit the subscript i in the following analysis.

Similar to ET–Net, the reader represents each input word using GloVe, POS, and NER embeddings, while each article word has additional relation embedding and feature embedding.

5.4.2.1 Relation embedding

ET–RR employs the large-scale knowledge graph ConceptNet to obtain the relation between each article word and words in the question/choice. For example, the relation between *car* and *move* is *capableOf*, and the relationship between *car* and *vehicle* is *isA*. ET–RR then assigns a 10D learnable embedding to each relation (including NoRelation). Suppose the article word w finds a relation r to any question/choice word, the relation embedding of r is appended to w's embedding. If there are multiple relations between w and question/choice, the model randomly selects one.

5.4.2.2 Feature embedding

The feature embedding includes a 1-bit exact match embedding, which encodes whether an article word w appears in the question or choice, and a logarithm of w's frequency in the text.

5.4.2.3 Attention layer

Denote the article word vectors by $W_Q \in R^{q \times d_Q}$, the question word vectors by $W_P \in R^{p \times d_P}$, and the choice word vectors by $W_C \in R^{c \times d_C}$. ET–RR calculates (1) the article-to-question attention vectors $W_P^Q \in R^{p \times d}$; (2) the choice-to-question attention vectors $W_C^Q \in R^{c \times d}$; and (3) the choice-to-article attention vectors $W_C^P \in R^{c \times d}$. The attention mechanism is similar to that in ET–Net.

5.4.2.4 Sequence modeling layer

ET-RR uses a bidirectional LSTM to calculate the contextual embedding for words in the question, choices, and article:

$$H^Q = \text{BiLSTM}([W_Q]) \in R^{q \times l}$$

$$H^C = \text{BiLSTM}([W_C; W_C^Q; W_C^P]) \in R^{c \times l}$$

$$H^P = \text{BiLSTM}([W_P; W_P^Q]) \in R^{p \times l}$$

5.4.2.5 Fusion layer

The word vectors in question and choice are separately condensed into a single vector q and c:

$$\alpha_Q = \text{softmax}\left([H^Q; w_e] w_{sq}^T\right)$$

$$q = H^{Q^T} \alpha_Q$$

$$\alpha_C = \text{softmax}\left(H^C w_{sc}^T\right)$$

$$c = H^{C^T} \alpha_C$$

where w_{sq} and w_{sc} are parameter vectors. The vector w_e is the output of the essential-term selector ET-Net, in which the ith component is 1 if ET-Net predicts the ith question word to be an essential term, and 0 otherwise.

The article word vectors H^P are then fused with the question vector q to obtain the *final representation of the article*, p:

$$\alpha_P = \text{softmax}\left(H^P q\right)$$

$$p = H^{P^T} \alpha_P$$

5.4.2.6 Choice interaction layer

Humans often extract useful information from the differences among the choices to solve multiple-choice questions. Similarly, ET-RR captures the difference in semantic information of the choices. Suppose

H^{C_i} stands for the word vectors for the ith choice generated by the sequence modeling layer. Then, the semantic difference between this choice and other choices are computed as follows:

$$c_i^{inter} = \text{Maxpool}\left(H^{C_i} - \frac{1}{N-1}\sum_{j\neq i} H^{C_j}\right)$$

Therefore suppose each choice contains c words (for shorter choices, ET-RR pads them with special symbols), the model computes the difference between the kth dimension of the first word vector in choice i and the average of the kth dimension of other choices' first word. Denote this difference by d_1. Similarly, $d_2, \ldots, d_c$ are computed for the words in other positions. The kth dimension of c_i^{inter} is set to $\max\{d_1, \ldots, d_c\}$. Thus if choice i is distinct from other choices, many components of c_i^{inter} will be large in scale. As a result, c_i^{inter} captures the distinctiveness between choice i and other choices. ET-RR takes $c_i^{final} = \left[c_i^{inter}; c_i\right]$ as the *final representation of choice i*.

5.4.2.7 Output layer

The input to this layer includes vectors of question, article, and choices: $\left\{q, p_n, c_n^{final}\right\}_{n=1}^N$. The output layer computes how likely the nth choice is to be the correct answer to the question, given the article's information p_n:

$$s_n^{pc} = p_n W^{pc} c_n^{final}, s_n^{qc} = q_n W^{qc} c_n^{final}$$

$$s_n = \frac{e^{s_n^{pc}}}{\sum_j e^{s_j^{pc}}} + \frac{e^{s_n^{qc}}}{\sum_j e^{s_j^{qc}}}$$

Then, the cross entropy loss function is calculated based on the scores $s_1, \ldots, s_N$.

The main contribution of the ET-RR model is the proposed deep learning model ET-Net to extract essential terms from the question. Using essential terms as the query can significantly improve the relevance of retrieved results, which is very important in corpus–based MRC tasks. In addition, similar to humans, ET-RR leverages the dissimilarity among the choices to answer multiple-choice questions. In August 2018 ET-RR achieved an accuracy of 36.36% and took the first place in AI2 reasoning challenge, a scientific MRC competition hosted by the Allen Institute for Artificial Intelligence.

5.5 Summary

- The bidirectional attention flow model, **BiDAF**, proposes the general architecture for MRC models: the encoding layer, interaction layer, and output layer. It applies article-to-question and question-to-article attention in the interaction layer. Most models following MRC focus on the design of the interaction layer, especially contextual embeddings and attention mechanisms.
- **R-NET** applies the **gating mechanism** in attention to dynamically control the flow of information.
- **FusionNet** uses **history-of-word** and **fully-aware attention**. To compress the dimension of output, FusionNet uses the complete history of word to calculate attention scores, but only computes the weighted sum of certain layers' output.
- The Essential-Term-Aware Retriever-Reader (**ET-RR**) is a corpus-based MRC model consisting of a retriever and a reader. The retriever extracts essential terms in the question to shorten the query and improve the quality of search results. The reader leverages the dissimilarity of semantic information between choices to improve the model's performance on multiple-choice questions.

References

[1] Seo M, Kembhavi A, Farhadi A, Hajishirzi H. Bidirectional attention flow for machine comprehension. arXiv preprint arXiv 2016; 1611.01603.
[2] Srivastava RK, Greff K, Schmidhuber J. Highway networks. arXiv preprint arXiv 2015; 1505.00387.
[3] Wang W, Yang N, Wei F, Chang B, Zhou M. Gated self-matching networks for reading comprehension and question answering. Proceedings of the 55th annual meeting of the association for computational linguistics, vol. 1. Long Papers; 2017. p. 189—98.
[4] Huang HY, Zhu C, Shen Y, Chen W. Fusionnet: Fusing via fully-aware attention with application to machine comprehension. arXiv preprint arXiv 2017; 1711.07341.
[5] Ni J, Zhu C, Chen W, McAuley J. Learning to attend on essential terms: an enhanced retriever-reader model for open-domain question answering. arXiv preprint arXiv 2018; 1808.09492.

CHAPTER 6

Pretrained language models

6.1 Pretrained models and transfer learning

Pretrained models were first applied in computer vision. In 2012 the deep learning model AlexNet achieved first place in the image recognition competition ImageNet, significantly outperforming other methods. Since then, AlexNet has been widely used in many computer vision tasks. Instead of retraining AlexNet's network architecture from scratch, many new models reuse its parameters and continue to fine-tune the network on target tasks. The experimental results show that the usage of the pretrained AlexNet significantly increases the accuracy on the target task, and dramatically shortens the new model's training time. The reason is that the pretrained model already has a strong capability of image understanding after being exposed to massive data in the original task. This method of transferring the model trained on one task to other related tasks is called **transfer learning**.

Transfer learning is similar to how humans integrate knowledge and skills in multiple similar tasks. For example, it is much faster for a car driver to learn to drive a truck than for a person who has no driving experience to do the same task, since the car driver can transfer and adjust their car-driving skills to accommodate the new vehicle. In machine learning, transfer learning first trains a model M on the source task(s) A, and then optimizes it on the target task B to get the final model M'. Here, to ensure the effectiveness of the model transfer, the task A and B must be related and share some similarity.

One primary reason that transfer learning becomes popular is that the target task often does not have enough data. For example, in many machine reading comprehension (MRC) tasks, the questions and answers need to be manually generated and edited, which is time- and labor-consuming. If a large model is trained from scratch on a small dataset, overfitting may occur which reduces the generalizability of the model. Transfer learning alleviates this problem by pretraining the model on large-scale data of one or more related tasks before adapting to the target task.

Meanwhile, transfer learning is gaining popularity as more and more pretrained models are open-sourced, so one can easily access the code and

Machine Reading Comprehension. DOI: https://doi.org/10.1016/B978-0-323-90118-5.00006-0
© 2021 Beijing Huazhang Graphics & Information Co., Ltd/China Machine Press.
Published by Elsevier Inc. All rights reserved.

trained parameters of these models. It saves a considerable amount of time and computing resources by directly starting from the pretrained model's checkpoint to further fine-tune it on the target task.

However, usually the source task A and target task B are not exactly the same. For example, the aforementioned AlexNet model was pretrained to categorize 1000 objects, but the target task B may only need to classify 10 objects. Therefore we cannot directly use the AlexNet architecture without modification. Instead, we need to modify the pretrained model to meet task B's requirements. One common solution is to replace the output layer of the pretrained model (which scores 1000 objects classes) with the output layer for the target task (which scores 10 objects classes). The new output layer may also include more complex architectures based on the nature of task B. Both the new layer and retained architecture are fine-tuned.

As shown in Fig. 6.1, the output layer of the pretrained model is replaced with one for task B plus an recurrent neural network (RNN) layer. This new output layer is randomly initialized while other parts inherit the parameters of the pretrained model.

It is worth noting that a pretrained model is fundamentally different from pretrained word vectors, for example, GloVe and word2vec. The reason is that the pretrained word vectors are a dictionary of embeddings, while a pretrained model is a computational module that includes both the network architecture and the parameters.

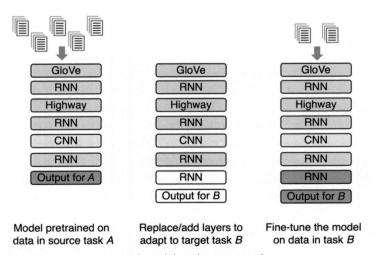

Figure 6.1 Adapting a pretrained model to the target task.

Pretrained language models have been applied in natural language processing (NLP) and MRC since 2015. Google proposed to pretrain RNN using autoencoders and language models [1]. Then, the CoVe and embeddings from language models (ELMo) models provide contextual embedding layers to target tasks. These pretrained language models are usually applied in MRC networks as part of the encoding layer, so one still needs to design and train the interaction and output layers. In October 2018 the BERT model was proposed and it can replace all the encoding and interaction layers in MRC models, so one only needs to design the output layer to achieve remarkable results in various MRC tasks.

6.2 Translation-based pretrained language model: CoVe

In 2017 researchers from Salesforce proposed a translation-based pretrained language model, CoVe (Contextualized Vector) [2], and opensourced the code and parameters on GitHub. CoVe is based on the widely adopted encoder—decoder architecture in machine translation, where the encoder produces vector representations of the text in the source language, and the decoder generates the text in the target language. As machine translation needs to faithfully express the semantics of the source language text, the representation generated by the encoder can be used as high-quality semantic embeddings. Therefore CoVe first pretrains the encoder and decoder on large-scale translation data, and then applies the encoder to other NLP tasks.

6.2.1 Machine translation model

CoVe adopts the canonical sequence-to-sequence architecture for machine translation. The pretraining task is to translate English into German. Suppose the English text is tokenized into $w^x = \left[w_1^x, \ldots, w_n^x\right]$, and each word is assigned its Glove representation $\text{GloVe}(w_i^x)$. This embedding is fed into a two-layer bidirectional long short-term memory (LSTM) to obtain the 600D contextual embeddings:

$$\boldsymbol{H} = \text{MT-LSTM}\left(\text{GloVe}\left(w_1^x\right), \ldots, \text{GloVe}\left(w_n^x\right)\right) = (\boldsymbol{h}_1, \boldsymbol{h}_2, \ldots, \boldsymbol{h}_n)$$

where MT-LSTM indicates that this LSTM is for machine translation.

The decoder is a two-layer unidirectional LSTM:

$$\boldsymbol{h}_t^{dec} = \text{LSTM}\left(\left[\boldsymbol{z}_{t-1}; \tilde{\boldsymbol{h}}_{t-1}\right], \boldsymbol{h}_{t-1}^{dec}\right)$$

where z_{t-1} is the embedding of the previously decoded word, $\tilde{h}_{t-1}$ is the attention vector, and h_{t-1}^{dec} is the previous hidden state. The new hidden attention vector $\tilde{h}_t$ is computed as follows:

$$\alpha_t = \text{softmax}\left(H\left(W_1 h_t^{dec} + b_1\right)\right)$$

$$\tilde{h}_t = \tanh\left(W_2\left[H^T \alpha_t; h_t^{dec}\right] + b_2\right)$$

Finally, the decoder predicts the next word in target language through the new decoder state $\tilde{h}_t$:

$$p\left(\tilde{w}_t^z | w_1^x, \ldots, w_n^x, w_1^z, \ldots, w_{t-1}^z\right) = \text{softmax}\left(W_{out}\tilde{h}_t + b_{out}\right)$$

where W_{out} and b_{out} are parameters.

6.2.2 Contextual embeddings

After massive pretraining on the machine translation task, CoVe's encoder can be used to generate contextual embeddings:

$$\text{CoVe}(w) = \text{MT} - \text{LSTM}(\text{GloVe}(w_1), \ldots, \text{GloVe}(w_n))$$

This contextual embedding is concatenated with the Glove embedding and used in the downstream network of the target task (Fig. 6.2):

$$\tilde{w} = [\text{GloVe}(w); \text{CoVe}(w)]$$

Experimental results show that the contextual embedding from CoVe's encoder can effectively improve the performance on various NLP tasks including sentiment analysis, question classification, and MRC. For example, in the SQuAD dataset, the F1 score of an MRC model increased by 3.9%

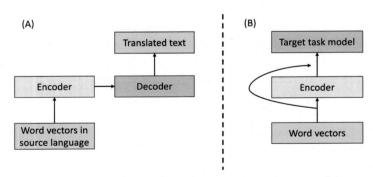

Figure 6.2 (A) Pretraining CoVe on a machine learning task. (B) Use of the pretrained encoder in the target task.

with CoVe's encoder. As a result, many MRC models including FusionNet adopt CoVe as the contextual embedder.

Code 6-1 exemplifies the usage of CoVe. First, one needs to install the CoVe package from GitHub. Then, the *MTLSTM* class generates CoVe's contextual embeddings given GloVe embeddings and word ids in the text.

Code 6-1 Use of the pretrained language model CoVe

```
# download source code of CoVe from GitHub
$ git clone https://github.com/salesforce/cove.git
$ cd cove
# install the required packages
$ pip install − r requirements.txt
# install CoVe
$ python setup.py develop
# Python code
import torch
from torchtext.vocab import GloVe
from cove import MTLSTM
# GloVe embeddings. Size: 2.1 M × 300
glove = GloVe (name = '840B', dim = 300, cache = '.embeddings')
# two input sentences with word ids
inputs = torch.LongTensor ([[ 10, 2, 3, 0] , [ 7, 8, 10, 3]] )
# length of the sentences
lengths = torch.LongTensor ([ 3, 4] )
# MTLSTM is the class for CoVe
cove = MTLSTM (n_vocab = glove.vectors.shape[ 0] ,
    vectors = glove.vectors, model_cache = '.embeddings')
# contextual embeddings from Cove for each word in each sentence.
  Size: 2 × 4 × 600
outputs = cove (inputs, lengths)
```

Compared with GloVe embeddings, the contextual embedding network of CoVe's encoder can be fine-tuned to adapt its parameters to the target task. This greatly increases the flexibility of the model.

However, we note that the CoVe model can only be used as part of the encoding layer for the target task's model. Thus one still needs to design other modules such as attention and RNN. Therefore CoVe cannot reduce the model complexity of the target network. In addition, only the pretrained encoder of CoVe is utilized in downstream tasks. In the next section, we will introduce the ELMo model which fully utilizes the pretrained parameters.

6.3 Pretrained language model ELMo

In 2018 the Allen Institute for Artificial Intelligence and the University of Washington proposed the pretrained language model ELMo [3] and open-sourced its code and parameters. ELMo is pretrained on the bidirectional language model task. Compared with CoVe, ELMo has a larger model size and is more flexible in applications.

6.3.1 Bidirectional language model

Suppose a piece of text is tokenized into $(t_1, t_2, \ldots, t_N)$. The forward language model factorizes the text probability into the probability of each word t_k given the previous words $t_1, \ldots, t_{k-1}$:

$$p(t_1, t_2, \ldots, t_N) = \prod_{k=1}^{N} p(t_k | t_1, t_2, \ldots, t_{k-1})$$

ELMo's encoding layer includes a character convolutional neural network (char-CNN) and two highway networks. This layer embeds each word into a contextually independent vector x_k^{LM}. These vectors are then fed into an L-layer forward LSTM:

$$\overrightarrow{h}_{k,0}^{LM} = x_k^{LM}, \quad 1 \le k \le N$$

$$\overrightarrow{h}_{1,j}^{LM}, \overrightarrow{h}_{2,j}^{LM}, \ldots, \overrightarrow{h}_{N,j}^{LM} = \text{LSTM}\left(\overrightarrow{h}_{1,j-1}^{LM}, \overrightarrow{h}_{2,j-1}^{LM}, \ldots, \overrightarrow{h}_{N,j-1}^{LM}\right), 1 \le j \le L$$

Finally, the last hidden state of the Lth layer, $\overrightarrow{h}_{k,L}^{LM} \in R^{d_{mn}}$, is used to predict the $(k + 1)$th word:

$$p(t_{k+1} | t_1, t_2, \ldots, t_k) = \text{softmax}(\overrightarrow{h}_{k,L}^{LM} M)$$

where $M \in R^{d_{mn} \times |V|}$ is a parameter matrix and $|V|$ is the size of the vocabulary.

Similarly, ELMo uses a backward LSTM to obtain $\overleftarrow{h}_{k,j}^{LM}$, $1 \le j \le L$, which are used to compute the probability for the backward language model:

$$p(t_1, t_2, \ldots, t_N) = \prod_{k=1}^{N} p(t_k | t_{k+1}, \ldots, t_N)$$

The forward and backward language models share the encoder's parameters Θ_x (char-CNN and highway network) and the final linear layer M. But they have separate LSTM parameters $\overrightarrow{\Theta}_{LSTM}$ and $\overleftarrow{\Theta}_{LSTM}$.

The goal of the pretraining is to maximize the bidirectional language model probability:

$$\sum_{k=1}^{N} \log p(t_k | t_1, \ldots, t_{k-1}; \Theta_x, \overrightarrow{\Theta}_{LSTM}, \boldsymbol{M}) + \log p(t_k | t_{k+1}, \ldots, t_n; \Theta_x, \overleftarrow{\Theta}_{LSTM}, \boldsymbol{M})$$

6.3.2 How to use ELMo

After pretraining, ELMo can produce contextual embedding R_k for each word t_k in the tokenized text:

$$R_k = \left\{ \boldsymbol{x}_k^{LM}, \overrightarrow{\boldsymbol{h}}_{k,j}^{LM}, \overleftarrow{\boldsymbol{h}}_{k,j}^{LM} \,|\, j = 1, \ldots, L \right\} = \left\{ \boldsymbol{h}_{k,j}^{LM} \,|\, j = 0, \ldots, L \right\}$$

where $\boldsymbol{h}_{k,0}^{LM} = \boldsymbol{x}_k^{LM}$ is contextually independent, and $\boldsymbol{h}_{k,j}^{LM} = [\overrightarrow{\boldsymbol{h}}_{k,j}^{LM}; \overleftarrow{\boldsymbol{h}}_{k,j}^{LM}]$ is the output of the jth layer of forward and backward LSTMs. Then, ELMo computes a parametrized weighted sum of these $L + 1$ vectors as the ELMo embedding:

$$ELMo_k = \gamma \sum_{j=0}^{L} s_j \boldsymbol{h}_{k,j}^{LM}$$

where γ and $s_0, \ldots, s_L$ are learnable parameters. In the open–sourced ELMo model, there are $L = 2$ layers of LSTM, and each direction has a 512D hidden state, that is, $\boldsymbol{h}_{k,j}^{LM} \in R^{1024}$. Therefore the ELMo embedding has a dimension of 1024.

Like CoVe, the ELMo embedding can be concatenated with the word embedding: $w_k = [\text{GloVe}(t_k); ELMo_k]$. In addition, experimental results show that it is beneficial to supplement the output layer's input with the ELMo embedding.

Code 6-2 shows how to get ELMo embeddings. The *batch_to_ids* function converts words into character ids. The embeddings from all layers of ELMo, represented by *all_layers*, are used to compute a weighted sum by the parameter s and γ.

Code 6-2 Get ELMo embeddings

```
# install the allennlp package
pip install allennlp
# Python code (version 3.6)
import torch
```

(Continued)

(Continued)

```
from torch import nn
import torch.nn.functional as F
from allennlp.modules.elmo import Elmo, batch_to_ids
from allennlp.commands.elmo import ElmoEmbedder
from allennlp.nn.util import remove_sentence_boundaries
# url to the pre-trained language model
options_file = "https://allennlp.s3.amazonaws.com/models/elmo/
  2x4096_512_2048cnn_2xhighway/elmo_2x4096_512_2048cnn_2x
  highway_options.json"
weight_file = "https://allennlp.s3.amazonaws.com/models/elmo/
  2x4096_512_2048cnn_2xhighway/elmo_2x4096_512_2048cnn_2x
  highway_weights.hdf5"
# the ELMo class
elmo_bilm = ElmoEmbedder(options_file, weight_file).elmo_bilm
elmo_bilm.cuda()
sentences = [['Today', 'is', 'sunny', '.'], ['Hello', '!']]
# obtain character ids for each word. Size: batch_size ×
  max_sentence_len × word_len
character_ids = batch_to_ids(sentences).cuda()
# ELMo's output
bilm_output = elmo_bilm(character_ids)
# ELMo embeddings for each layer
layer_activations = bilm_output['activations']
# indicate whether there is a word at each position
mask_with_bos_eos = bilm_output['mask']
# remove the special sentence start and end symbols added by ELMo
without_bos_eos = [remove_sentence_boundaries(layer, mask_with_
  bos_eos) for layer in layer_activations]
# three layers of 1024D ELMo embeddings. Size: 3 × batch_size ×
  max_sentence_len × 1024
all_layers = torch.cat([ele[0].unsqueeze(0) for ele in
  without_bos_eos], dim=0)
# parameters for weighted sum
s = nn.Parameter(torch.Tensor([1., 1., 1.]), requires_grad=True).
  cuda()
# normalize the weights
s = F.softmax(s, dim=0)
# the multiplier γ
gamma = nn.Parameter(torch.Tensor(1, 1), requires_grad=True).cuda()
# ELMo embedding. Size: batch_size × max_sentence_len × 1024
res = (all_layers[0]*s[0] + all_layers[1]*s[1] + all_layers[2]*s
  [2]) * gamma
```

In summary, ELMo is pretrained in the language model task on a massive corpus to provide contextual embeddings. Compared with CoVe, ELMo effectively utilizes all pretrained parameters. Therefore ELMo replaced CoVe as the standard contextual embedder for various NLP tasks such as MRC, named entity recognition, and sentence similarity.

6.4 The generative pretraining language model: generative pre-training (GPT)

In June 2018 OpenAI introduced the generative pretraining language model GPT [4]. Like ELMo, GPT is a left-to-right language model. What makes GPT distinctive is that its model architecture can be applied to a target task with a relatively small network layer at the top.

The GPT model does not use the traditional RNN unit. Instead, it adopts the attention-based model, that is, Transformer. In this section, we will first introduce the architecture of the Transformer model and then analyze the GPT model.

6.4.1 Transformer

Transformer [5] is an advanced attention-based model proposed by Google in 2017 to generate contextual embeddings. Traditionally, the RNN-based contextual embedder is limited by its sequential style of computation. For example, a forward RNN's hidden vector of the 10th word cannot be obtained before the first to ninth words are all processed. As a result, it is difficult to parallelize RNN. In addition, due to the decay of information, the interaction between two words far apart in the text is hard to be analyzed by RNN. This is actually why RNN often works with the self-attention mechanism.

To alleviate these problems, the Transformer model uses an improved self-attention mechanism to generate contextual embeddings, including multihead attention, position encoding, layer normalization, and feedforward neural networks.

6.4.1.1 Multihead attention

The attention mechanism calculates the relevance scores between a word (defined as the query) and a sequence of words (defined as the keys), and then uses the normalized scores to compute the weighted sum of a sequence of words (defined as the values).

Suppose the input contains n queries, m keys, and m values. The query vectors are $\boldsymbol{Q} \in R^{n \times d_{model}}$, the key vectors are $\boldsymbol{K} \in R^{m \times d_{model}}$, and the value vectors are $V \in R^{m \times d_v}$. The attention vector of a transformer is computed as follows:

$$\text{Attention}(\boldsymbol{Q}, \boldsymbol{K}, \boldsymbol{V}) = \text{softmax}\left(\frac{\boldsymbol{Q}\boldsymbol{K}^T}{\sqrt{d_{model}}}\right)\boldsymbol{V} \in R^{n \times d_v}$$

Here, d_{model} is the dimension of query and key vectors, while d_v is the dimension of the value vector. In the case of self-attention, $m = n$, $d_{model} = d_v$. $\boldsymbol{Q}\boldsymbol{K}^T$ are the attention scores computed by the inner product, which are then normalized by the scaling factor $1/\sqrt{d_{model}}$ to control the effect of dimension.

Multihead attention is to repeat the above process by h times, and then concatenate all the results. Each time, it first projects $\boldsymbol{Q}$ and $\boldsymbol{K}$ to a space of dimension d_k and $\boldsymbol{V}$ to a space of dimension d_v, through three matrix parameters $\boldsymbol{W}_i^Q \in R^{d_{model} \times d_k}, \boldsymbol{W}_i^K \in R^{d_{model} \times d_k}$, and $\boldsymbol{W}_i^V \in R^{d_{model} \times d_v}$. Then, it concatenates the h resulting vectors and projects it back to the space of dimension d_{model} by $\mathbf{W}^O \in R^{hd_v \times d_{model}}$:

$$\text{MultiHead}(\boldsymbol{Q}, \boldsymbol{K}, \boldsymbol{V}) = \text{Concat}(\text{head}_1, \ldots, \text{head}_h)\mathbf{W}^O \in R^{n \times d_{model}}$$

$$\text{head}_i = \text{Attention}\left(\boldsymbol{Q}\boldsymbol{W}_i^Q, \boldsymbol{K}\boldsymbol{W}_i^K, \boldsymbol{V}\boldsymbol{W}_i^V\right) \in R^{n \times d_v}$$

6.4.1.2 Positional encoding

Compared with RNN, one disadvantage of self-attention is that the word order does not affect the result. However, the arrangement of words in text is strongly related to the semantics, for example, the object is often preceded by the subject, a pronoun usually refers to a close-by entity. To solve this problem, Transformer applies **positional encoding** to preserve the word order information. Positional encoding assigns each position a unique embedding of dimension d_{model}. There are two general forms of positional encoding: functional and tabular.

A functional position encoding is a function of the word position *pos* and output dimension d_{model}. For example, a trigonometry function for positional encoding can be:

$$\text{PE}_{pos,2i} = \sin(pos/10,000^{2i/d_{model}})$$

$$\text{PE}_{pos,2i+1} = \cos(pos/10,000^{2i/d_{model}})$$

where $\text{PE}_{pos,j}$ stands for the value of the jth component in the embedding for the posth word position. Functional positional encoding can naturally extend to word positions beyond the range in the training data, that is, it can compute embedding for arbitrary values of pos. However, without trainable parameters, the fixed form of the functional positional encoding limits its flexibility.

The tabular positional encoding establishes an embedding table of size $L \times d_{model}$, where L is a predefined maximum length of input text. The embeddings in the table are trainable parameters, so they can be optimized to adapt to the target task. However, it cannot accept input text longer than L words.

6.4.1.3 Layer normalization

In neural networks, the output from a layer can cause changes in the distribution of input to upper layers. As a result, the top layers are oversensitive to the network's input, resulting in an unstable training of their parameters due to a shift in the input distribution.

To alleviate this problem, **layer normalization** normalizes the input to each layer. Suppose the input is $(x_1, \ldots, x_d)$, the mechanism calculates the mean and standard deviation of each component and normalizes the input into $(x'_1, \ldots, x'_d)$:

$$\mu = \frac{1}{d}\sum_{i=1}^{d} x_i, \sigma = \sqrt{\frac{1}{d}\sum_{i=1}^{d}(x_i - \mu)^2 + \epsilon}$$

$$x'_i = f\left(g\frac{x_i - \mu}{\sigma} + b\right)$$

where g, b are parameters and f is a nonlinear function.

6.4.1.4 Feed-forward network

The Transformer contains a feed-forward network comprising two linear layers and a nonlinear activation function. Given an input vector $x \in R^{d_{model}}$, the network computes $\text{FFN}(x)$ as follows:

$$\text{FFN}(x) = \text{ReLU}(xW_1 + b_1)W_2 + b_2$$

where $W_1 \in R^{d_{model} \times d_{hidden}}, b_1 \in R^{d_{hidden}}, W_2 \in R^{d_{hidden} \times d_{model}}, b_2 \in R^{d_{model}}$ are parameters.

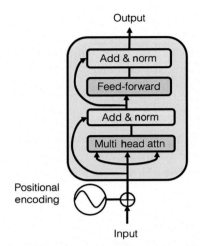

Figure 6.3 The architecture of a Transformer layer, with positional encoding, multi-head attention, layer normalization, and a feed-forward network.

The architecture of the Transformer model is shown in Fig. 6.3. It adds the positional encodings to the word embeddings and feeds them to a multi-head self-attention module. The module's output is added to its input and goes through layer normalization and the feed-forward network. The transformer again adds the output to the input and conducts layer normalization. It is worth noting that the method of adding the output of a network layer to its input is from the **residual network**. The goal is to reduce the average chain length when computing the gradient using the chain rule.

The Transformer has an important characteristic: the input and output vectors have the same dimensions. As a result, we can stack multiple Transformers like multilayer RNN to obtain deeper semantic information. The multilayer Transformer architecture has outperformed RNN in many NLP tasks.

6.4.2 GPT

GPT is a language model based on n layers of Transformers. The model first tokenizes the input text via byte pair encoding (BPE). Then, it predicts the next word using a sliding window: predict the ith word using the $(i-1)$th, ..., $(i-k)$th words. If the input text is tokenized into $U = \{u_1, u_2, \ldots, u_m\}$, the cross entropy loss function is:

$$L_1(U) = \sum_i logP(u_i|u_{i-k}, \ldots, u_{i-1}; \Theta)$$

where k is the window size and Θ indicates the network parameters.

In detail, the input $\boldsymbol{h}_0$ to the first Transformer in GPT is the representations of the words in the window. We denote the representation of the ith word by a vector $\boldsymbol{h}_0^i$ of dimension d:

$$\boldsymbol{h}_0 = \left(\boldsymbol{h}_0^{i-k}, \ldots, \boldsymbol{h}_0^{i-1}\right) = U\boldsymbol{W}_e + \boldsymbol{W}_p$$

where U is the one-hot matrix, $\boldsymbol{W}_e$ is the embedding matrix for all dictionary words, and $\boldsymbol{W}_p$ is the position encoding matrix. Then, $\boldsymbol{h}_0$ passes through n Transformer layers and the last layer's output is used to predict the next word u_i:

$$\boldsymbol{h}_l = \text{transformer}(\boldsymbol{h}_{l-1}) \in R^{k \times d}, \forall l \in [1, n]$$

$$P(u_i) = \text{softmax}(\boldsymbol{h}_n^{i-1} \boldsymbol{W}_e^T)$$

The open-sourced pretrained GPT model has $n = 12$ layers of Transformers with 12-head attention. The word embedding has a dimension of 768. The whole model has been trained on the BooksCorpus dataset for 100 epochs.

6.4.3 Apply GPT

Unlike CoVe and ELMo, the pretrained GPT model is not used as part of the encoding layer for target tasks. Instead, with a task-specific output layer, GPT can quickly adapt to the target task after a few epochs of fine-tuning.

For example, suppose the target task is K-class text classification. If the input text C is tokenized into $\{u_1, u_2, \ldots, u_m\}$ and the category label is y, one only needs to add an output layer $\boldsymbol{W}_y$ on top of the GPT network to make predictions:

$$P(y|u_1, u_2, \ldots, u_m) = \text{softmax}\left(\boldsymbol{h}_n^m \boldsymbol{W}_y\right) \in R$$

where $\boldsymbol{W}_y \in R^{d \times K}$. The output layer converts the GPT's output vector for the last input word, $\boldsymbol{h}_n^m$, into scores for each category. The cross entropy loss function is then used for fine-tuning:

$$L_2(C) = \sum_{(u,y)} logP(y|u_1, \ldots, u_m)$$

Experiments show that it is beneficial to add a language model loss during fine-tuning to further improve the accuracy on the target task:

$$L_3(C) = L_2(C) + \lambda \times L_1(C)$$

where λ is a weight coefficient and set to 0.5 in the GPT paper.

GPT can also be applied to target tasks with multiple inputs. For the entailment task, we can concatenate the premise and hypothesis separated by the *Delim* symbol as the input. In addition, all input texts to GPT are prepended with the *Start* symbol and appended with the *Extract* symbol.

Because the language model is an unsupervised learning task, GPT can effectively leverage a massive unlabeled corpus to obtain a strong semantic understanding capability. Compared with CoVe and ELMo, GPT is used as the main part of models for target tasks for the first time, and only an additional output layer is required to adapt to downstream tasks. Experimental results show that GPT achieves state-of-the-art results in various NLP tasks including natural language inference, question answering, and text classification.

In February 2019 OpenAI further introduced GPT-2, which had the same architecture as GPT but is 10 times larger. GPT-2 is pretrained on a corpus 10 times larger than that for GPT. GPT-2 significantly outperforms its predecessor and demonstrates amazing text generation capability. For example, given a random beginning, it can generate a news article with very high quality. This has led to a heated discussion about artificial intelligence.

6.5 The phenomenal pretrained language model: BERT

In October 2018 a paper from Google [6] shocked the NLP community. It proposed the pretrained Bidirectional Encoder Representations from Transformers (BERT), which won the first place in 11 NLP tasks, and surpassed the human level performance in SQuAD v1.0 and situations with adversarial generations (SWAG) common sense reasoning datasets. After the code and pretrained model was released, BERT was immediately adopted in various NLP models and achieved remarkable results. For example, in the CoQA dataset, the top 10 models are all based on BERT; in the SQuAD v2.0 dataset, the top 20 models are all based on BERT. In both datasets, the best model's score has surpassed the human level.

Like GPT, BERT also has a multilayer Transformer structure. Its input text is tokenized by WordPiece, a tokenization method similar to BPE, and its output is the BERT contextual embeddings, which encode a word's meaning and contextual information. In the pretraining, the BERT model leverages two tasks: masked language model (MLM) and next sentence prediction (NSP). Both tasks belong to the **self-supervised**

learning category, which only requires the text corpus without any manual labels.

6.5.1 Masked language model

The GPT model in the previous section is a forward language model, which predicts the next word based on the information of preceding words. Although the ELMo model contains an additional backward language model, the language models in both directions are independent of each other. In other words, the word prediction in ELMo does not simultaneously utilize information in both directions.

However, a word is usually related to its context in both directions. For instance, to predict [WORD] in *Tom is a [WORD] in our school*, we know that [WORD] should be a description of the preceding word *Tom*, and it is also related to the following word *school*. Based on this information, [WORD] could be *student* or *teacher*, instead of *apple* of *play*. Thus a good design should leverage context in both directions in language modeling.

One seemingly viable solution is by modifying the self-attention mechanism in the Transformer. We can add an attention mask to make the output embedding y_i of the ith word depend on all words except itself, that is, $y_i = f(x_1, \ldots, x_{i-1}, x_{i+1}, \ldots, x_n)$, where x_i is the embedding of word i. The vector y_i can then be used to predict the word in the ith position. However, this masking technique only works with a single layer of this modified Transformer. The reason is that the output embedding for the ith position of the second layer is $z_i = f(y_1, \ldots, y_{i-1}, y_{i+1}, \ldots, y_n)$, which already contains the information from x_i. This information leakage makes the solution invalid for bidirectional language modeling.

To solve this problem, BERT proposes to mask the input words. It randomly selects 15% of the input words to be replaced by the special symbol [MASK]. It then uses the multilayer Transformer model to predict the masked words. As these words have been completely masked in input, it is valid to use the input to predict them. As a result, BERT is a bidirectional language model.

However, since there is no [MASK] symbol in a normal text, the masking technique creates discrepancy between the pretraining task and target tasks. Therefore after the masked words are selected, BERT replaces them by [MASK] 80% of the time, by random words 10% of the time, and by the original words 10% of the time. Experiments show that this approach improves the model's accuracy on target tasks.

6.5.2 Next sentence prediction

As many target tasks of BERT are classification problems, BERT designs the second pretraining task: NSP. Given two sentences A and B, BERT determines whether B is the actual next sentence of A in the original text. To take more context into consideration, the total length of A and B can be up to 512 tokens. During pretraining, the positive and negative samples each take 50% of the data. In negative samples, B is randomly selected from the corpus.

Since the Transformer model only accepts one input sequence, BERT concatenates A with B and adds the start symbol [CLS] and the separation symbol [SEP]. To distinguish between A and B, different segment embeddings are added to tokens in A and B. Suppose the final BERT embedding for the token [CLS] is x_{CLS}, BERT predicts $\sigma(Wx_{CLS}) \in [0, 1]$ as the probability that B is the next sentence after A, where W is a parameter matrix and σ is the sigmoid function.

6.5.3 Configurations of BERT pretraining

BERT is pretrained on public corpus including BooksCorpus (800 M words) and English Wikipedia (2500 M words). There are two versions of BERT models available online:

- **BERT$_{BASE}$**: 12-layer Transformers, input and output dimension of 768, 12 attention heads with 110 M parameters;
- **BERT$_{LARGE}$**: 24-layer Transformers, input and output dimension of 1024, 24 attention heads with 340 M parameters.

The BERT$_{BASE}$ model is of a similar size with GPT for fair comparison. Both BERT$_{BASE}$ and BERT$_{LARGE}$ models were trained for 40 epochs over 4 days. BERT$_{BASE}$ was trained on four Cloud TPUs, and BERT$_{LARGE}$ was trained on 16 Cloud TPUs. It is worth noting that compared with GPU, the TPU is better optimized in hardware and algorithms for deep learning. It is estimated that it would take about 100 days to train BERT$_{LARGE}$ on four GPUs. As a result, BERT is the largest ever pretrained language model which also consumes the most computing resources.

6.5.4 Fine-tuning BERT

The influence of BERT is primarily from its excellent performance in many targeted tasks. In the BERT paper, the fine-tuned BERT model achieved the first place in 11 NLP tasks including language inference task MNLI, sentence similarity task STS-B, paraphrasing task MRPC, and reading comprehension task SQuAD. Both BERT$_{\text{BASE}}$ and BERT$_{\text{LARGE}}$ significantly outperformed the GPT model. BERT has been widely used by researchers in a variety of NLP tasks to achieve state-of-the-art results. In this section, we will introduce how BERT is fine-tuned on target tasks.

6.5.4.1 Text classification tasks

In such tasks, BERT needs to score or classify a given input text, which is similar to the pretraining task of NSP. First, all the input information is concatenated into one piece of text. The BERT embedding of [CLS] is then fed into a feed-forward network to obtain the score for each class.

For example, in a multichoice MRC task, the model needs to assign a score to each choice. Suppose the article is P, the question is Q, and the ith choice is C_i. BERT defines the input as [CLS] Q C_i [SEP] P. Suppose the BERT embedding of [CLS] is $h_0^{(i)} \in R^d$. It then goes through a feed-forward network $W \in R^{d \times 1}$ to obtain the score $s^{(i)} = h_0 W$. The scores of all K options, that is, $[s^{(1)}, \ldots, s^{(K)}]$, are normalized by softmax to give the probability that each choice is correct. The cross entropy is used as the loss function.

6.5.4.2 Sequence labeling tasks

In such tasks, BERT needs to assign scores to each token in the input text. First, all the input information is concatenated into one piece of text. The BERT embedding of each token to be labeled is fed into a feed-forward network to obtain the score for each class.

For example, in an MRC task for extractive answers, BERT should output the probability that the answer starts from and ends at each token in the article. Suppose the article is P and the question is Q, BERT defines the input as [CLS] Q [SEP] P. We denote the BERT embeddings of the article words by $[h_1, \ldots, h_n]$, $h_i \in R^d$. These embeddings are fed into a linear layer $W^S \in R^{d \times 1}$ to obtain scores $s_i = h_i W^S$, which are normalized by softmax into the probabilities that the answer starts from each token in the article:

$$p_1^S, \ldots, p_n^S = \text{softmax}(s_1, \ldots s_n)$$

Similarly, the BERT embeddings of the article words are fed into another linear layer $W^E \in R^{d \times 1}$ to get the probability that the answer ends at each token in the article:

$$p_1^E, \ldots, p_n^E = \text{softmax}(e_1, \ldots e_n)$$

The cross entropy loss function is then computed based on these probabilities and ground-truth answers.

During the above fine-tuning processes, the parameters from both BERT and the added layers are updated. And the fine-tuning only takes 2—4 epochs on the target task.

Similar to GPT, BERT can be applied to many NLP tasks with a simple output layer. Since BERT has been well trained on a massive corpus, it already has strong language understanding capabilities. Therefore BERT can quickly adapt to various types of target tasks by appending a simple output layer with a modest amount of fine-tuning. It can achieve great results even if only a small amount of data is available, which is ideal for tasks which require labor-intensive labeling, including MRC.

6.5.5 Improving BERT

Because of BERT's characteristics, many studies in NLP focus less on new model architectures. More innovations are proposed on data collection, pretraining tasks, and fine-tuning techniques.

6.5.5.1 Better pretraining tasks
There are studies which improve the masking technique in the pretraining of BERT. For example, phrases or sentences are masked instead of individual words, making the model focus on more contextual information. Also, some studies modify the masking to enable BERT to carry out language generation tasks.

6.5.5.2 Multitask fine-tuning
During the fine-tuning phase, one can simultaneously train on multiple target tasks by mixing the data. These tasks share the underlying BERT structure, but each has its designated output layer. Furthermore, these target tasks do not need to be inherently similar. For instance, MRC, sentence similarity, and paraphrasing can be fine-tuned together. Experiments show that multitask training can improve the performance on each individual task.

6.5.5.3 Multiphase pretraining
The data for pretraining BERT is BooksCorpus and English Wikipedia. However, these corpora may not be similar to the language in the target domains, such as medical and legal language understanding tasks. Therefore BERT can be further pretrained on text from the target domains and then fine-tuned to improve its performance on these domains.

6.5.5.4 Use BERT as an encoding layer

Since the BERT model is massive in scale, its fine-tuning on target tasks usually requires a significant amount of computing resources. When such resources are limited, one option is to leverage BERT as an encoding layer. In this case, the parameters in BERT's structure are fixed, that is, no gradients are calculated. Similar to ELMo, the final BERT embedding is obtained as a parametrized weighted sum of each BERT layer's output and used in subsequent network layers. This approach is used in the MRC model SDNet described in the next chapter.

6.5.6 Implementing BERT fine-tuning in MRC

One of the reasons for the popularity of BERT is that the authors open-sourced the TensorFlow version of code and shared the parameters of the pretrained language model. Afterwards, the HuggingFace company converted the code to PyTorch and provided various APIs including tokenization, pretraining, and fine-tuning. Code 6-3 shows how to fine-tune BERT in MRC to generate extractive answers.

Code 6-3 Fine-tune BERT in MRC to generate extractive answers

```
# install the transformer package which includes BERT
$ pip install pytorch-transformers
# Python code
import torch
from pytorch_transformers import *
# use the case insensitive BERT-base model
config = BertConfig.from_pretrained('bert-base-uncased')
# the tokenization API used by BERT
tokenizer = BertTokenizer.from_pretrained('bert-base-uncased')
# load the BERT model including a dedicated output layer for
    extractive-answer question answering
model = BertForQuestionAnswering(config)
# preprocess the training data
# obtain the tokenized word id. Size: batch_size (1) × seq_length (4)
input_ids = torch.tensor(tokenizer.encode("This is an example")).
    unsqueeze(0)
# record the start and end positions of the ground-truth answers in
    the article. Size: batch_size
start_positions = torch.tensor([ 1] )
```

(Continued)

```
(Continued)
end_positions = torch.tensor ([3] )
# get the output from the model
outputs = model (input_ids, start_positions = start_positions, end_
    positions = end_positions)
# get the cross entropy loss and the predicted scores for each article
    token being the start and end position of the answer. Size: batch_size
    (1) x seq_length
loss, start_scores, end_scores = outputs
```

Although the basic idea of self-supervised training on large-scale corpora in BERT is similar to that in GPT, there are two major innovations of BERT. First, it employs masking to implement a bidirectional language model, which better aligns with how humans analyze text. Second, the pretraining task of NSP enhances BERT's capability in many related downstream classification tasks.

Since the advent of BERT, numerous studies in NLP follow the pretraining + fine-tuning strategy. In many areas, the era of designing and training a specific model for each task has passed. BERT essentially breaks the barrier between various NLP problems by a shared massive pretrained language model. There is no doubt that BERT is one of the most important milestones in the history of NLP.

6.6 Summary

- The **pretraining** strategy first trains the model on related tasks, and then fine-tunes it on the target task to transfer the knowledge. The pretrained language model can help with target tasks which lack training data.
- The **CoVe** model is pretrained on a machine translation task. Its encoder is then used to produce contextual embeddings.
- **ELMo** is a language model based on RNN. It can be used as a contextual embedder for downstream tasks.
- The **Transformer** architecture leverages **multihead attention** and **positional encoding** to produce contextual embeddings.
- The **GPT** model is a Transformer-based language model. It can adapt to target tasks by adding an output layer.

- The **BERT** model is a bidirectional language model based on Transformer. BERT is pretrained on two self-supervised learning tasks: MLM and NSP. BERT has excelled in many NLP tasks and is one of the most important milestones in the history of NLP.

References

[1] Dai AM, Le QV. Semi-supervised sequence learning. Advances in neural information processing systems. 2015. p. 3079−87.
[2] McCann B, Bradbury J, Xiong C, Socher R. Learned in translation: contextualized word vectors. Advances in neural information processing systems. 2017. p. 6294−305.
[3] Peters ME, Neumann M, Iyyer M, Gardner M, Clark C, Lee K, et al. Deep contextualized word representations. arXiv preprint arXiv 2018; 1802.05365.
[4] Radford A, Narasimhan K, Salimans T, Sutskever I. Improving language understanding by generative pretraining; 2018.
[5] Vaswani A, Shazeer N, Parmar N, Uszkoreit J, Jones L, Gomez AN, et al. Attention is all you need. Advances in neural information processing systems. 2017. p. 5998−6008.
[6] Devlin J, Chang MW, Lee K, Toutanova K. Bert: pretraining of deep bidirectional transformers for language understanding. arXiv preprint arXiv 2018; 1810.04805.

PART III

Application

CHAPTER 7

Code analysis of the SDNet model

7.1 Multiturn conversational machine reading comprehension model: SDNet

SDNet [1] is an machine reading comprehension (MRC) model that handles multiturn conversational reading comprehension tasks in 2018. SDNet won first place in the MRC competition conversational question answering (CoQA) and open-sourced its PyTorch version of code at https://github.com/microsoft/sdnet. The SDNet model contains an encoding layer, an interaction layer, and an output layer. It uses the pre-trained model Bidirectional Encoder Representations from Transformers (BERT). This section describes the network structure of SDNet and interprets its design principles and innovations.

7.1.1 Encoding layer

In a multiturn conversational reading comprehension task, there are multiple rounds of questions and answers for an article. To answer the kth question Q_k, the model needs to analyze the article C and the information from the previous $k-1$ rounds of questions and answers: $Q_1, A_1, \ldots, Q_{k-1}, A_{k-1}$. Thus SDNet proposes to concatenate the previous two rounds of questions and answers with the current question as the new context-aware question: $Q_{new} = \{Q_{k-2}; A_{k-2}; Q_{k-1}; A_{k-1}; Q_k\}$. In this way, the task is converted into a classic single-turn reading comprehension task.

SDNet uses the GloVe embeddings to represent words in the question and article. Additionally, each article word is represented by 12D part-of-speech (POS) embeddings, 8D named entity recognition (NER) embeddings, 3D exact match embeddings, and 1D word frequency embedding.

SDNet leverages the state-of-the-art BERT model to generate contextual embeddings for each word. Instead of fine-tuning BERT with a simple output layer, SDNet locks the parameters of BERT and leverages a parametrized weighted sum of each Transformer layer's embedding. Specifically, suppose BERT has L Transformer layers, SDNet defines L weight parameters: $\alpha_1, \ldots, \alpha_L$. When a word is fed into BERT, define $\boldsymbol{h}^t$ as its contextual embedding given by the tth Transformer layer. SDNet

Machine Reading Comprehension. DOI: https://doi.org/10.1016/B978-0-323-90118-5.00007-2
© 2021 Beijing Huazhang Graphics & Information Co., Ltd/China Machine Press.
Published by Elsevier Inc. All rights reserved.

then uses the linear combination of these layers' encodings: $\sum_{t=1}^{L} \alpha_t \boldsymbol{h}^t$. Note that only the weights $\alpha_1, \ldots, \alpha_L$ are updated, whereas all BERT parameters are locked.

However, there is one issue in the process above. BERT uses WordPiece for tokenization, which may generate subwords, but the GloVe embedding, POS embedding, and NER embedding are all based on words. Thus it is not possible to directly these embeddings with BERT embeddings. To solve this problem, SDNet applies WordPiece to each tokenized word to get a number of subwords. Then, the original word's BERT embedding is defined to be the average of these subwords' BERT embeddings. In detail, suppose a word w is tokenized by WordPiece into s subwords: $b_1, b_2, \ldots, b_s$, and the tth Transformer layer embeds b_i into a vector $\boldsymbol{h}_i^t$. The BERT embedding for w is then:

$$\text{BERT}(w) = \sum_{t=1}^{L} \alpha_t \frac{\sum_{i=1}^{s} \boldsymbol{h}_i^t}{s}$$

Since SDNet does not fine-tune BERT's parameters, the total number of parameters in SDNet is greatly reduced, which saves computing resources and speeds up timization. Moreover, this approach goes beyond the traditional fine-tuning method with an added output layer, which provides a new direction for applying BERT in natural language processing (NLP) models.

7.1.2 Interaction layer and output layer

The interaction layer of SDNet is similar to that of FusionNet in Section 5.3. It also uses word-level attention layer, reading layer, question understanding layer, fully-aware multilevel fusion layer, and fully-aware self-boosted fusion layer. However, since SDNet integrates previous rounds of questions and answers into the input question, the model implements a self-attention layer for the question to accommodate it at greater length. The final result of the interaction layer is the contextual embeddings of each article word, that is, $\{\boldsymbol{u}_i^C\}_{i=1}^m$, and the contextual embeddings of each question word, that is, $\{\boldsymbol{u}_i^Q\}_{i=1}^n$.

The CoQA task includes four types of answers: extractive, Yes, No, and unknown. Thus the output layer produces $2m + 3$ probability scores: $2m$ scores for each article word being the start and end position of the answer and 3 scores for Yes/No/unknown. SDNet is optimized by the cross entropy loss function.

7.2 Introduction to code

This section describes the structure of SDNet's open-source code and how to run the code.

7.2.1 Code structure

The code of SDNet contains two sections: Model and Function, which define network computation and common functions, respectively.

1. Model Section (Folder: Models)
   a. BaseTrainer.py: the base class of trainer, which initializes the trainer, produces logs, and so on.
   b. SDNetTrainer.py: trainer of SDNet, which defines the training/optimization/testing process and the saving/loading of models.
   c. SDNet.py: the SDNet network, which defines the network architecture and forward computation.
   d. Layers.py: all custom network layers.
   e. Folder Bert: code related to BERT
      i. Bert.py: use BERT in SDNet, which includes averaging subword embeddings.
      ii. modeling.py, optimization.py, tokenization.py: the PyTorch version of BERT by Huggingface, which loads the pretrained model and computes embeddings.
2. Function Section (Folder: Utils)
   a. Arguments.py, which reads the configuration file.
   b. Constants.py, which defines the constants used in the code, such as the id of out-of-vocabulary symbol <UNK>.
   c. CoQAPreprocess.py, which preprocesses the raw data of CoQA, tokenizes words, and sets up the dictionary.
   d. CoQAUtils.py, GeneralUtils.py, which define functions used in the trainer and network code of SDNet.

The main.py in the root folder is the entry code that performs the training and testing of SDNet.

7.2.2 How to run the code

7.2.2.1 Configuring the docker

The code of SDNet requires relevant packages, including PyTorch 0.4.1 and spaCy 2.0.16. To facilitate reproduction, all required packages have been encapsulated into a docker and uploaded to Docker Hub. Readers can choose between v3.0 or v4.0 from https://hub.docker.com/r/zcgzcgzcg/squadv2/tags.

Code 7-1 shows how to download and use the docker in Linux.

Code 7-1 Download and use the docker

```
docker login # then enter your account and password on Docker Hub
# download the docker
docker pull zcgzcgcg/squadv2:4.0
# enter the docker with nVidia GPU support. Map the local directory
   to /workspace/ in the docker
nvidia-docker run -it --mount src = '/',target = /workspace/,type =
   bind zcgzcgzcg/squadv2:4.0
# enter the mapped folder
cd /workspace
```

7.2.2.2 Download data

The open-sourced SDNet separates code from data and places them into two folders. This can facilitate code development and experimentation. In detail, one can create a folder *coqa*, and download the training and validation data (*coqa-train-v1.0.json* and *coqa-dev-v1.0.json*) from https://stanfordnlp.github.io/coqa/ into the subfolder *coqa/data*.

Since SDNet contains the BERT module, the pretrained model needs to be downloaded from Huggingface (https://github.com/huggingface/pytorch-transformers) into the BERT directory: *coqa/bert-large-uncased* (for BERT-large) or *coqa/bert-base-cased* (for BERT-base). Then, the BERT WordPiece files *bert-*-uncased-vocab.txt* (in the *bert_vocab_files* folder of SDNet) also need to be downloaded to the BERT directory.

Finally, create a *glove* folder in the same location as *coqa* to store the GloVe embedding file glove.840B.300d.txt downloadable from https://nlp.stanford.edu/projects/glove/.

Now, the folder structure is like the following:
1. sdnet/ (code)
    a. main.py
    b. other Python code
2. coqa/ (data)
    a. data/
        i. coqa-train-v1.0.json
        ii. coqa-dev-v1.0.json

    b. bert–large–uncased/
        i. bert–large–uncased–vocab.txt
        ii. bert_config.json
        iii. pytorch_model.bin
    c. conf
3. glove/: glove.840B.300d.txt

Note that the *coqa* folder contains the configuration file *conf*, which includes the definitions of various hyperparameters and data paths. We will introduce the configuration file in the next section.

7.2.2.3 Execute the code

In the code folder *sdnet*, the training can be started with the following command:

```
CUDA_VISIBLE_DEVICES = 0  python  main.py  train  [ path  to  coqa
                         folder] /conf
```

where CUDA_VISIBLE_DEVICES refers to the id of GPU to be used. In the Linux system, the id and status of each GPU can be monitored by the *nvidia-smi* command. *Main.py* is the entry code to SDNet, which requires two arguments: the command (train) and the path to the configuration file.

During the first time of training, the code will tokenize the input text, create the dictionary and store it in *coqa/conf~ /spacy_intermediate_feature~ /*. During each running, a new folder *run_[id]* will be created in *conf~ /*, which contains a copy of the configuration file, *conf_copy*, the log file *log.txt*, and the best model, *best_model.pt*, which has the highest performance on the validation set.

7.2.3 Configuration file

The SDNet model has many tunable hyperparameters, such as the number of recurrent neural network (RNN) layers, dimension of hidden states, and random seeds. As a result, we often need to try different combinations of these hyperparameters in experiments. The SDNet employs a configuration file to set all hyperparameters.

The configuration file should be placed in the data folder, such as *coqa/*. The path to the configuration file is an argument of *main.py*.

The code will use the path to locate the data folder. Each line in the configuration file defines a hyperparameter in one of two formats:

1 *Parameter_name Parameter_value*, for example, *SEED 1033*, indicating the initial seed value is 1033
2 *Property_name*, for example, *BERT* indicates that the model uses BERT's embedding

The first format is a key-value pair separated by a tab, indicating the name and value of the hyperparameter. The second format is a property name, indicating that the corresponding switch is on.

Code 7-2 shows the content of the configuration file in the open-sourced SDNet code, which can be used to reproduce the optimal result in the paper.

Code 7-2 Default configuration file for SDNet

```
# name of the raw training file
CoQA_TRAIN_FILE    data/coqa-train-v1.0.json
# name of the raw validation file
CoQA_DEV_FILE    data/coqa-dev-v1.0.json
# concatenate the previous PREV_ANS rounds of answers with the
  current question
PREV_ANS    2
# concatenate the previous PREV_QUES rounds of questions with the
  current question
PREV_QUES    2
# the dropout probability of word embeddings and BERT embeddings
dropout_emb    0.4
# the dropout probability in other modules, e.g. RNN.
DROPOUT    0.3
# variational dropout applies the same dropout mask to the inputs of
  each RNN unit
VARIATIONAL_DROPOUT
# use BERT model and its embeddings
BERT
# use the BERT-LARGE model
BERT_LARGE
# lock BERT's parameters during fine-tuning
LOCK_BERT
# compute the weighted sum of each BERT layer's output
BERT_LINEAR_COMBINE
# the pre-trained model and tokenization file for BERT-BASE and
  BERT-LARGE
```

(Continued)

```
(Continued)
BERT_tokenizer_file    bert-base-cased/bert-base-cased-vocab.txt
BERT_model_file    bert-base-cased/
BERT_large_tokenizer_file
   bert-large-uncased/bert-large-uncased-vocab.txt
BERT_large_model_file    bert-large-uncased/
# randomization seed
SEED    1033
# use spaCy for tokenization
SPACY_FEATURE
# path to GloVe embedding file
INIT_WORD_EMBEDDING_FILE    ../glove/glove.840B.300d.txt
# batch size
MINI_BATCH    32
# number of training epochs
EPOCH    30
# apply self-attention for question words
QUES_SELF_ATTN
# maximum number of words in the predicted answer
max_len    15
# whether to concatenate each RNN layer's output
concat_rnn    False
# range of gradient clipping
grad_clipping    10
# dimension of word embedding
embedding_dim    300
# dimension of hidden states in the word-level attention layer
prealign_hidden    300
# dimension of hidden states in the question self-attention layer
query_self_attn_hidden_size    300
# dimension of POS embedding
pos_dim    12
# dimension of NER embedding
ent_dim    8
# dimension of hidden states in the reading layer
hidden_size    125
# dimension of hidden states in the fully-aware cross-attention layer
deep_att_hidden_size_per_abstr    250
# number of layers in the fully-aware cross-attention RNN
in_rnn_layers    2
# dimension of the final article and question word representations
```

(Continued)

```
(Continued)
highlvl_hidden_size      125
# number of RNN layers in the question understanding layer
question_high_lvl_rnn_layers     1
```

The entry code *main.py* reads the information from the configuration file through the *Arguments* class and stores the content in the dictionary variable *opt*. As a result, for the above configuration file, opt['SEED'] = 1033, opt['pos_dim'] = 12, opt['SPACY_FEATURE'] = True, etc.

In addition, *main.py* defines the data folder as the folder that contains the configuration file:

```
opt['datadir'] = os.path.dirname(conf_file)
```

7.3 Preprocessing

The preprocessor file *Utils/CoQAPreprocess.py* converts the raw data into a format convenient for model training, including dictionary generation, text tokenization, and so on. The converted data is stored at the following path:

```
[ data folder] /conf~/spacy_intermediate_feature~/
```

7.3.1 Initialization

The initialization function *__init__* first checks whether the folder *spacy_intermediate_feature~* exists. If not, it starts the conversion process:

```
self.data_prefix = 'coqa-'
# labels for training and development datasets
dataset_labels = [ 'train', 'dev']
# check whether all data of the new format has been generated
allExist = True
# the data of new format is saved in coqa-train-preprocessed.json
  and coqa-dev-preprocessed.json
for dataset_label in dataset_labels:
```
(Continued)

(*Continued*)

```
    # self.spacyDir is the data folder
    if not os.path.exists(os.path.join(self.spacyDir, self.data_
        prefix + dataset_label + '-preprocessed.json')):
        allExist = False
# quit if the data of new format already exists
if allExist:
    return
print('Processed results not found, creating preprocessed files
    now...')
# load GloVe embeddings
self.glove_vocab = load_glove_vocab(self.glove_file, self.glove_
    dim, to_lower = False)
# make a new directory spacy_intermediate_feature~
if not os.path.isdir(self.spacyDir):
    os.makedirs(self.spacyDir)
    print('Directory created: ' + self.spacyDir)
# convert training and development data
for dataset_label in dataset_labels:
    self.preprocess(dataset_label)


# the load_glove_vocab function loads GloVe embeddings (function is
    defined in Utils/GeneralUtils.py)
def load_glove_vocab(file, wv_dim, to_lower = True):
    glove_vocab = set()
    with open(file, encoding = 'utf-8') as f:
        for line in f:
            elems = line.split()
            # in the GloVe file, each line has a word and its 300D
                embedding
            token = normalize_text(''.join(elems[ 0:-wv_dim] ))
            if to_lower:
                token = token.lower()
            glove_vocab.add(token)
    return glove_vocab
```

7.3.2 Preprocessing

7.3.2.1 Tokenization

The preprocessing function converts the raw text into word ids for subsequent training. The function first tokenizes the article, question, and answer:

```
# read the data in json format
with open(file_name, 'r') as f:
    dataset = json.load(f)
data = []
tot = len(dataset['data'])
# the tqdm package displays the progress bar
for data_idx in tqdm(range(tot)):
    # datum contains one article (context) with all rounds of
      questions and answers (qa)
    datum = dataset['data'][data_idx]
    context_str = datum['story']
    _datum = {'context': context_str,
               'source': datum['source'],
               'id': datum['id'],
               'filename': datum['filename']}
    # tokenization, NER and POS
    # get spaCy instance (defined in Utils/GeneralUtils.py)
    # nlp = spacy.load('en', parser = False)
    nlp_context = nlp(pre_proc(context_str))
    _datum['annotated_context'] = self.process(nlp_context)
    # obtain the start and end character location for each word in the
      original text, e.g. in I am fine, fine has a range of [5, 9)
    _datum['raw_context_offsets'] = self.get_raw_context_offsets
      (_datum['annotated_context']['word'], context_str)
    _datum['qas'] = []
    # additional_answer is similarly processed (omitted here)
    ......
    for i in range(len(datum['questions'])):
        # obtain the current round of question and answer
        question, answer = datum['questions'][i], datum['answers'][i]
        idx = question['turn_id']
        _qas = {'turn_id': idx,
            'question': question['input_text'],
            'answer': answer['input_text']}
        if idx in additional_answers:
            _qas['additional_answers'] = additional_answers[idx]
        # tokenize the question
        _qas['annotated_question'] = self.process(nlp(pre_proc
          (question['input_text'])))
        # tokenize the answer
```

(Continued)

(Continued)

```
        _qas[ 'annotated_answer'] = self.process(nlp(pre_proc
        (answer[ 'input_text']) ) )

# the pre_proc function converts punctuations into spaces (defined
  in Utils/GeneralUtils.py):
def pre_proc(text):
    # convert punctuations to spaces by regular expression
    text = re.sub(u'-|\u2010|\u2011|\u2012|\u2013|\u2014|\u2015|
        %|\[ |\] | : |\ (|\) |/|\t', space_extend, text)
    text = text.strip(' \n')
    # remove consecutive spaces
    text = re.sub('\s + ', ' ', text)
    return text
```

The raw data gives the ground-truth answer with the article sentence containing it. Here, the code locates the ground-truth answer within the article to get the start and end positions:

```
# input_text is the ground-truth answer
    _qas[ 'raw_answer'] = answer[ 'input_text']
    # span_start and span_end are the start and end positions of
      the article sentence containing the answer
    _qas[ 'answer_span_start'] = answer[ 'span_start']
    _qas[ 'answer_span_end'] = answer[ 'span_end']
    # look for input_text between span_start and span_end
    start = answer[ 'span_start']
    end = answer[ 'span_end']
    chosen_text = _datum[ 'context'][ start:end] .lower()
    # remove leading and trailing spaces
    while len(chosen_text) > 0 and chosen_text[ 0] in string.
        whitespace:
            chosen_text = chosen_text[ 1:]
            start + = 1
    while len(chosen_text) >0 and chosen_text[ - 1] in string.
        whitespace:
            chosen_text = chosen_text[ :-1]
            end - = 1
```

(Continued)

(Continued)

```
    input_text = _qas[ 'answer'] .strip () .lower ()
    # if the ground-truth answer appears between span_start and
      span_end, record its location; otherwise find a segment with
      the highest overlapping ratio
    if input_text in chosen_text:
        p = chosen_text.find(input_text)
        _qas[ 'answer_span'] = self.find_span (_datum[ 'raw_context_
            offsets'], start + p, start + p + len (input_text))
    else:
        _qas[ 'answer_span'] = self.find_span_with_gt ( _datum
          [ 'context'],
            _datum[ 'raw_context_offsets'] , input_text)
```

SDNet concatenates previous rounds of questions and answers with the current question, and computes its features including POS embedding, NER embedding, and exact match embedding.

```
    # concatenate the current question with the previous 2 rounds of
      question and answers
    long_question = ''
    for j in range (i - 2, i + 1):
        if j < 0:
            continue
        long_question += '' + datum[ 'questions'][ j][ 'input_text']
        if j < i:
            long_question += ' ' + datum[ 'answers'][ j][ 'input_text']
        long_question = long_question.strip ()
        # tokenize the new long_question
        nlp_long_question = nlp (long_question)
        # compute features
        _qas[ 'context_features'] = feature_gen (nlp_context,
          nlp_long_question)
        _datum[ 'qas'] .append ( _qas)
    data.append (_datum)

  # the feature_gen function generates features for words (defined in
    Utils/CoqaUtils.py)
```
(Continued)

```
(Continued)
def feature_gen(context, question):
    counter_ = Counter(w.text.lower() for w in context)
    total = sum(counter_.values())
    # compute word frequencies in the article
    term_freq =[ counter_[ w.text.lower()] / total for w in context]
    question_word = { w.text for w in question}
    question_lower = { w.text.lower() for w in question}
    # lemma is the word's lemma (e.g. the lemma of does is do)
    question_lemma = { w.lemma_ if w.lemma_ != '-PRON-' else w.text.
        lower() for w in question}
    match_origin = [ w.text in question_word for w in context]
    match_lower = [ w.text.lower() in question_lower for w in context]
    match_lemma = [ (w.lemma_ if w.lemma_ != '-PRON-' else w.text.
        lower()) in question_lemma for w in context]
    # word features include word frequencies and 3 exact match
        embeddings
    C_features = list(zip(term_freq, match_origin, match_lower,
        match_lemma))
    return C_features
```

7.3.2.2 Build the vocabulary

After tokenizing the words, the preprocessing code builds the dictionary to convert words into ids. To do that, all the words in GloVe are sorted in decreasing order of frequencies in the article, and likewise for all the words not in GloVe.

```
# build the vocabulary on training data
if dataset_label == 'train':
    contexts = [ _datum[ 'annotated_context'][ 'word'] for _datum in
        data]
    qas =[ qa[ 'annotated_question'][ 'word'] + qa[ 'annotated_
        answer'][ 'word'] for qa in _datum[ 'qas'] for _datum in data]
    self.train_vocab = self.build_vocab(contexts, qas)

def build_vocab(self, contexts, qas):
    # compute word frequencies
    counter_c = Counter(w for doc in contexts for w in doc)
    counter_qa = Counter(w for doc in qas for w in doc)
```
(Continued)

(Continued)

```
counter = counter_c + counter_qa
# sort words in GloVe in decreasing frequencies in the text
vocab = sorted([ t for t in counter_qa if t in self.glove_vocab] ,
    key = counter_qa.get, reverse = True)
# sort words not in GloVe in decreasing frequencies in the text
vocab += = sorted([ t for t in counter_c.keys() - counter_qa.keys()
    if t in self.glove_vocab] , key = counter.get, reverse = True)
# the first 4 dictionary words are special symbols
# <PAD> is for padding
vocab.insert(0, " < PAD > ")
# <UNK> is for out-of-vocabulary words
vocab.insert(1, " < UNK > ")
# questions from previous rounds are prepended with <Q>
vocab.insert(2, " < Q > ")
# answers from previous rounds are prepended with <A>
vocab.insert(3, " < A > ")
return vocab
```

7.3.2.3 Get word ids

After obtaining the dictionary, all words are converted into word ids:

```
# dictionary from words to ids
w2id = { w: i for i, w in enumerate(self.train_vocab)}
for _datum in data:
    # convert word into ids and save into wordid
    _datum[ 'annotated_context'][ 'wordid'] = token2id_sent (_datum
    [ 'annotated_context'][ 'word'] , w2id, unk_id = 1, to_lower = False)
    for qa in _datum[ 'qas'] :
        qa[ 'annotated_question'][ 'wordid'] = token2id_sent (qa
        [ 'annotated_question'][ 'word'] , w2id, unk_id = 1, to_lower
        = False)
        qa[ 'annotated_answer'][ 'wordid'] = token2id_sent
        (qa[ 'annotated_answer'][ 'word'] , w2id, unk_id = 1,
        to_lower = False)

# obtain id from word
def token2id_sent(sent, w2id, unk_id = None, to_lower = False) :
    if to_lower:
        sent = sent.lower()
```

(Continued)

(Continued)

```
    w2id_len = len(w2id)
    # return id if the word is in the dictionary, otherwise return
      unk_id
    ids = [ w2id[ w] if w in w2id else unk_id for w in sent]
    return ids
```

7.3.2.4 Save the dictionary and data of new format

If a dictionary word is in GloVe, the code assigns it its GloVe embedding. Otherwise the code assigns it a random embedding. The embeddings, dictionary, and data of the new format are stored in the folder *conf~ / spacy_intermediate_feature~ /*. The embeddings and dictionary are stored in MessagePack format and the new data is stored in json format:

```
if dataset_label == 'train':
    # obtain 300D embedding for each word
    embedding = build_embedding(self.glove_file, self.train_vocab,
      self.glove_dim)
    meta = { 'vocab': self.train_vocab, 'embedding': embedding.
      tolist()}
    meta_file_name = os.path.join(self.spacyDir, dataset_label +
      '_meta.msgpack')
    # store dictionary and embeddings in MessagePack format
    with open(meta_file_name, 'wb') as f:
        msgpack.dump(meta, f, encoding = 'utf8')
dataset[ 'data'] = data
# store the new format data in json
with open(output_file_name, 'w') as output_file:
    json.dump(dataset, output_file, sort_keys = True, indent = 4)
# get embeddings for words
def build_embedding(embed_file, targ_vocab, wv_dim) :
    vocab_size = len(targ_vocab)
    # random embeddings are uniform from -1 to 1 in each dimension
    emb = np.random.uniform(-1, 1, (vocab_size, wv_dim))
    # no. 0 word, <PAD>, has an all-zero embedding
    emb[ 0] = 0
    w2id = { w: i for i, w in enumerate(targ_vocab)}
    # read GloVe embeddings
```

(Continued)

```
(Continued)
    with open(embed_file, encoding = "utf8") as f:
        for line in f:
            elems = line.split()
            token = normalize_text(''.join(elems[ 0:-wv_dim] ))
            # it the word is in GloVe, it is assigned its GloVe embedding
            if token in w2id:
                emb[ w2id[ token]] = [ float(v) for v in elems[ -wv_dim:]]
    return emb
```

7.3.2.5 Load the dictionary and embeddings

The function *load_data* loads the dictionary and embeddings in *conf~ / spacy_intermediate_feature ~ /*.

```
def load_data(self):
    # loads the dictionary and embeddings
    meta_file_name = os.path.join(self.spacyDir, 'train_meta.
        msgpack')
    with open(meta_file_name, 'rb') as f:
        meta = msgpack.load(f, encoding = 'utf8')
    embedding = torch.Tensor(meta[ 'embedding'] )
    # store the size of dictionary and dimension of embeddings
    self.opt[ 'vocab_size'] = embedding.size(0)
    self.opt[ 'vocab_dim'] = embedding.size(1)
    return meta[ 'vocab'] , embedding
```

7.4 Training

The training code of SDNet adopts a two-level structure: the base class in *BaseTrainer.py* and the subclass in *SDNetTrainer.py*, both in the folder *Models*.

7.4.1 Base class

The file *Models/BaseTrainerTrainer.py* defines basic functions in the trainer, such as setting up a new folder to save the model, configuration file, and logs. The function *getSaveFolder* looks for the smallest number id such that *run_[id]* folder does not exist in *conf~ /*, and then creates the folder. Thus the first time the code runs, this function creates the folder *run_1*; the second time the code runs, this function creates the folder *run_2*, and so on.

```
def getSaveFolder(self):
    runid = 1
    # starting from run_1, it looks for the smallest id such that the
      folder run_id does not exist, and then creates the folder
    while True:
        saveFolder = os.path.join(self.opt['datadir'], 'conf~',
          'run_' + str(runid))
        if not os.path.exists(saveFolder):
            self.saveFolder = saveFolder
            os.makedirs(self.saveFolder)
            return
        runid = runid + 1
```

7.4.2 Subclass

The subclass in *Models/SDNetTrainer.py* inherits from the base class in *Models/BaseTrainer.py*. The subclass controls the training and testing of SDNet.

7.4.2.1 Training function

The training proceeds in batches, that is, the gradients are computed and the model is updated based on the current batch of data. For every 1500 batches, the code evaluates the model's performance on the validation set. The model with the highest accuracy score so far is saved in the *run_id* folder as *best_model.pt*. Here's the code analysis for the training function *train*:

```
def train(self):
    # set the training mode
    self.isTrain = True
    self.getSaveFolder()
    self.saveConf()
    # get the dictionary and embeddings from the preprocessor
    self.vocab, vocab_embedding = self.preproc.load_data()
    # initialize the model
    self.setup_model(vocab_embedding)
    # if it's in RESUME mode, load the saved model
    if 'RESUME' in self.opt:
        model_path = os.path.join(self.opt['datadir'], self.opt
          ['MODEL_PATH'])
        self.load_model(model_path)
```
(Continued)

(Continued)

```
# read preprocessed data in the new format
with open(os.path.join(self.opt['FEATURE_FOLDER'], self.data_
    prefix + 'train-preprocessed.json'), 'r') as f:
    train_data = json.load(f)
print('Loading dev json...')
with open(os.path.join(self.opt['FEATURE_FOLDER'], self.data_
    prefix + 'dev-preprocessed.json'), 'r') as f:
    dev_data = json.load(f)
# record the highest F1 score on the validation set so far
best_f1_score = 0.0
# get the number of training epochs
numEpochs = self.opt['EPOCH']
for epoch in range(self.epoch_start, numEpochs):
    # set the training model, which enables functions like Dropout
    self.network.train()
    # the batch generator for training data
    train_batches = BatchGen(self.opt, train_data['data'],
        self.use_cuda, self.vocab)
    # the batch generator for validation data
    dev_batches = BatchGen(self.opt, dev_data['data'], self.
        use_cuda, self.vocab, evaluation = True)
    for i, batch in enumerate(train_batches):
        # evaluate on the validation data every 1,500 batches, or at
            the end of each epoch, or the 1st batch under RESUME mode
        if i == len(train_batches) − 1 or (epoch == 0 and i == 0
            and ('RESUME' in self.opt)) or (i > 0 and i % 1500 == 0):
            predictions = []
            confidence = []
            dev_answer = []
            final_json = []
            for j, dev_batch in enumerate(dev_batches):
                # the prediction includes the answer text, proba-
                    bilities, and json-format answers
                phrase, phrase_score, pred_json = self.predict
                    (dev_batch)
                final_json.extend(pred_json)
                predictions.extend(phrase)
                confidence.extend(phrase_score)
                dev_answer.extend(dev_batch[ − 3]) # answer_str
            # compute exact match and F1 scores
```

(Continued)

(Continued)

```
            result,  all_f1s  =  score(predictions,  dev_answer,
                final_json)
            f1 = result['f1']
            if f1 > best_f1_score:
                # if the current F1 score is higher than previous
                    results, save the current model
                model_file = os.path.join(self.saveFolder,
                    'best_model.pt')
                self.save_for_predict(model_file, epoch)
                best_f1_score = f1
                pred_json_file = os.path.join(self.saveFolder,
                    'prediction.json')
                with open(pred_json_file, 'w') as output_file:
                    json.dump(final_json, output_file)
        # compute gradient and update the model based on the
            current batch
        self.update(batch)
```

7.4.2.2 Forward function

The previous function *train* calls the function *update* at the end, which conducts forward calculation of SDNet on the batch of data. Additionally, the function *update* computes the loss function value and updates the parameters. The parameter update uses the Autograd function in PyTorch, which automatically calculates gradients based on the computation graph.

Since the answer in the CoQA task includes extractive form, Yes, No, and No answer, the *update* function generates the probabilities for all cases: suppose there are m words in the article, the network produces $m^2 + 3$ scores, corresponding to all article intervals with the three special answers.

Here's the *update* function:

```
def update(self, batch):
    # enter training mode
    self.network.train()
    self.network.drop_emb = True
```

(Continued)

(Continued)

```
# obtain articles, questions and answers from the batch, including
  word ids, POS and NER embeddings, BERT word ids, etc.
x, x_mask, x_features, x_pos, x_ent, x_bert, x_bert_mask,
  x_bert_offsets, query, query_mask, query_bert, query_bert_
  mask, query_bert_offsets, ground_truth, context_str, context_
  words, _, _, _, _ = batch
# forward calculation to get predictions:
# 1. the probability that the answer starts from and ends at
  each location in the article: score_s, score_e. Size: batch ×
  context_word_num
# 2. the probability of Yes/No/No answer: score_yes, score_no,
  score_no_answer. Size: batch × 1
score_s, score_e, score_yes, score_no, score_no_answer = self.
  network(x, x_mask, x_features, x_pos, x_ent, x_bert, x_bert_
  mask, x_bert_offsets, query, query_mask, query_bert, query_
  bert_mask, query_bert_offsets, len(context_words))
# get the pre-defined maximum answer length
max_len = self.opt[ 'max_len'] or score_s.size(1)
batch_size = score_s.shape[ 0]
m = score_s.size(1)
# the function gen_upper_triangle calculates a 2D matrix A based
  on score_s and score_e
# A[ i,j] = score_s[ i] × score_e[ j] , for i< = j< = i+max_len-1,
  otherwise A[ i,j] = 0
# A is then converted to a 1D array of size max_len × max_len
  expand_score = gen_upper_triangle(score_s, score_e, max_len,
  self.use_cuda)
# concatenate probabilities of extractive answers with those of
  Yes/No/No answer
scores = torch.cat((expand_score, score_no, score_yes, score_
  no_answer), dim = 1)
# the ground-truth answer's position in the article is converted
  into a position id to align with expand_score, e.g.:
#[ 0, 3] becomes 0 × m + 3 = 3
#[ 3, 5] becomes 3 × m + 5
# No becomes m × m
# Yes becomes m × m + 1
# No answer becomes m × m + 2
targets = [ ]
span_idx = int(m * m)
```

(Continued)

(Continued)

```
    for i in range(ground_truth.shape[ 0] ):
        if ground_truth[ i][ 0] == −1 and ground_truth[ i][ 1] == −1:
            # No answer
            targets.append(span_idx + 2)
        if ground_truth[ i][ 0] == 0 and ground_truth[ i][ 1] == −1: # No
            targets.append(span_idx)
        if ground_truth[ i][ 0] == −1 and ground_truth[ i][ 1] == 0:
            # Yes
            targets.append(span_idx + 1)
        if ground_truth[ i][ 0] != −1 and ground_truth[ i][ 1] != −1:
            # extractive
            targets.append(ground_truth[ i][ 0] * m + ground_truth[ i]
              [ 1] )
    targets = torch.LongTensor(np.array(targets) )
    if self.use_cuda:
        targets = targets.cuda()
    # cross entropy loss
    loss = self.loss_func(scores, targets)
    # clear all gradients
    self.optimizer.zero_grad()
    # automatic gradient computation using PyTorch function
    loss.backward()
    # gradient clipping to avoid gradient explosion
    torch.nn.utils.clip_grad_norm(self.network.parameters(),
      self.opt[ 'grad_clipping'] )
    # update parameters
    self.optimizer.step()
    self.updates += 1
```

7.4.2.3 Evaluation

SDNet evaluates the model on the validation set every 1500 batches via the *predict* function. Similar to the *update* function, *predict* conducts forward calculation to obtain model's predictions. Then, it selects the answer with the highest probability. Here's the code analysis of the *predict* function:

```
# set the model to evaluation mode, i.e. no gradient is computed and
  dropout is disabled
```

(Continued)

(Continued)

```
self.network.eval()
self.network.drop_emb = False
# forward calculation to get model predictions
x, x_mask, x_features, x_pos, x_ent, x_bert, x_bert_mask, x_bert_
    offsets, query, query_mask, query_bert, query_bert_mask, query_
    bert_offsets, ground_truth, context_str, context_words, context_
    word_offsets, answers, context_id, turn_ids = batch
m = len(context_words)
score_s, score_e, score_yes, score_no, score_no_answer = self.
    network(x, x_mask, x_features, x_pos, x_ent, x_bert, x_bert_
    mask, x_bert_offsets, query, query_mask, query_bert, query_
    bert_mask, query_bert_offsets, len(context_words))
# get batch size
batch_size = score_s.shape[0]
# get maximum answer length
max_len = self.opt['max_len'] or score_s.size(1)
# get a 1D probability vector of size m × m + 3
expand_score = gen_upper_triangle(score_s, score_e, max_len,
    self.use_cuda)
scores = torch.cat((expand_score, score_no, score_yes, score_
    no_answer), dim = 1) # batch × (m × m + 3)
# put the result in CPU for numpy operations
prob = F.softmax(scores, dim = 1).data.cpu()
# store the text of      predicted answer
predictions = []
# store the probability of predicted answer
confidence = []
# store answers in json format
pred_json = []
for i in range(batch_size):
    # sort all answer candidates in decreasing probabilities
    _, ids = torch.sort(prob[i, :], descending = True)
    idx = 0
    # best_id is the id with the maximum probability
    best_id = ids[idx]
    # record the maximum probability
    confidence.append(float(prob[i, best_id]))
    # case 1: extractive answer
```

(Continued)

(Continued)

```
    if best_id < m * m:
        # convert best_id to start position st and end position ed
        st = best_id / m
        ed = best_id % m
        # context_word_offsets provides the positions of the first
          and last character of each word in the article
        st = context_word_offsets[ st][ 0]
        ed = context_word_offsets[ ed][ 1]
        # obtain the text of the predicted answer
        predictions.append(context_str[ st:ed] )
    # case 2: No
    if best_id == m * m:
        predictions.append('no')
    # case 3: Yes
    if best_id == m * m + 1:
        predictions.append('yes')
    # case 4: No answer
    if best_id == m * m + 2:
        predictions.append('unknown')
    # store answer in json format
    pred_json.append({
        'id': context_id,
        'turn_id': turn_ids[ i] ,
        'answer': predictions[ − 1]
    } )
return (predictions, confidence, pred_json)
```

7.5 Batch generator

The SDNet training and testing functions in the previous section are based on data batches. During training, we usually reshuffle all the training data at the beginning of each epoch, and then sequentially generate batches of data. For example, suppose there are 10 data samples of which the reshuffled order in this epoch is [3,7,4,1,9,10,2,6,5,8], and the batch size is 2. Then the data batches are [3,7], [4,1], [9,10], [2,6] and [5,8]. During training, the gradients are computed using one batch and the network parameters are updated. If we use the gradient descent optimizer, this approach is also called the **Stochastic Gradient Descent (SGD)**.

To implement the above process, SDNet employs a batch generator, *BatchGen*. At the beginning of each epoch, *BatchGen* reshuffles all articles. Then, one batch is defined as an article and its related questions and answers in all rounds. As the questions in one batch may have varying lengths, we use the following padding technique.

7.5.1 Padding

In the batch generation for NLP data, there is an important concept: **padding**. Usually, the text in the same batch forms an input matrix, composed of all word ids. However, since different inputs may have varying lengths, each line of the matrix is not equal in length. PyTorch, on the other hand, requires that each dimension of a tensor has the same length. Thus we need to pad the representations.

Suppose there are *batch_size* input texts, and the maximum length is *L* words. The word ids form a matrix of size *batch_size* × *L*. If one input instance contains fewer than *L* words, the special word <PAD> with word id 0 will fill the gaps. Meanwhile, to indicate the paddings, we create a mask matrix of *batch_size* × *L*, which contains 1 if the corresponding position has an input word, and 0 otherwise. Fig. 7.1 shows an example.

The *BatchGen* class in *Utils/CoQAUtils.py* constructs the batch data including the padding. Note that we will defer the introduction to the batch generation for BERT to the next section.

The first function in *BatchGen* is the constructor ___init___:

Maximum length *L*=5

I	am	happy		
he	goes	to	the	gym
this	is	a	good	book
come	home			

Batch_size=4

Word ids

3	20	4	0	0
16	5	2	7	32
6	9	15	17	28
12	26	0	0	0

Mask matrix

1	1	1	0	0
1	1	1	1	1
1	1	1	1	1
1	1	0	0	0

Figure 7.1 Word ids and the mask matrix in one batch.

```
def __init__(self, opt, data, use_cuda, vocab, evaluation = False):
    self.data = data
    self.use_cuda = use_cuda
    # vocab is the vocabulary, sorted by word ids
    self.vocab = vocab
    # evaluation indicates whether it's evaluation mode
    self.evaluation = evaluation
    self.opt = opt
    # each question is concatenated with certain previous rounds of
      questions and answers
    if 'PREV_ANS' in self.opt:
        self.prev_ans = self.opt['PREV_ANS']
    else:
        self.prev_ans = 2
    if 'PREV_QUES' in self.opt:
        self.prev_ques = self.opt['PREV_QUES']
    else:
        self.prev_ques = 0
    # upper limit for the length of the concatenated question
    self.ques_max_len = (30 + 1) * self.prev_ans + (25 + 1) * (self.
      prev_ques + 1)
    # shuffle the data
    if not evaluation:
        indices = list(range(len(self.data)))
        random.shuffle(indices)
        self.data = [self.data[i] for i in indices]
```

BatchGen provides an iterator to be directly used in loop statements. In Python, *__iter__* is a predefined name of an iterator function, which uses the *yield* command to produce information for the caller loop. In SDNet, the iterator in *BatchGen* provides information such as article word ids, question word ids, mask matrix, and features in a batch. These are later used in the network's forward calculation. Here's the analysis for the code of the iterator function:

```
def __iter__(self):
    data = self.data
    # the maximum number of words in the answer
```

                                                                (Continued)

(Continued)

```
MAX_ANS_SPAN = 15
for datum in data:
    if not self.evaluation:
        # ignore exceedingly long answers during training
        datum['qas'] = [ qa for qa in datum['qas'] if len(qa
            ['annotated_answer']['word']) == 1 or qa['answer_
            span'][1] - qa['answer_span'][0] < MAX_ANS_SPAN]
    if len(datum['qas']) == 0:
        continue
    # context_len is the number of words in the article of this batch
    context_len = len(datum['annotated_context']['wordid'])
    x_len = context_len
    # qa_len is the number of rounds, which is equal to batch_size
    qa_len = len(datum['qas'])
    batch_size = qa_len
    # x contains article word ids
    x = torch.LongTensor(1, x_len).fill_(0)
    # x_pos contains POS ids of article words
    x_pos = torch.LongTensor(1, x_len).fill_(0)
    # x_pos contains NER ids of article words
    x_ent = torch.LongTensor(1, x_len).fill_(0)
    # query contains the question word ids. Size: batch_size ×
      ques_max_len
    query = torch.LongTensor(batch_size, self.ques_max_len).
      fill_(0)
    # the start and end positions of the ground-truth answer in
      the article
    ground_truth = torch.LongTensor(batch_size, 2).fill_(-1)
    # article ID
    context_id = datum['id']
    # the original article text
    context_str = datum['context']
    # the article words
    context_words = datum['annotated_context']['word']
    # the position of the first and last character of each word in
      the article
    context_word_offsets = datum['raw_context_offsets']
    # the ground-truth answer text
    answer_strs = []
    turn_ids = []
```

(Continued)

(Continued)

```
# obtain pre-processed word ids
x[ 0, :context_len] = torch.LongTensor(datum[ 'annotated_
  context'] [ 'wordid'])
x_pos[ 0, :context_len] = torch.LongTensor(datum[ 'annotated_
  context'][ 'pos_id'])
x_ent[ 0, :context_len] = torch.LongTensor(datum[ 'annotated_
  context'][ 'ent_id'])
# process each round of QA
for i in range(qa_len):
    # obtain features for article words, including word
      frequencies and exact match embedding
    x_features[ i, :context_len, :4] = torch.Tensor(datum
      [ 'qas'][ i] [ 'context_features'])
    turn_ids.append(int(datum[ 'qas'][ i][ 'turn_id']))
    # concatenate the question with previous rounds of
      questions and answers
    # p indicates the number of words in the current concatenation
    p = 0
    ques_words = []
    for j in range(i - self.prev_ans, i + 1):
        if j < 0:
            continue;
        # questions with "No answer" is not concatenated
        if not self.evaluation and datum[ 'qas'][ j][ 'answer_
          span'][ 0] == - 1:
            continue
        # each question is prepended with <Q> (word id 2)
        q = [ 2] + datum[ 'qas'][ j][ 'annotated_question']
          [ 'wordid']
        if j >= i - self.prev_ques and p + len(q) <= self.
          ques_max_len:
            ques_words.extend([ '<Q>']  +  datum[ 'qas'][ j]
              [ 'annotated_question'][ 'word'])
            query[ i, p: (p + len(q))] = torch.LongTensor(q)
            ques = datum[ 'qas'][ j][ 'question'] .lower()
            p + = len(q)
            # each answer is prepended with <A> (word id 3)
            a = [ 3] + datum[ 'qas'][ j][ 'annotated_answer']
              [ 'wordid']
```

(Continued)

```
                    if j < i and j >= i - self.prev_ans and p + len(a)
                    <= self.ques_max_len:
                        ques_words.extend([ '<A>'] + datum[ 'qas'][ j]
                        [ 'annotated_answer'][ 'word'])
                        query[ i, p:(p + len(a))] = torch.LongTensor(a)
                        p += len(a)
                # the start and end positions of the ground-truth answer
                  in the article
                ground_truth[ i, 0] = datum[ 'qas'][ i][ 'answer_span'][ 0]
                ground_truth[ i, 1] = datum[ 'qas'][ i][ 'answer_span'][ 1]
                answer = datum[ 'qas'][ i][ 'raw_answer']
                # answer of special types
                # define "Yes" as start = -1, end = 0
                if answer.lower() in[ 'yes', 'yes.'] :
                    ground_truth[ i, 0] = −1
                    ground_truth[ i, 1] = 0
                    answer_str = 'yes'
                # define "No" as start = 0, end = −1
                    ground_truth[ i, 0] = 0
                    ground_truth[ i, 1] = −1
                    answer_str = 'no'
                # define "No Answer" as start = -1, end = −1
                if answer.lower() == [ 'unknown', 'unknown.'] :
                ground_truth[ i, 0] = −1
                    ground_truth[ i, 1] = −1
                    answer_str = 'unknown'
                if ground_truth[ i, 0] >= 0 and ground_truth[ i, 1] >= 0:
                    answer_str = answer
                # CoQA also provides additional answer candidates
                all_viable_answers = [ answer_str]
                if 'additional_answers' in datum[ 'qas'][ i] :

                    all_viable_answers.extend(datum[ 'qas'][ i]
                    [ 'additional_answers'])
                answer_strs.append(all_viable_answers)
        # generate the mask matrix based on padding (<PAD> has word id 0)
        x_mask = 1 - torch.eq(x, 0)
        query_mask = 1 - torch.eq(query, 0)
        # put tensors into GPU
        x = Variable(x.cuda(async = True))
        x_mask = Variable(x_mask.cuda(async = True))
```

(Continued)

```
        x_features = Variable(x_features.cuda(async = True))
        x_pos = Variable(x_pos.cuda(async = True))
        x_ent = Variable(x_ent.cuda(async = True))
        query = Variable(query.cuda(async = True))
        query_mask = Variable(query_mask.cuda(async = True))
        ground_truth = Variable(ground_truth.cuda(async = True))
        # the iterator yields all related data in the batch
        yield(x, x_mask, x_features, x_pos, x_ent, x_bert, x_bert_
            mask, x_bert_offsets, query, query_mask, query_bert, query_
            bert_mask, query_bert_offsets, ground_truth, context_str,
            context_words, context_word_offsets, answer_strs, context_
            id, turn_ids)
```

7.5.2 Preparing data for Bidirectional Encoder Representations from Transformers

Since the SDNet model employs BERT to produce contextual embeddings, it provides the BERT model with the required input format. BERT uses its own tokenization tool based on WordPiece and comes with a predefined dictionary of subwords. However, SDNet uses spaCy for tokenization, which may not align with the WordPiece tokens.

To address this inconsistency problem, SDNet firstly uses spaCy to obtain individual words, and then leverages BERT's tokenizer to split each word into subwords. In this way, each word corresponds to one or more WordPiece subwords. For example, if the result from spaCy is [*Johanson, 's, house*], the subwords will be [[CLS], *johan, ##son, ', s, house*, [SEP]], where [CLS] and [SEP] are the start and end symbols defined in BERT. # indicates that this subword, together with previous subwords, make one word.

Here's the analysis for the part of code in *BatchGen* for generating BERT subwords.

```
def __init__(self):
    ...
    self.bert_tokenizer = None
    if 'BERT' in self.opt:
        # use BERT-Large pre-trained model
        if 'BERT_LARGE' in opt:
```

(Continued)

(Continued)

```
        tkz_file = os.path.join(opt[ 'datadir'] , opt[ 'BERT_
            large_tokenizer_file'] )
        # use the WordPiece tokenizer from BERT
        self.bert_tokenizer = BertTokenizer.from_pretrained
            (tkz_file)
    else:
    # use BERT-Base pre-trained model
        tkz_file = os.path.join(opt[ 'datadir'] , opt[ 'BERT_
            tokenizer_file'] )
        self.bert_tokenizer = BertTokenizer.from_pretrained
            (tkz_file)
```

The bertify function then continues to tokenize each word into BERT subwords:

```
# BERT tokenization on each word in a list
# Input:
# words: a list of words, which is the tokenized result of spaCy
def bertify(self, words):
    if self.bert_tokenizer is None:
        return None
    # subwords contains the subwords tokenized by BERT, starting
      with [ CLS]
    subwords = [ '[ CLS]']
    # x_bert_offsets stores the position of the first and last sub-
      word of each word
    x_bert_offsets = [ ]
    for word in words:
        # split each word into sub-words by BERT' s tokenizer
        now = self.bert_tokenizer.tokenize(word)
        # store the position of the first and last sub-word for word
        x_bert_offsets.append([ len(subwords), len(subwords) + len
            (now)] )
        subwords.extend(now)
    # the last sub-word is [ SEP]
    subwords.append('[ SEP] ')
    # convert sub-words into ids in BERT tokenizer
    x_bert = self.bert_tokenizer.convert_tokens_to_ids(subwords)
    return x_bert, x_bert_offsets
```

Finally, the iterator __*iter*__ yields the result from *bertify* function in the batch data.

```
def __iter__(self):
    ...
    if 'BERT' in self.opt:
        # obtain results from the bertify function
        x_bert, x_bert_offsets = self.bertify(datum[ 'annotated_
            context'][ 'word'] )
        # the article is shared in one batch
        x_bert_mask = torch.LongTensor(1, len(x_bert)).fill_(1)
        x_bert = torch.tensor([ x_bert] , dtype = torch.long)
        x_bert_offsets = torch.tensor([ x_bert_offsets] , dtype =
            torch.long)
    # tokenize each question using the BERT tokenizer
    query_bert_offsets = torch.LongTensor(batch_size, self.ques_
        max_len, 2).fill_(0)
    # save the BERT tokenization results in q_bert_list to get the
        maximum length
    q_bert_list = [ ]
    if 'BERT' in self.opt:
        now_bert, now_bert_offsets = self.bertify(ques_words)
        query_bert_offsets[ i,:len(now_bert_offsets),:]  = torch.
            tensor(now_bert_offsets, dtype = torch.long)
        q_bert_list.append(now_bert)
    if 'BERT' in self.opt:
        # obtain the maximum question length bert_len in the batch
        bert_len = max([ len(s) for s in q_bert_list] )
        # create PyTorch tensors to store question word ids
        query_bert = torch.LongTensor(batch_size, bert_len).
            fill_(0)
        query_bert_mask = torch.LongTensor(batch_size, bert_len).
            fill_(0)
        # put the tokenized sub-word ids into the tensors
        for i in range(len(q_bert_list)):
            query_bert[ i,:len(q_bert_list[ i] )]  = torch.LongTensor
                (q_bert_list[ i] )
            query_bert_mask[ i,:len(q_bert_list[ i] )] = 1
        # put the tensors into GPU
        x_bert = Variable(x_bert.cuda(async = True))
        x_bert_mask = Variable(x_bert_mask.cuda(async = True))
```

(Continued)

(Continued)

```
        query_bert = Variable(query_bert.cuda(async = True))
        query_bert_mask = Variable(query_bert_mask.cuda
            (async = True))
```

7.6 SDNet model

The core part of the implementation, *SDNet.py*, defines the network structure and forward computation. As a PyTorch network class, the *SDNet* class inherits from *nn.Module* to register parameters to be optimized. Also, it implements the constructor function *__init__* and the *forward* function.

7.6.1 Network class

The network class *SDNet* is defined in *Models/SDNet.py*. The constructor *__init__* defines the network layers. Here's an analysis of the code:

```
# Input:
# word_embedding contains the Glove embeddings for words in the
  dictionary
def __init__(self, opt, word_embedding):
    super(SDNet, self).__init__()
    self.opt = opt
    # set the dropout probability
    set_dropout_prob(0. if not 'DROPOUT' in opt else float(opt
      ['DROPOUT']))
    set_seq_dropout('VARIATIONAL_DROPOUT' in self.opt)
    # x_input_size stores the dimension of each article word's
      feature
    # ques_input_size stores the dimension of each question word's
      feature
    x_input_size = 0
    ques_input_size = 0
    # size of vocabulary
    self.vocab_size = int(opt['vocab_size'])
    # dimension of GloVe embeddings
    vocab_dim = int(opt['vocab_dim'])
    # nn.Embedding is the embedder module in PyTorch
```

(Continued)

(Continued)

```
self.vocab_embed = nn.Embedding(self.vocab_size,vocab_dim,
  padding_idx = 1)
# initialize the embedder weights using GloVe
self.vocab_embed.weight.data = word_embedding
x_input_size + = vocab_dim
ques_input_size + = vocab_dim
# the embedding layer' s parameters are locked, i.e. no gradients
  are required
self.vocab_embed.weight.requires_grad = False
if 'BERT' in self.opt:
    self.Bert = Bert(self.opt)
    if 'LOCK_BERT' in self.opt:
        # lock BERT' s parameters
        for p in self.Bert.parameters():
            p.requires_grad = False
    if 'BERT_LARGE' in self.opt:
        bert_dim = 1024
        bert_layers = 24
    else:
        bert_dim = 768
        bert_layers = 12
    if 'BERT_LINEAR_COMBINE' in self.opt:
        # define alpha and gamma for linear combination of BERT
          layers' output
        self.alphaBERT = nn.Parameter(torch.Tensor
          (bert_layers), requires_grad = True)
        self.gammaBERT = nn.Parameter(torch.Tensor(1, 1),
          requires_grad = True)
        torch.nn.init.constant(self.alphaBERT, 1.0)
        torch.nn.init.constant(self.gammaBERT, 1.0)
    x_input_size + = bert_dim
    ques_input_size + = bert_dim
# word-level attention layer
self.pre_align = Attention(vocab_dim, opt[ 'prealign_hidden'] ,
  do_similarity = True)
x_input_size + = vocab_dim
# POS and NER embeddings
pos_dim = opt[ 'pos_dim']
ent_dim = opt[ 'ent_dim']
self.pos_embedding = nn.Embedding(len(POS), pos_dim)
self.ent_embedding = nn.Embedding(len(ENT), ent_dim)
```

(Continued)

(Continued)

```
# article word features, e.g. word frequencies and exact match
x_feat_len = 4
x_input_size + = pos_dim+ ent_dim+ x_feat_len
addtional_feat = 0
# RNN layer for the article
self.context_rnn, context_rnn_output_size = RNN_from_opt(x_
   input_size, opt[ 'hidden_size'] , num_layers = opt[ 'in_rnn_
   layers'] , concat_rnn = opt[ 'concat_rnn'] , add_feat = addtional_
   feat)
# RNN layer for the question
self.ques_rnn, ques_rnn_output_size = RNN_from_opt(ques_input_
   size, opt[ 'hidden_size'] , num_layers = opt[ 'in_rnn_layers'] ,
   concat_rnn = opt[ 'concat_rnn'] , add_feat = addtional_feat)
# fully-aware cross-attention layer
self.deep_attn = DeepAttention(opt, abstr_list_cnt = opt
   [ 'in_rnn_layers'] , deep_att_hidden_size_per_abstr = opt
   [ 'deep_att_hidden_size_per_abstr'] , word_hidden_size = vocab_
   dim+ addtional_feat)
self.deep_attn_input_size = self.deep_attn.rnn_input_size
self.deep_attn_output_size = self.deep_attn.output_size
# question understanding layer
self.high_lvl_ques_rnn, high_lvl_ques_rnn_output_size = RNN_
   from_opt (ques_rnn_output_size * opt[ 'in_rnn_layers'] ,
   opt[ 'highlvl_hidden_size'] , num_layers = opt[ 'question_high_
   lvl_rnn_layers'] , concat_rnn = True)
# calculate the dimension of history of word vectors
self.after_deep_attn_size = self.deep_attn_output_size +
   self.deep_attn_input_size + addtional_feat + vocab_dim
self.self_attn_input_size = self.after_deep_attn_size
self_attn_output_size = self.deep_attn_output_size
#  self-attention layer for article
self.highlvl_self_att = Attention(self.self_attn_input_size,
   opt[ 'deep_att_hidden_size_per_abstr')
# high level RNN layer for article
self.high_lvl_context_rnn,   high_lvl_context_rnn_output_size
   = RNN_from_opt (self.deep_attn_output_size + self_attn_
   output_size,    opt[ 'highlvl_hidden_size'] ,
   num_layers = 1, concat_rnn = False)
# final dimension of article word vectors
context_final_size = high_lvl_context_rnn_output_size
# question self-attention layer
```

(Continued)

(Continued)

```
self.ques_self_attn = Attention(high_lvl_ques_rnn_output_
  size, opt[ 'query_self_attn_hidden_size'] )
# final dimension of question word vectors
ques_final_size = high_lvl_ques_rnn_output_size
# linear attention layer to get the question vector
self.ques_merger = LinearSelfAttn(ques_final_size)
# output layer
self.get_answer = GetFinalScores(context_final_size,
  ques_final_size)
```

Then, the *forward* function takes the batch data generated by *BatchGen* as input and calculates the scores via the network layers. Here's an analysis of the code:

```
def forward(self, x, x_single_mask, x_features, x_pos, x_ent,
  x_bert, x_bert_mask, x_bert_offsets, q, q_mask, q_bert, q_bert_
  mask, q_bert_offsets,    context_len):
    batch_size = q.shape[ 0]
    # as the batch shares the article, x_single_mask only has 1 row
    # the code repeats x_single_mask by batch_size times to align
      with the question tensors
    x_mask = x_single_mask.expand(batch_size, -1)
    # the article word embeddings are also repeated by batch_size
      times
    x_word_embed=self.vocab_embed(x).expand(batch_size, - 1, - 1)
    # obtain question word embeddings
    ques_word_embed = self.vocab_embed(q)
    # history of word (concept in FusionNet) for article words
    x_input_list =[ dropout(x_word_embed, p= self.opt[ 'dropout_
      emb'] , training = self.drop_emb)]
    # history of word for question words
    ques_input_list  =  [ dropout(ques_word_embed,  p= self.opt
      [ 'dropout_emb'] , training = self.drop_emb)]
    # contextual embedding layer
    x_cemb = ques_cemb = None
    if 'BERT' in self.opt:
        if 'BERT_LINEAR_COMBINE' in self.opt:
            # obtain output from each BERT layers
```

(Continued)

(Continued)

```
            x_bert_output = self.Bert(x_bert, x_bert_mask, x_
              bert_offsets, x_single_mask)
            # calculate the weighted sum
            x_cemb_mid = self.linear_sum(x_bert_output, self.
              alphaBERT, self.gammaBERT)
            ques_bert_output = self.Bert(q_bert, q_bert_mask,
              q_bert_offsets, q_mask)
            ques_cemb_mid = self.linear_sum(ques_bert_output,
              self.alphaBERT, self.gammaBERT)
            x_cemb_mid = x_cemb_mid.expand(batch_size, -1, -1)
        else:
            # no weighted sum is computed
            x_cemb_mid = self.Bert(x_bert, x_bert_mask,
              x_bert_offsets, x_single_mask)
            x_cemb_mid = x_cemb_mid.expand(batch_size, -1, -1)
            ques_cemb_mid = self.Bert(q_bert, q_bert_mask, q_
              bert_offsets, q_mask)
        # add contextual embeddings into history of word
        x_input_list.append(x_cemb_mid)
        ques_input_list.append(ques_cemb_mid)
    # word-level attention layer
    x_prealign = self.pre_align(x_word_embed, ques_word_
      embed, q_mask)
    x_input_list.append(x_prealign)
    # POS embeddings
    x_pos_emb = self.pos_embedding(x_pos).expand
      (batch_size, -1, -1)
    # NER embeddings
    x_ent_emb = self.ent_embedding(x_ent).expand
      (batch_size, -1, -1)
    x_input_list.append(x_pos_emb)
    x_input_list.append(x_ent_emb)
    # add article word features
    x_input_list.append(x_features)
    # concatenate history of word vectors for article words
    x_input = torch.cat(x_input_list, 2)
    # concatenate history of word vectors for question words
    ques_input = torch.cat(ques_input_list, 2)
    # obtain RNN layer's output
    _, x_rnn_layers = self.context_rnn(x_input, x_mask,
      return_list=True, x_additional=x_cemb)
```

(Continued)

(Continued)

```
_, ques_rnn_layers = self.ques_rnn(ques_input, q_mask,
    return_list = True,  x_additional = ques_cemb)  # layer  x
    batch x q_len x ques_rnn_output_size
# question understanding layer
ques_highlvl = self.high_lvl_ques_rnn(torch.cat(ques_rnn_
    layers, 2), q_mask) # batch x q_len x high_lvl_ques_rnn_
    output_size
ques_rnn_layers.append(ques_highlvl)
# input to fully-aware cross-attention layer
if x_cemb is None:
    x_long = x_word_embed
    ques_long = ques_word_embed
else:
    x_long = torch.cat([x_word_embed, x_cemb], 2)
    ques_long = torch.cat([ques_word_embed, ques_cemb], 2)
# fully-aware cross-attention layer processes the
    article word vectors
x_rnn_after_inter_attn, x_inter_attn = self.deep_attn
    ([x_long], x_rnn_layers, [ques_long], ques_rnn_layers,
    x_mask, q_mask, return_bef_rnn = True)
# input to fully-aware self-attention layer
if x_cemb is None:
    x_self_attn_input = torch.cat([x_rnn_after_inter_attn,
        x_inter_attn, x_word_embed], 2)
else:
    x_self_attn_input = torch.cat([x_rnn_after_inter_attn,
        x_inter_attn, x_cemb, x_word_embed], 2)
# fully-aware self-attention layer processes the article
    word vectors
x_self_attn_output = self.highlvl_self_att(x_self_
    attn_input, x_self_attn_input, x_mask, x3 = x_rnn_after_
    inter_attn, drop_diagonal = True)
# high-level RNN layer
x_highlvl_output = self.high_lvl_context_rnn(torch.cat
    ([x_rnn_after_inter_attn, x_self_attn_output], 2), x_mask)
# final article word vectors x_final
x_final = x_highlvl_output
# question self-attention layer
ques_final = self.ques_self_attn(ques_highlvl, ques_
    highlvl, q_mask, x3 = None, drop_diagonal = True)
# obtain the question vector
```

(Continued)

(*Continued*)

```
        q_merge_weights = self.ques_merger(ques_final, q_mask)
        ques_merged = weighted_avg(ques_final, q_merge_weights) #
          batch x ques_final_size
        # get the scores for extractive answers/Yes/No/No answer
        score_s, score_e, score_no, score_yes, score_noanswer =
          self.get_answer(x_final, ques_merged, x_mask)
        return score_s, score_e, score_no, score_yes, score_noanswer
```

The code above employs the *linear_sum* function to calculate the weighted sum of each BERT layer's output. Here's the code of the *linear_sum* function:

```
def linear_sum(self, output, alpha, gamma):
    # normalize alpha using softmax
    alpha_softmax = F.softmax(alpha)
    for i in range(len(output)):
        # the weight for the i-th layer is alpha_softmax[ i] X gamma
        if i == 0:
            res = t
        else:
            res += t
    # dropout layer
    res = dropout(res, p = self.opt[ 'dropout_emb'] , training =
      self.drop_emb)
    return res
```

7.6.2 Network layers

In the previous section, SDNet leverages the classes such as *Attention*, *DeepAttention*, *GetFinalScores*. These classes are defined in *Models/ Layers.py* and encapsulate subnetwork structures to implement various functions.

7.6.2.1 Attention layer

Layers.py defines two classes to compute the attention scores and attention vectors respectively. The *AttentionScore* class calculates the attention scores, that is, $\text{score}(x_1, x_2) = \text{ReLU}(\mathbf{U}x_1)^{\mathrm{T}}\mathbf{D}\text{ReLU}(\mathbf{U}x_2)$:

```
class AttentionScore(nn.Module):
    def __init__(self, input_size, hidden_size, do_similarity =
      False):
        super(AttentionScore, self).__init__()
        # dimension of hidden state, i.e. number of rows in the matrix U
        self.hidden_size = hidden_size
        # self.linear corresponds to the matrix U
        self.linear = nn.Linear(input_size, hidden_size, bias =
          False)
        # self.diagonal is the diagonal matrix D
        # if do_similarity = True, the result is normalized by the
          square root of dimension and D is updated
        if do_similarity:
            self.diagonal = Parameter(torch.ones(1, 1, 1) /
                (hidden_size ** 0.5), requires_grad = False)
        else:
            self.diagonal = Parameter(torch.ones(1, 1, hidden_
                size), requires_grad = True)

    # Input:
    # attention scores for vector groups x1 and x2
    # Size of x1: batch X word_num1 X dim
    # Size of x2: batch X word_num2 X dim
    # Output:
    # attention scores between all pairs of vectors. Size: batch X
      word_num1 X word_num2
    def forward(self, x1, x2):
        x1 = dropout(x1, p = dropout_p, training = self.training)
        x2 = dropout(x2, p = dropout_p, training = self.training)
        x1_rep = x1
        x2_rep = x2
        batch = x1_rep.size(0)
        word_num1 = x1_rep.size(1)
        word_num2 = x2_rep.size(1)
        dim = x1_rep.size(2)
        # compute Ux_1
        x1_rep = self.linear(x1_rep.contiguous().view(-1, dim)).
          view(batch, word_num1, self.hidden_size)
        # compute Ux_2
```

(Continued)

(*Continued*)

```
        x2_rep = self.linear(x2_rep.contiguous().view(-1, dim)).
          view(batch, word_num2, self.hidden_size)
        x1_rep = F.relu(x1_rep)
        x2_rep = F.relu(x2_rep)
        # compute Relu(Ux₁)ᵀD
        x1_rep = x1_rep * self.diagonal.expand_as(x1_rep)
        # compute Relu(Ux₁)ᵀDRelu(Ux₂)
        scores = x1_rep.bmm(x2_rep.transpose(1, 2))
        return scores
```

The *Attention* class takes vector groups x_1, x_2, x_3 as input, and then computes the attention scores between x_1 and x_2 via the *AttentionScore* function. After normalization by softmax, it computes the weights sum of the vectors in x_3 to get the attention vectors. This is analogous to the query, key, and value in multihead attention in Section 6.4.1. Here's the analysis of the code:

```
class Attention(nn.Module):
    def __init__(self, input_size, hidden_size, do_similarity =
      False):
        super(Attention, self).__init__()
        # the function to calculate attention scores
        self.scoring = AttentionScore(input_size, hidden_size,
          correlation_func, do_similarity)

    def forward(self, x1, x2, x2_mask, x3 = None, drop_
        diagonal = False):
        batch = x1.size(0)
        word_num1 = x1.size(1)
        word_num2 = x2.size(1)
        # if x₃ is None, x₂ is used as x₃
        if x3 is None:
            x3 = x2
        # obtain attention scores
        scores = self.scoring(x1, x2)
        # set attention scores to minus infinity at padded positions
          in x₂
        empty_mask = x2_mask.eq(0).unsqueeze(1).expand_as(scores)
        scores.data.masked_fill_(empty_mask.data, -float('inf'))
```
(*Continued*)

(Continued)

```
    # when drop_diagonal = True, the attention scores at the
        diagonal is set to minus infinity, i.e. each word does not
        compute attend to itself
    if drop_diagonal:
        diag_mask = torch.diag(scores.data.new(scores.size(1)).
            zero_() + 1).byte().unsqueeze(0).expand_as(scores)
        scores.data.masked_fill_(diag_mask, -float('inf'))
    # normalize attention weights via softmax, where positions
        with minus infinity are assigned a weight of 0
    alpha_flat = F.softmax(scores.view(-1, x2.size(1)), dim = 1)
    alpha = alpha_flat.view(-1, x1.size(1), x2.size(1))
    # multiply the attention weights with x3 to obtain the
        attention vectors
    attended = alpha.bmm(x3)
    return attended
```

7.6.2.2 Fully-aware attention layer

The fully-aware attention layer is defined in the class *DeepAttention*. It compresses dimensions to calculate attention scores from the history of word. It then computes the weighted sum of only a part of the history of word. Here's the code analysis:

```
class DeepAttention(nn.Module):
    def __init__(self, opt, abstr_list_cnt, deep_att_hidden_size_
        per_abstr, word_hidden_size = None):
        super(DeepAttention, self).__init__()
        word_hidden_size = opt['embedding_dim'] if word_hidden_
            size is None else word_hidden_size
        abstr_hidden_size = opt['hidden_size'] * 2
        att_size = abstr_hidden_size * abstr_list_cnt +
            word_hidden_size
        # multiple network layers are put into nn.ModuleList
        self.int_attn_list = nn.ModuleList()
        # the number of times for attention computation in the fully-
            aware attention layer is abstr_list_cnt + 1
        for i in range(abstr_list_cnt + 1):
            self.int_attn_list.append(Attention(att_size,
                deep_att_hidden_size_per_abstr))
```

(Continued)

(Continued)
```
        rnn_input_size = abstr_hidden_size * abstr_list_cnt * 2
          + (opt[ 'highlvl_hidden_size'] * 2)
      self.rnn_input_size = rnn_input_size
  # RNN layer
      self.rnn, self.output_size = RNN_from_opt(rnn_input_size,
        opt[ 'highlvl_hidden_size'] , num_layers = 1)
      self.opt = opt

  def forward(self, x1_word, x1_abstr, x2_word, x2_abstr, x1_
      mask, x2_mask, return_bef_rnn = False):
      # get history of word via concatenation of word vectors from
        previous layers
      x1_att = torch.cat(x1_word + x1_abstr, 2)
      x2_att = torch.cat(x2_word + x2_abstr[ :-1] , 2)
      x1 = torch.cat(x1_abstr, 2)
      x2_list = x2_abstr
      for i in range(len(x2_list)):
          # attention vectors
          attn_hiddens  =  self.int_attn_list[ i] (x1_att,  x2_att,
            x2_mask, x3 = x2_list[ i] )
          # concatenate the results
          x1 = torch.cat((x1, attn_hiddens), 2)
      # go through the RNN layer
      x1_hiddens = self.rnn(x1, x1_mask)
      if return_bef_rnn:
          return x1_hiddens, x1
      else:
      return x1_hiddens
```

7.6.2.3 Question vector layer
The question vector is computed by the *LinearSelfAttn* class and *weighted_avg* function. The computation employs the parametrized weighted sum described in Section 3.1.3.

Specifically, given the input vectors $(x_1, \ldots, x_n)$, the *LinearSelfAttn* class computes

$$o_i = \text{softmax}\left(b^T x_i\right), \ 1 \leq i \leq n$$

where b is a parameter vector. The *weighted_avg* function then outputs the weighted sum $\sum_i o_i x_i$. Here's the code analysis:

```
class LinearSelfAttn(nn.Module):
    def __init__(self, input_size):
        super(LinearSelfAttn, self).__init__()
        # self.linear corresponds to the parameter vector b
        self.linear = nn.Linear(input_size, 1)

    def forward(self, x, x_mask):
        # empty_mask has 1 in padded positions
        empty_mask = x_mask.eq(0).expand_as(x_mask)
        x = dropout(x, p=dropout_p, training=self.training)
        x_flat = x.contiguous().view(-1, x.size(-1))
        # compute b^T x_i
        scores = self.linear(x_flat).view(x.size(0), x.size(1))
        # set attention scores to minus infinity at padded positions
        scores.data.masked_fill_(empty_mask.data, -float('inf'))
        # compute attention scores o
        alpha = F.softmax(scores, dim=1)
        return alpha

def weighted_avg(x, weights):
    # compute the weighted sum of vectors in x
    return weights.unsqueeze(1).bmm(x).squeeze(1)
```

7.6.2.4 Output layer

The *GetFinalScores* class produces SDNet's output scores for extractive answers and special answers (Yes/No/No Answer). The *get_single_score* function computes the scores for the special answer. Here's the analysis of the code:

```
class GetFinalScores(nn.Module):
    def __init__(self, x_size, h_size):
        super(GetFinalScores, self).__init__()
        # parameter vectors for special answer: Yes/No/No answer
        self.noanswer_linear = nn.Linear(h_size, x_size)
        self.noanswer_w = nn.Linear(x_size, 1, bias=True)
        self.no_linear = nn.Linear(h_size, x_size)
        self.no_w = nn.Linear(x_size, 1, bias=True)
        self.yes_linear = nn.Linear(h_size, x_size)
```

(Continued)

(Continued)

```
        self.yes_w = nn.Linear(x_size, 1, bias = True)
        # compute the probability of each extractive answer
        self.attn = BilinearSeqAttn(x_size, h_size)
        self.attn2 = BilinearSeqAttn(x_size, h_size)
        # the GRU unit between the computation of start position and
          end position probabilities
        self.rnn = nn.GRUCell(x_size, h_size)

    # Input:
    # x: the final article word vectors
    # h0: the question vector
    # x_mask: the mask
    # Output:
    # scores of all types of answers
    def forward(self, x, h0, x_mask):
        # the probability that the answer starts from each position
          in the article
        score_s = self.attn(x, h0, x_mask)
        # compute a weighted sum of article word vectors using
          score_s
        ptr_net_in  =  torch.bmm(F.softmax(score_s, dim = 1).
          unsqueeze(1), x).squeeze(1)
        ptr_net_in = dropout(ptr_net_in, p = dropout_p, training =
          self.training)
        h0 = dropout(h0, p = dropout_p, training = self.training)
        # get a new hidden state for end position computation via GRU
        h1 = self.rnn(ptr_net_in, h0)
        # the probability that the answer ends at each position in the
          article
        score_e = self.attn2(x, h1, x_mask)
        # calculate the probability of Yes/No/No answer
        score_no  =  self.get_single_score(x, h0, x_mask, self.
          no_linear, self.no_w)
        score_yes  =  self.get_single_score(x, h0, x_mask, self.
          yes_linear, self.yes_w)
        score_noanswer  =  self.get_single_score(x, h0, x_mask,
          self.noanswer_linear, self.noanswer_w)
        return score_s, score_e, score_no, score_yes, score_noanswer

    # calculate the probability of Yes/No/No answer
    def get_single_score(self, x, h, x_mask, linear, w):
```

(Continued)

(Continued)

```
        # convert h into the same dimension of x
        Wh = linear(h)
        # compute the attention score xᵀWh
        xWh = x.bmm(Wh.unsqueeze(2)).squeeze(2)
        # set the attention scores to minus infinity where x is padded
        empty_mask = x_mask.eq(0).expand_as(x_mask)
        xWh.data.masked_fill_(empty_mask.data, -float('inf'))
        # normalize by softmax and compute the weighted sum of x
        attn_x = torch.bmm(F.softmax(xWh, dim = 1).unsqueeze(1), x)
        # get the output score
        single_score = w(attn_x).squeeze(2)
        return single_score
```

The *BilinearSeqAttn* class used in *GetFinalScores* computes attention scores between a vector group and a single vector. Given vectors $x_1, x_2, \ldots, x_n$ and the vector y, it computes:

$$o_i = x_i^T W y, \ 1 \le i \le n$$

where W is a parameter matrix. Here's the code of *BilinearSeqAttn* class:

```
class BilinearSeqAttn(nn.Module):
    def __init__(self, x_size, y_size, identity = False):
        super(BilinearSeqAttn, self).__init__()
        if not identity:
            # if x and y are of different dimensions, the dimension of
              y is converted to that of x
            self.linear = nn.Linear(y_size, x_size)
        else:
            self.linear = None

    def forward(self, x, y, x_mask):
        empty_mask = x_mask.eq(0).expand_as(x_mask)
        # dropout layer
        x = dropout(x, p = dropout_p, training = self.training)
        y = dropout(y, p = dropout_p, training = self.training)
        # compute Wy
        Wy = self.linear(y) if self.linear is not None else y
        # compute the attention score xᵀWy
```

(Continued)

(Continued)

```
xWy = x.bmm(Wy.unsqueeze(2)).squeeze(2)
# set the attention scores to minus infinity where x is padded
xWy.data.masked_fill_(empty_mask.data, -float('inf'))
return xWy
```

7.6.3 Generate Bidirectional Encoder Representations from Transformers embeddings

The contextual embedding from BERT is computed in *Bert/Bert.py*. In *BatchGen*, each word has been tokenized into one or more WordPiece subwords. BERT generates multilayer contextual embeddings for each subword. The SDNet model averages the contextual embeddings of all subwords of a word in a layer to obtain the word embedding for that layer.

One subtlety in the process is that BERT only accepts inputs of up to 512 subwords, but some articles in CoQA exceed this limit. Thus SDNet divides the article into segments of 512 subwords (the last segment may contain fewer than 512 subwords). It then calculates the BERT embedding for each segment and concatenates the embeddings.

Here's the analysis of *Bert.py*:

```
def forward(self, x_bert, x_bert_mask, x_bert_offset, x_mask):
    all_layers = []
    # number of sub-words
    bert_sent_len = x_bert.shape[1]
    # each time process a segment of up to self.BERT_MAX_LEN = 512
      subwords
    p = 0
    while p < bert_sent_len:
        # obtain sub-word embeddings for all layers
        all_encoder_layers, _ = self.bert_model(x_bert[:, p:
        (p + self.BERT_MAX_LEN)], token_type_ids = None, attention_
        mask = x_bert_mask[:, p:(p + self.BERT_MAX_LEN)])
        all_layers.append(torch.cat(all_encoder_layers, dim = 2))
        p += self.BERT_MAX_LEN
    # concatenate the embeddings from all segments
    bert_embedding = torch.cat(all_layers, dim = 1)
```

(Continued)

(Continued)

```
batch_size = x_mask.shape[ 0]
max_word_num = x_mask.shape[ 1]
tot_dim = bert_embedding.shape[ 2]
output = Variable(torch.zeros(batch_size, max_word_num,
  tot_dim))
# if a word has T sub-words, the sub-word embeddings are divided
  by T and then added together to get the word' s BERT embedding
for i in range(batch_size):
    for j in range(max_word_num):
        if x_mask[ i, j] == 0:
            continue
        # the sub-words for this word range from st to ed-1
        st = x_bert_offset[ i, j, 0]
        ed = x_bert_offset[ i, j, 1]
        if st + 1 == ed:
            output[ i, j, :] = bert_embedding[ i, st, :]
        else:
            subword_ebd_sum = torch.sum(bert_embedding[ i, st:
              ed, :] , dim = 0)
            # divide the sub-word embeddings by the number of
              sub-words: ed-st
            if st < ed:
                output[ i, j, :] = subword_ebd_sum / float(ed - st)
outputs = [ ]
# output each word' s BERT embedding for every layer
for i in range(self.bert_layer):
    now = output[ :,:, (i * self.bert_dim): ((i + 1) * self.
      bert_dim)]
    now = now.cuda()
    outputs.append(now)
return outputs
```

7.7 Summary

- **SDNet** is a model for multiturn conversational MRC. It adopts the architecture of encoding layer, interaction layer, and output layer. SDNet for the first time incorporates BERT as a contextual embedder into the network structure.

- The implementation of SDNet separates code from data, sets hyper-parameters via configuration files, and provides the docker for reproducing experiments.
- **CoQAPreprocess.py** preprocesses the data and generates the dictionary.
- **SDNetTrainer.py** specifies the training and evaluation process. The data is processed in batches and the model with the highest accuracy on the validation dataset is saved.
- The **BatchGen** class in **Utils/CoQAUtils.py** produces batch data for training and evaluation. It employs padding and the BERT tokenizer.
- **SDNet.py** defines the network structure and computation process of SDNet.
- **Layers.py** contains many custom layers and functions.

Reference

[1] Zhu C, Zeng M, Huang X. Sdnet: contextualized attention-based deep network for conversational question answering. arXiv preprint arXiv 2018; 1812.03593.

CHAPTER 8

Applications and future of machine reading comprehension

8.1 Intelligent customer service

Customer service is a very important component in business operations. Currently, most customer services heavily rely on human agents. On the one hand, customers have to wait for a long time to be served and the satisfaction rates of different agents may vary a lot. On the other hand, the customer service department is a huge cost center for enterprises. Therefore it can be immensely helpful to automate the customer service through efficient and intelligent computer-based models.

Early intelligent customer services usually take the form of **Interactive Voice Response (IVR)**. The IVR system prerecords or produces speech for various services. Users can navigate the system and obtain the information by pressing buttons during phone calls. An IVR system can automatically handle simple user questions, while more complex requests are transferred to human agents. This can save a lot of costs for enterprises and waiting time for users.

However, in many cases, due to the complex nature of products, user questions are typically involved, which requires deeper communication for solutions. These problems are out of the scope of a simple IVR system. As a result, there has emerged the customer support chatbot to realize complex engagement with users via AI technologies.

A customer service chatbot can communicate with users through text or voice to obtain relevant information and offer solutions. Therefore the chatbot should match the user's question to product documentation and have conversations with humans (Fig. 8.1). It is worth noting that a customer service chatbot is very different from an open–domain chatbot. A customer service chatbot must quickly find the solution based on the user's information, with the sole goal of solving the user's product-related questions. An open–domain chatbot (e.g., XiaoIce) focuses more on interacting with the user from different aspects, and it can freely change the theme of conversation to adapt to users' emotions. A successful open-domain chatbot usually tries to maximize the time of engagement.

Machine Reading Comprehension. DOI: https://doi.org/10.1016/B978-0-323-90118-5.00008-4
© 2021 Beijing Huazhang Graphics & Information Co., Ltd/China Machine Press.
Published by Elsevier Inc. All rights reserved.

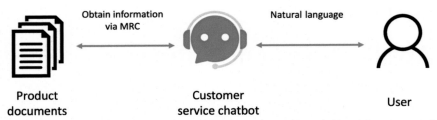

Figure 8.1 The relationship between the customer service chatbot, the user, and product documents.

To build an intelligent customer service model, there are in general three parts: building a knowledge base for the product, understanding the user's intent, and generating answers, as shown in the following sections.

8.1.1 Building product knowledge base

The product questions arising in customer service are often predictable and limited in scope, for example, usage, repair, and registration. The corresponding solutions can be provided by the enterprise in forms like FAQ, or by historic customer service records. These questions and solutions form the product knowledge base for customer service.

There are two kinds of product knowledge base: table-based or graph-based (Fig. 8.2). The table-based design is simpler, analogous to the questions and answers in an FAQ. With this design, the chatbot can conduct a single-turn conversation with the user that resembles a search engine: find the most similar question to the user's query and return the answer. The graph-based design organizes the questions and answers into a graph structure. Usually there is one graph for each intent. Once the user's intent is determined based on the question, the chatbot starts from the corresponding graph's starting node, which represents a conversation state. At each node, the chatbot asks a clarification question and follows an edge to another node based on the user's reply. Once at the answer state node, the chatbot returns the predefined answer. Therefore the graph-based knowledge base supports multiple dialogue turns and can be used for a more natural interaction with customers.

8.1.2 Intent understanding

The most critical part of a customer service chatbot is to understand the user's intent based on the question, and then to find related items in the

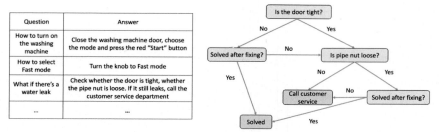

Question	Answer
How to turn on the washing machine	Close the washing machine door, choose the mode and press the red "Start" button
How to select Fast mode	Turn the knob to Fast mode
What if there's a water leak	Check whether the door is tight, whether the pipe nut is loose. If it still leaks, call the customer service department
...	...

Figure 8.2 Left: A table-based knowledge base contains pairs of product-related questions and answers. Right: In a graph-based knowledge base, each node represents the current state of the chatbot and contains the clarifying question to ask. The chatbot follows the edge corresponding to the user's reply. This knowledge graph is for the question *What to do if the washing machine leaks.*

product knowledge base. This section describes the modeling and training of this module.

8.1.2.1 Modeling

The core technology in understanding the user's intent is to compute the semantic correlation between text. For example, in a table-based knowledge base, if the model finds that the user's input text is semantically close to a question in the table, it can directly output the corresponding answer.

One simple approach for semantic correlation is keyword matching. For example, for the knowledge base in Fig. 8.2, if the user's input contains the word *leak*, the model can retrieve the answer to the question *What if there's a water leak*. Typically, the rules for keyword matching are manually designed, such as logical expressions (for example, containing *leak* and *washing machine*). Although keyword matching has a high precision, it is difficult to achieve a satisfying recall rate, that is, many related questions are not covered by these rules. The fundamental reason is that the same question may have multiple semantically equivalent but different expressions in natural language. Therefore keyword matching is often used as the basic-level module for intent understanding.

To understand the variations in language, a more robust semantic analysis model is required. One such method [1] is based on deep learning as shown in Fig. 8.3. The model takes two text segments A and B as input, for example, the user's input and an intent's description text. The model returns a correlation score between these two text segments. This amounts to a classification task which returns the probability that the two input texts are semantically equivalent.

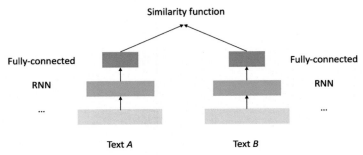

Figure 8.3 Semantic similarity model.

The natural language understanding model introduced in Chapter 3, Deep Learning in Natural Language Processing, can be used here to compute semantic similarities. It uses word vectors and network layers such as recurrent neural network (RNN) to obtain the text vectors a and b for A and B, respectively. Then, the similarity between a and b is computed via a function, such as the following cosine similarity function, where a larger value indicates a closer semantic similarity:

$$cos(a, b) = \frac{a^T b}{\sqrt{a^T a}\sqrt{b^T b}} \in [-1, 1]$$

8.1.2.2 Training

To train the semantic similarity model, both positive (semantically similar pairs of text) and negative (semantically different pairs of text) samples are required. In fact, one only needs to collect positive data from which the negative data is generated. For example, given two positive data instances:

my washing machine is leaking; what to do if my washing machine leaks

I've put my clothes in the washing machine and how to it on; how to turn the washing machine on

The negative text pairs can be randomly drawn from different positive pairs, such as (*my washing machine is leaking; how to turn the washing machine on*).

The training data is usually collected from publicly available paraphrasing corpus or historic customer service records. For the latter case, labelers can categorize the user's questions into intents, and each question and its corresponding intent's description text form a semantically similar pair.

During testing, the model selects the intent that has the highest similarity score with the user's question. If the score is above a predefined threshold, the chatbot returns the answer from the table-based knowledge base, or asks a clarifying question in the graph for that intent. Otherwise, the chatbot can ask the user to rephrase the question or forward it to a human agent.

8.1.3 Answer generation

After obtaining adequate information from the user, the customer service chatbot needs to return a solution in forms including but not limited to text, links, images, and videos. However, because many products have complex functions and are constantly upgraded, it is difficult to write all answers in advance. Moreover, the tedious process of answer editing requires considerable human efforts, which greatly limits the deployment of chatbot systems. Therefore manually edited answers usually cover only the most frequent user intents. When a user's question is not covered by predefined intents, that is, in the long tail of question distribution, answers can be dynamically generated from the product documents. The task to return relevant answers from the product documentation based on the user's question falls into the category of corpus-based machine reading comprehension (MRC). The model can first retrieve relevant paragraphs and then extract appropriate answers. Therefore the MRC technology can effectively supplement the manually edited knowledge base and flexibly provides solutions for customers.

8.1.4 Other modules

8.1.4.1 Application programming interface (API) integration

In real applications, the user's input is not limited to the text format. Services such as registration and fee inquiry require login information like username, password, and verification codes. The system needs to communicate with back-end APIs to verify the user's identity and obtain related information. Thus the chatbot should integrate both front end (for example, login interface) and back end (e.g., API integration) functions.

8.1.4.2 Contextual understanding

The graph knowledge base facilitates multiturn conversations, which requires the model to understand the context. For example, suppose the chatbot asks "Is the washing machine door closed?" and the user answers "Just tried this method, it didn't work." The model needs to understand that *this method* refers to *close the washing machine door*, and *doesn't work* corresponds to *No* in the knowledge base. To correctly interpret context, the chatbot can leverage coreference resolution technologies to interpret context. Another solution is to employ user-friendly user interface designs such as yes/no buttons to obtain precise input.

8.1.4.3 Chit-chat

To make a chatbot more user-friendly, an intelligent customer service chatbot should have the chit-chat functionality, such as greeting and comforting, for example, *Don't worry, let us try another method*. At the same time, the system needs to identify whether the user's input is chit-chat. This will greatly improve the usability of customer service systems.

As an early commercialized natural language processing (NLP) application, intelligent customer service has a huge market value. According to a market survey in 2017, the global customer service industry is worth about $350 billion. There is no doubt that intelligent customer service will revolutionize industries across all domains. Therefore as one of the key supporting technologies, MRC will have a great prospect in this field.

8.2 Search engine

Since its inception in the early 1990s, search engines have served users around the world to query the vast amount of information on the internet. Early search engines were mostly directory navigation systems which provided web page links in a manually maintained directory, for example, Yahoo! Directory. In 1995 the first natural language-based search engine, AltaVista, went online to enable users to search with natural language queries, which greatly improved the efficiency and usability.

In 1998 Google was founded, and it is still the world's largest and most popular search engine today. It employs PageRank (PR) technology to model the importance of web pages and build large-scale indices to provide highly relevant results to user queries. Meanwhile, other search engines such as Bing and Baidu came to light. These search engines immensely facilitate global information exchange and gave birth to a variety of booming industries like online advertising, e-commerce, and cloud computing.

In this section, we will introduce the key supporting technologies of search engines including MRC.

8.2.1 Search engine technology

A search engine matches user queries with related web pages to return relevant content. To accomplish this task, a search engine usually has three modules in its architecture: crawling, indexing, and ranking.

8.2.1.1 Crawling

The search engine obtains the information about online web pages via a crawler. A crawler is a program that browses and navigates web content. The crawler starts from highly visited page links, and continuously collects page content and follows the hyperlinks in it to jump to more pages. Because of the massive scale of the Internet, hundreds of web crawlers may need to work simultaneously to crawl web pages.

8.2.1.2 Indexing

Theoretically, given a user query, the search engine can be iterative over all crawled web pages and select the relevant ones. However, this method is too slow to work in real time. Therefore a search engine needs to index web pages to facilitate fast content-based retrieval. A popular technique is the **Inverted Index**. The inverted index builds a key-value store to map keywords to pages that contain the keyword. In this way, the search engine can quickly return relevant pages using the keywords in the user query. In addition, due to the timeliness of web pages and user queries, a search engine usually maintains multiple levels of indices in chronological order, for example, inverted index of pages of today, within a week, and so on.

8.2.1.3 Ranking

A search engine can extract keywords and logical relationships from natural language queries. It then uses these keywords to get candidate pages from the inverted index and processes them according to the logical relationship. For example, if the query is *Italian restaurant in New York*, the returned web pages should contain both keywords *Italian restaurant* and *New York*. Thus the search engine can conduct an intersection operation on the web page lists from the *Italian restaurant* entry and the *New York* entry of the inverted index.

However, it is very likely that there are still many remaining web pages. So the search engine needs to rank the pages for display. The basic criteria for page ranking are twofold: its relevance to the query and its importance. Here are some typical methods to quantify these two aspects.

Intuitively, if a query word appears multiple times in a web page, it is more likely that this page is related to the query. This can be measured by the **term frequency** (**TF**) in the page. However, some common words like *this* or *you* may have a high term frequency even in irrelevant pages. Such common words should be discounted for their appearance, which can be quantified by **inverse document frequency** (**IDF**). IDF is computed by taking the opposite of the logarithm of the word's frequency in all web pages. For example, if there are 100 pages in total, and the word *machine* appears in 20 pages, then its IDF is $-\log(20/100) = \log 5$. Apparently, common words have a low IDF score. The term frequency and IDF of each query word are multiplied and then summed together to obtain the TF-IDF score of each page. TF-IDF has been widely used by search engines to measure the relevance of a page to the query.

To measure the importance of a web page, one can leverage the hyperlink graph. The intuition is that when an important web page A has a link to another web page B, page B is considered important as well. And the importance of B increases if there are more important pages linking to it. Based on this principle, the founders of Google, Larry Page and Sergey Brin, among others, designed the PR algorithm [2]. PR assigns each page X an importance weight $PR(X)$. Suppose X contains links to three other pages A, B, and C, then each of these three pages receives a vote of value $PR(X)/3$. Every page collects and sums up the votes it receives to get an updated PR score. This process goes on until convergence. The final PR score is used to measure the importance of each web page. Apparently, a junk page which has a lot of outgoing links but few incoming links will end up with a very low PR score.

To take both relevance and importance into consideration, a search engine ranks and displays the web pages in decreasing order of the product of the relevance score (e.g., TF-IDF) and the importance score (e.g., PR) of each web page. In real applications, the search engine has many additional measures to further improve the accuracy of returned results.

The approach above is largely based on keyword matching. However, in any language, there are many semantically similar words/phrases, which cannot be captured by simple word matching. To improve the quality of search engines, deep learning and other semantic analysis have been widely used. In this process, it is critical to collect adequate training data for model building. One popular approach is to leverage historic click data. The click data contains the records of user's queries and the pages that the user clicks. Statistically, many queries are semantically similar to the title and content of clicked pages. Therefore many search engines utilize the massive click data to significantly enhance the quality of retrieved results.

8.2.2 Machine reading comprehension in search engine

In search engines, one important application is question and answering (QA). When the user's query is in the form of a question, the search engine should

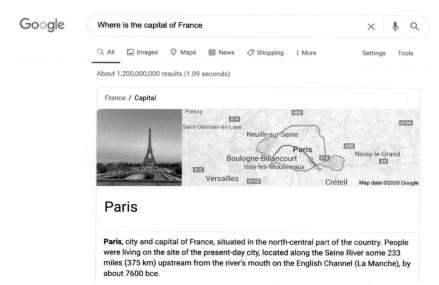

Figure 8.4 The Google search engine directly answers the query *Where is the capital of France*.

return the answer. In this case, the content of a web page is considered as an article, and the user's query is considered as a question. Thus the search engine can leverage MRC technologies to extract answers in the web page and directly display the result if the confidence score is high. As shown in Fig. 8.4, the Google search engine returns the answer *Paris* with introductory information for the query *Where is the capital of France*.

Besides directly answering user queries, MRC can also be used to display related text segments in the retrieved web pages, also known as snippets, to provide richer information in addition to the title and URL (Fig. 8.5). The snippet can be generated as the extractive answer to the query given a web page. As the snippet has a great impact on users' impression of the system, many search engine companies have introduced MRC tasks and competitions to encourage development of MRC algorithms. For example, the MS MARCO dataset introduced in Section 1.5.2 contains real user queries from the Bing search engine.

8.2.3 Challenges and future of machine reading comprehension in search engine

With the increasing popularity of search engines and the massive amount of information, MRC has broad prospects in the search engine industry. At the same time, it is facing various challenges.

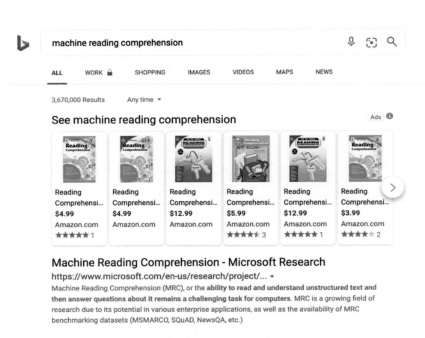

Figure 8.5 The Bing search engine returns a list of web pages given the query *machine reading comprehension*, which include snippets from the web page's content.

First, although search engine provides massive amount of data like click records, most data is not manually labeled. Therefore it is important to design MRC models that can take advantage of large-scale unlabeled or weakly labeled data. The pretrained model Bidirectional Encoder Representations from Transformers (BERT) in Chapter 6, Pretrained Language Model, is proving to be a promising approach, but models better suited for the searching scenario remain to be explored.

Second, a prominent feature of search engine is that it runs in real time. Typically, search results have to be returned within hundreds or even tens of milliseconds. Traditional keyword matching methods, although not as accurate as deep learning models, have a great advantage in speed. Therefore it remains a big challenge to significantly improve the computational efficiency of MRC models with increasing data volumes. Parallel computing, network optimization, and model compression are among the various techniques to speed up computation. This is also an interdisciplinary area requiring efforts from both science and engineering.

Third, in recent years, multimodality has greatly revolutionized the way humans interact with computers. As an important entry to the world's information, search engines need to adopt and process information in forms beyond text, for example, voice, video, gestures, and gaze. Thus MRC should be able to process semantic information in various modalities to accommodate future scenarios of human—computer interaction.

8.3 Health care

Health care has long been the focus of scientific explorations. The fast development in computer science has brought new vitality to this field. For instance, computer vision algorithms can analyze images from medical instruments such as MRI machines to conduct automatic diagnosis. The computerized modeling of biological and chemical reactions greatly speeds up discoveries of new drugs. Digitalization of hospitals significantly increases the efficiency and reduces the chance of medical accidents. Recently, the MRC technology also begins to play an important role in medical applications.

First, with the prevalence of search engines, many patients will first search online to query symptoms and treatments. Therefore the MRC technique in the search engine can help offer more accurate answers.

Second, professional medical practitioners can use MRC to assist diagnosis. Due to the fast development of medical technologies, a massive amount of medical documents, terminologies, and drugs are produced every day. Therefore doctors need to quickly retrieve similar medical records based on the patient's symptoms and medical history for diagnosis and treatment. This involves efficient NLP technologies including MRC for effective semantic analysis. Clearly, a highly accurate medical MRC model can greatly facilitate the daily work of doctors.

In order to promote the development of MRC research in this area, there are several MRC datasets in the medical domain. The QAngaroo dataset (Section 1.5.2) contains the MedHop dataset, which is derived from the abstract of medical research papers from pubMed. In MedHop, the model needs to search for clues in given paragraphs based on the question and selects the correct answer option. In 2018 researchers from Belgium introduced the medical MRC dataset CliCR [3]. CliCR contains 100K cloze-style reading comprehension questions collected from anonymized case reports of patients. These questions range from diagnosis to treatment.

We believe that with the booming of intelligent medicine, the MRC technology will take a more important role in reducing the burden of doctors and improving the service for patients.

8.4 Laws

The modern law system is both vast and highly complex. Legal professionals spend a significant amount of time to read and analyze legal files, which makes the litigation process costly and time-consuming. For example, in China, there are around 250 national laws, nearly 10,000 local laws, more than 5500 judicial interpretations, and 20 million court verdicts.

With the MRC technology, massive documents can be automatically and efficiently analyzed. Moreover, computerized models can to a large extent reduce the bias and prejudice in human processing. As a result, there has emerged research leveraging MRC in legal domains in recent years.

8.4.1 Automatic judgement

Automatic judgement employs AI models to predict the judicial results based on cases and laws. In 2018 researchers from Peking University and Tsinghua University proposed an automatic judgement model, AutoJudge [4]. AutoJudge converts the judgement task into a legal reading comprehension problem: given the fact descriptions, pleas, and law articles, predict whether the pleas should be supported.

AutoJudge first performs semantic analysis on inputs via an encoding layer, which includes the contextualized embedder ELMo and BERT. It then uses self-attention and cross attention to analyze the relationship between the plea and facts and the relationship between facts and law articles. Finally, the output layer produces the probability that the plea should be supported.

The AutoJudge model is trained on large-scale data consisting of legal cases and provisions. Experiments show that the model can successfully predict the outcome of 82.2% cases, significantly higher than the baseline support vector machine (SVM) model, which has an accuracy of 55.5%. The result demonstrates that, with sufficient training data, MRC models can achieve remarkable performances without the expertise of legal professionals.

Moreover, the AutoJudge paper points out that automatic judgement can help to predict judgement details such as the amount of compensation. This is an important direction for future exploration.

8.4.2 Crime classification

To give accurate judgement, the judges need to first determine the corresponding laws and articles given fact descriptions. This process is also known as crime classification. Since each case is unique, the decision has to be made based on the expertise and experience of the judges, which is both labor-intensive and time-consuming, yet not error-proof.

In 2019 researchers from Beijing University of Posts and Telecommunications and the Chinese Academy of Sciences proposed the Hierarchical Matching Network (HMN) [5] for crime classification. HMN adopts the concept of the two-level hierarchical structure of laws and articles. The encoding layer obtains representations of the laws, articles, and fact descriptions. The model then uses the attention mechanism to analyze the relationship between these inputs. Finally, the output layer generates the probability that each law/article can be applied to the fact description. The law/article with the highest probability is the predicted result.

Although the research on MRC in the law domain is still in the early stages, the results are very promising. It is very likely that with the fast development of models and algorithms, fully automatic judges will appear in the court and assume the sacred responsibility of judgement in the foreseeable future.

8.5 Finance

The financial sector covers a broad range of industries such as banking, investment, insurance, and leasing. The financial industry is characterized by rapid response to real-time information like political and economic news. Therefore financial analysis heavily depends on an accurate interpretation of this information, including news, corporate earnings reports, social media, etc. The analysis in turn greatly affects the profits of financial products. As a result, many financial firms invest in artificial intelligence and NLP to extract valuable information from various information sources.

8.5.1 Predicting stock prices

Accurate stock price forecasts can effectively increase the return of investment. Traditional stock price prediction methods are based on time series analysis. However, stock price fluctuations are often affected by real-time information such as policies and public opinion. Therefore it has long been a great challenge to improve the accuracy of stock price prediction.

The MRC technology can be leveraged to analyze various sources of information to better predict stock prices. In 2014 researchers from the University of Edinburgh proposed a deep learning model, StockNet [6], which can predict stock prices based on price history and related tweets. StockNet uses a GRU to encode stock prices and relevant news over a period of time. The representations then enter a variational movement decoder to characterize the distribution of stock prices. Finally, the model employs temporal attention to predict whether the stock price will rise or fall. Experimental results show that StockNet can outperform the statistical model autoregressive integrated moving average (ARIMA) by nearly 7% in prediction accuracy, demonstrating the effectiveness of text analysis for stock price forecasting.

Stock prices can also be predicted via sentiment analysis of news and social media. Sentiment analysis refers to the process of identifying and extracting subjective information from text, that is, the author's opinion and attitude. Analyzing the public opinion about an event or a company can often help improve the accuracy of stock price prediction.

In machine learning, sentiment analysis is framed as a classification problem. Early models are usually based on keyword extraction, such as computing the frequency of signal words (e.g., great, bad) in the text. However, due to the complexity of language, the accuracy of keyword-based methods is often below expectation. For instance, a negation word can completely change the sentiment of the sentence, for example, *I don't think this company will be profitable in the short term.*

In recent years, many sentiment analysis models based on MRC and deep learning have been proposed. One method is to build a semantic network using long short-term memory (LSTM) or Transformer, and then use self-attention to predict the probability of each emotion category. These models have greatly improved the accuracy of emotional analysis.

8.5.2 News summarization

In modern society, with the prevalence of smartphones and social media, the impact of information on finance is often measured in minutes, if not seconds. Meanwhile, the amount of information is beyond what any individual can digest. This highlights the importance of automatic models to collect and summarize related information.

Therefore it is critical to generate succinct summaries containing salient information in the text, which is known as the task of **text summarization**. There are two types of summarization: extractive and abstractive. Extractive summarization selects a subset of sentences from the text to form a summary; abstractive summarization reorganizes the language in the text and adds novel words/phrases into the summary if necessary. In general, extractive summarization models are relatively simple, which frames the task as a binary classification problem for each sentence in the text: whether to select it into the summary. It follows that extractive summarization can be objectively evaluated by accuracy. Abstractive summarization models must contain a text generation module, for example, decoder in freestyle-answer MRC. The quality of generated summaries is manually evaluated or automatically measured by the ROUGE metric introduced in Section 1.4.2.

To promote the development in this field, Google, DeepMind, and the University of Oxford published a summarization dataset based on articles from convolutional neural network (CNN) and Daily Mail in 2015. This dataset contains more than 280K news articles and human-edited summaries. In 2018 Cornell University introduced a dataset of 1.3 million news and summaries from 38 major media outlets. These large-scale datasets have spawned numerous high-quality models for MRC and text summarization, which are in turn employed in financial applications such as Bloomberg Terminal.

8.6 Education

While we can train computers to understand text, a trained MRC model can also assist humans in language learning. Therefore MRC has been used in the education domain.

One such education application is automatic essay scoring. Reading and scoring essays usually take a lot of effort by teachers, due to the complexity and length of essays. MRC can significantly expedite the process and enable students to get feedback anytime and anywhere. The evaluation of an essay is usually based on two criteria: correctness and coherence. The correctness of language includes spelling and grammar, which can be assessed using a dictionary and a language model. Coherence, on the other hand, measures whether an article is logically consistent, which is much harder to evaluate.

In 2018 researchers from the University of Cambridge proposed an automated essay scoring model [7]. The model employs RNN to evaluate the correctness of language usage, and uses a three-layer structure of word—sentence—clique to measure the semantic coherence. This model can detect correct yet incoherent essays, such as one made of reshuffled sentences of a good essay.

Automatic essay scoring models can become a writing assistant for students by pointing out grammatical errors, offering writing suggestions, and providing a personalized improvement plan. With additional speech recognition and synthesis technologies, it can help students improve language skills including listening, speaking, reading, and writing. With computer vision, the handwritten essays can also be evaluated in a timely manner. These technologies, combined with online education, are likely to revolutionize the education industry in the near future.

8.7 The future of machine reading comprehension

With the rapid development of NLP technologies, there has been great progress in MRC research. However, numerous problems still exist in this area, which impede the commercialization of MRC. This section describes the challenges in MRC research and points to the future directions.

8.7.1 Challenges

Although various models have achieved remarkable results on many MRC datasets, even surpassing the human level in some tasks, their performance is often below expectation in real-world applications. In this section, we list existing challenges in MRC research, which are also the focus of future directions.

8.7.1.1 Knowledge and reasoning

In Section 1.6.3, we introduced an experiment to evaluate MRC models using misleading context. The experiment added manually designed statements that contain certain question keywords but have no semantic relationship to the question. When these confusing statements are added to the article, the accuracy of almost all models decreased significantly. This demonstrates that most MRC models heavily rely on keyword matching rather than a deep understanding of the text.

In comparison, the reading ability of humans includes various aspects beyond keyword matching, such as analyzing the relationship between sentences, making inference based on clues in the article, and understanding the implied meaning in the text. These capabilities are exactly what is missing in computer models. Here are some examples:

> **Article:** David is upstairs with an apple in his pocket. He plays for a while, and then goes downstairs.
>
> **Q:** Is the apple upstairs?

As humans, we can infer that the answer is *No*, since we deduct from (1) David goes downstairs, and (2) apple in his pocket, that the apple must still be in David's pocket and hence downstairs. However, by simple keyword matching, the computer model is very likely to give the wrong answer *Yes* as the word *apple* is close to the word *upstairs*.

Also, one's reading ability is closely related to their life experience and knowledge. In many cases, the author of an article assumes that the reader is equipped with relevant knowledge. For example:

> **Article:** Tom is in Hangzhou. Because he's not familiar with the local language, he finds it very difficult to communicate with people there.
>
> **Q:** Why can't Tom communicate with others?

To answer such a question, one needs to know that Hangzhou is a city in China, and Chinese is the primary language used in the country. Then, the reader can infer that Tom cannot communicate since he does not understand Chinese. Thus a MRC model must acquire and apply knowledge and common sense before achieving human-level performance.

8.7.1.2 Interpretability

The vast majority of MRC models are based on deep learning. Many researchers have pointed out that despite their outstanding performance, deep learning models usually lack **interpretability**. Due to the large number of parameters and complex network structures, deep learning models are often referred to as black boxes. It is nearly impossible to find the root cause when the model makes a wrong prediction, let alone correct the model to fix a specific error.

In many applications of reading comprehension, for example, medical and legal domains, merely giving an answer is not enough. So the interpretability of model is vital. For example, if an MRC model gives a diagnosis based on the patient's medical history, laboratory results, and medical text, it must also come with a logical medical explanation.

Some machine learning models provide strong interpretability. For instance, if a decision tree makes an prediction, the path from the root to the corresponding leaf node contains the satisfied conditions which lead the model to this decision, for example, *there is a hospital and a high school in the neighborhood and the house is within 500 feet to a subway station → the house price is above $200 per square feet.* In comparison, the study of the interpretability of deep learning is just starting, and there is a lack of a rigorous theoretical framework to perfectly explain the behaviors of complex deep networks.

Another application of interpretability is to study the vulnerability of models. In 2017 researchers from Google proposed adversarial attacks on deep learning models [8]. The experiments showed that although deep learning models can achieve a high accuracy in many tasks, a little noise indiscernible to humans can drastically affect the model's prediction. In one example given by the paper, the original image is correctly recognized as a panda by a computer vision model. However, when the image is combined with white noises, the model predicts with a probability of 99.3% that the new image contains a gibbon. In NLP there are also numerous similar adversarial attacks. This vulnerability is attributed to the complexity of deep networks which can amplify the effects of small disturbances in the input, resulting in dramatic changes in output values. Apparently, in the absence of a plausible explanation to the prediction, the vulnerability of the MRC model makes it hard to be readily deployed in many industrial applications.

8.7.1.3 Low-resource machine reading comprehension
Advances in MRC research owe a lot to the proliferation of relevant datasets. Nevertheless, these manually collected and labeled datasets are very costly. Take SQuAD v1.0 as an example, the dataset contains more than 23,000 paragraphs and more than 100,000 questions. All questions and answers were written by labelers hired from the Amazon Mechanical Turk platform. Each labeler took 4 minutes to read a paragraph and write questions and answers. Each labeler was paid $9 per hour. After data collection, the authors carefully cleaned the data and verified the quality of answers. Therefore the development of any MRC dataset is both costly and time-consuming.

Meanwhile, in many practical applications, there is little or no labeled data. For instance, to build an intelligent customer service chatbot (Section 8.1), the available historical customer service data may be very limited. Without adequate training data, it is very hard to train an effective MRC model.

In recent years, low-resource NLP has drawn an increasing amount of attention. Many approaches have been proposed to improve models' performance in target domains with little training data. These methods range over unsupervised learning, semisupervised learning, and transfer learning. For example, one can pretrain a model on the SQuAD dataset before fine-tuning it on the small amount of labeled data in the target domain, such as customer service. Another solution is to conduct multitask learning, that is, the model is trained both for question answering and unsupervised tasks such as language modeling. In this way, the model can effectively leverage additional unlabeled data in the target domain.

Moreover, to read articles from new domains, humans can both employ their reading abilities developed in existing domains, and learn entities and relations in the new domain. Thus an MRC model can be pretrained for its reading capability on a large-scale corpus and then distilled with knowledge about new terminologies and relations in the target domain.

8.7.1.4 Multimodality
Currently, MRC primarily targets text data, especially unstructured text. However, there are many more data forms with different modalities and structures in practice. Therefore multimodal MRC is one of the important directions for research.

8.7.1.4.1 Question and answering on structured data
Structured text data, especially database, contains a great amount of information. With the prevalence of SQL technologies, there are emerging many table-based databases. In a database table, each column represents a property, and each row represents a data point. The QA task on databases can be seen as an MRC task: the tables are treated as articles from which information is extracted to answer questions. In 2017 Salesforce introduced the table-based QA dataset WikiSQL [9], which includes more than 24,000 tables and more than 80,000 related questions. A table-based QA model needs to analyze the properties of each table column, generate SQL queries based on the natural language question, and return the result from the SQL engine. This process of generating SQL statements from natural language is called NL2SQL. The paper also proposes an Seq2SQL algorithm which achieves an accuracy of 59.4% on the dataset.

An NL2SQL model should understand the question semantics, and then find its relationship with the table columns to determine the commands, arguments, and conditions according to SQL syntax.

8.7.1.4.2 Visual question answering

NLP and computer vision have been two relatively independent research branches. With the recent development of deep learning, there are many commonalities between the network architectures and optimization algorithms from both directions. As a result, a new research direction is emerging: **Visual Question Answering (VQA)**. In VQA, the input is an image and a question, and the model needs to be answer the question based on the image's content. To process multimodal information, a VQA model first encodes both the image and question into vector representations in the same semantic space. Then, it then uses attention to fuse information from two modalities before generating the text answer with a decoder.

In 2015 Virginia Tech and Microsoft Research introduced a large-scale VQA dataset containing 25,000 images and 760,000 questions [10]. The questions are about the position, color, shape, and number of objects, as well as the action and emotion of people in the image.

Examples of MRC in other modalities include:

1. Video QA, that is, analyze the content of a video to give a summary or answer relevant questions;
2. Reading text with multimedia, such as a news article with pictures and videos;
3. QA in virtual reality, that is, answer questions in **Virtual Reality (VR)** or **Augmented Reality (AR)**. This can be used in the scenario where a customer service chatbot instructs a user to use or fix the product via a VR headset.

With the evolution of media and related technology, multimodal data is produced at an unprecedented speed. Therefore it is an important research direction to adapt the existing MRC models to multimodality scenarios.

8.7.2 Commercialization

In general, the landing of any AI technology requires at least one of the following conditions:

- Optimize the product development/deployment and save costs.
- Provide users with higher quality services and/or generate new profitable domains.
- Continuous model improvement and iteration by using feedbacks from users.

The fundamental purpose of MRC technology is to use computers to analyze text, answer questions, and make decisions. Therefore it is most appropriate to land MRC in labor-intensive text-processing industries. In customer service, a high-quality chatbot can considerably save operational cost; in education, automatic essay scoring can provide students with immediate writing feedback in the place of teachers.

In the commercialization process, there are two modes to deploy MRC: (1) assisting or partially replacing humans, and (2) completely replacing humans.

8.7.2.1 Assisting or partially replacing humans

If the model's quality is not completely satisfiable in all cases, we can train the model to effectively handle relatively simple and frequent scenarios. The remaining cases can be taken over by humans. For instance, we can train a customer service chatbot to focus on the most asked questions by users, while transferring other questions to human agents. An intelligent financial MRC model can filter and summarize related news from the web, in order for the traders to make transaction decisions based on the digested information. As long as the saved labor cost outweighs the cost of development and deployment of models, the MRC technology can be industrialized to assist humans and improve the efficiency.

8.7.2.2 Completely replacing humans

Some applications require a computerized model to completely replace humans. For example, search engines need to automatically return results relevant to user queries; automatic essay scoring services should directly give scores and feedbacks to students. Typically, an MRC model in these applications has to be equipped with a high level of language understanding capability before commercialization. However, the model can continuously improve its parameters and architectures by leveraging users' feedback, through technologies such as **reinforcement learning (RL)**. RL adjusts the model to maximize the desired return by giving incentives and penalties from the environment. Reinforcement learning has played a significant role in decision-making, planning, and gaming. For example, the deep reinforcement learning model AlphaGo beat the world champion Li Sedol in a series of five Go matches in 2016. By using reinforcement learning in MRC, the model's quality can be further improved based on real-time feedback on the prediction results, as demonstrated in the dynamic coattention networks (DCN +) model [11] which uses self-critical policy learning in MRC.

In the commercialization process, MRC can be integrated with other related technologies to broaden its application. For example, in a smart speaker, speech recognition technology converts the user's voice into text to be analyzed by the NLP/MRC module. Then, the smart speaker will take various actions according to the user's commands. This greatly simplifies the communication between machine and users, and can be employed in applications such as over-the-phone customer service.

Finally, it is worth noting that although the MRC technology is just starting to land in various industries, any application requiring automatic text analysis can benefit from this technology, including but not limited to retail, education, finance, law, and health care. On the one hand, MRC models can be optimized for applications where NLP has achieved much success, for example, search engines, advertising, recommendation. On the other hand, we believe that with the continuous progress of MRC technologies, the gap between machines and humans will continue to shrink until we enter the era of technology singularity when MRC will revolutionize more industries.

8.8 Summary

- **Intelligent customer service** uses MRC technology to analyze the product documentation and user queries to solve users' questions about products.
- **Search engines** match user queries to related web pages, and adopt the crawl—index—rank pipeline. MRC can improve the accuracy of text analysis and provide intelligent question-and-answer capabilities for search engines.
- In diagnostics, MRC can analyze massive medical records and knowledge bases to provide smart health care services.
- MRC technology can parse legal files for **automatic judgement** and **crime classification**.
- The financial sector relies on real-time information processing, including **stock price prediction** and **news summarization**, which can be automated by MRC.
- MRC-based **automatic essay scoring** can help students learn to write by providing automatic feedbacks and suggestions.
- The challenges of MRC include **knowledge and reasoning**, **interpretability**, **low-resource MRC**, and **multimodality**.
- The commercialization of MRC has two modes: **assisting or partially replacing humans**, and **completely replacing humans**. Reinforcement learning can help continuously improve the model's performance with users' feedback.

References

[1] Huang PS, He X, Gao J, Deng L, Acero A, Heck L. Learning deep structured semantic models for web search using clickthrough data. Proceedings of the 22nd ACM international conference on information & knowledge management. 2013. p. 2333–8.

[2] Page L, Brin S, Motwani R, Winograd T. The PageRank citation ranking: bringing order to the web. Stanford InfoLab; 1999.

[3] Šuster S, Daelemans W. CliCR: a dataset of clinical case reports for machine reading comprehension. arXiv preprint arXiv 2018; 1803.09720.

[4] Long S, Tu C, Liu Z, Sun M. Automatic judgment prediction via legal reading comprehension. China national conference on Chinese computational linguistics. Cham: Springer; 2019. p. 558–72.

[5] Wang P, Fan Y, Niu S, Yang Z, Zhang Y, Guo J. Hierarchical matching network for crime classification. Proceedings of the 42nd international ACM SIGIR conference on research and development in information retrieval. 2019. p. 325–34.

[6] Xu Y, Cohen SB. Stock movement prediction from tweets and historical prices. Proceedings of the 56th annual meeting of the association for computational linguistics, vol. 1. Long Papers; 2018. p. 1970–9.

[7] Farag Y, Yannakoudakis H, Briscoe T. Neural automated essay scoring and coherence modeling for adversarially crafted input. arXiv preprint arXiv 2018; 1804.06898.

[8] Goodfellow IJ, Shlens J, Szegedy C. Explaining and harnessing adversarial examples. arXiv preprint arXiv 2014; 1412.6572.

[9] Zhong V, Xiong C, Socher R. Seq2sql: generating structured queries from natural language using reinforcement learning. arXiv preprint arXiv 2017; 1709.00103.

[10] Antol S, Agrawal A, Lu J, Mitchell M, Batra D, Lawrence Zitnick C, et al. Vqa: visual question answering. Proceedings of the IEEE international conference on computer vision. 2015. p. 2425–33.

[11] Xiong C, Zhong V, Socher R. Dcn + : mixed objective and deep residual coattention for question answering. arXiv preprint arXiv 2017; 1711.00106.

Appendix A: Machine learning basics

Machine learning is a science discipline that learns patterns from data to continuously improve model performance. As a machine learning problem, machine reading comprehension (MRC) follows the same methodology. In this section, we will introduce the basics of machine learning to build the foundation for the rest of the book.

A.1 Types of machine learning

According to whether and how labeled data is used, there are three main types of machine learning: **Supervised Learning**, **Unsupervised Learning**, and **Semisupervised Learning**.

In supervised training, each training data sample includes the input and corresponding labeled output. For example, an MRC data sample includes a paragraph, a question, and a ground-truth answer edited by labelers. Supervised learning models leverage the statistical relationship between the input and output, and update model parameters according to the difference between the ground-truth answer and the prediction. Given sufficient training data, supervising learning methods generally have better performance than unsupervised learning and semisupervised learning methods. The majority of the models introduced in this book belong to supervised learning. However, the data labeling process is both time-consuming and costly. One solution is to automatically obtain label signals from collected data. For instance, search engines record the clicked web pages for each user query and use them as training data for relevance models. The reason is that there is a statistical semantic correlation between the query's text and the title and content of the clicked pages.

In unsupervised learning, the training data does not contain labels, so the model needs to define its training criteria. For example, for the task of clustering news by categories, the model can maximize the similarity between news in the same predicted category while minimizing the similarity between news in different predicted categories. Usually, unsupervised learning is harder to train than supervised learning, and has inferior performances. However, unsupervised learning can effectively utilize large amounts of unlabeled data, which is particularly suitable for natural language processing applications.

Semisupervised learning uses both labeled and unlabeled data to build models. A typical example is to pretrain the model on massive unlabeled data and then fine-tune it with a modest amount of labeled data in the target domain.

A.2 Model and parameters

The most common concept in machine learning is the **model**. Here is an example of a supervised machine learning model.

Given the information of a house, for example, living area, number of bedrooms, and proximity to public transport, the model needs to predict the house price. We can treat the d pieces of house information as the independent variable $x = (x_1, x_2, \ldots, x_d)$, and the house price as the dependent variable y. The model aims to find the relationship between x and y. However, there can be countless possible ways to characterize this relationship. Thus we should first set a range of relationships from which the model selects. One example is the linear regression model which assumes a linear relationship between x and y:

$$y = \beta_0 + \beta_1 x_1 + \beta_2 x_2 + \cdots + \beta_d x_d$$

where $\beta_0, \beta_1, \ldots, \beta_d$ are **parameters** to be learned. A quadratic model would assume a quadratic relationship between x and y:

$$y = \beta_{0,0} + \sum_i \sum_j \beta_{i,j} x_i x_j$$

As shown, any model predefines a range of hypotheses between the input and output. Different models may set hypotheses ranges of varying complexities and number of parameters.

Once we decide which model to use, its parameters are then adjusted to appropriate values to improve the prediction performance. Therefore the training process is to update the value of model parameters based on the training data, and end up with a model with a high accuracy. We refer to this process as parameter optimization. Appendix B.1.2 and B.1.3 will introduce ways to systematically optimize model parameters.

A.3 Generalization and overfitting

The data for model training is called the **training set**. However, if the model is evaluated on the same set, one cannot distinguish between a high-quality model and a model that merely stores the whole training data to directly retrieve answers. Therefore a machine learning model must be evaluated on a separate **test set**. The test set includes data in the same distribution as that the training set, but is unseen during training. In other words, we care about a model's ability to generalize its prediction power on unseen data, also known as **generalization**.

Since the test set is not visible during training, how should one select from the various versions of model during training? One idea is to pick the model that works best on the training set. Unfortunately, in many cases, after the model exceeds a certain accuracy threshold in the training set, its performance on the test set becomes *worse* as its performance on the training set further improves. This phenomenon is referred to as **overfitting**.

The reason for overfitting is that the trained model not only fits the relationship between the input and output, but also fits the noise, that is, labeling errors, in the output signal in the training data. This makes the model achieve a particularly high accuracy on the training set, but its predictive power on unseen data is greatly reduced. As Fig. A.1 shows, the model's error rate on the test set begins to rise past the dashed line.

To observe overfitting in training, one can reserve a portion of the training data as the **validation set**. The validation data is not used to update model parameters. Instead, the model regularly evaluates its accuracy on the validation set. Once the accuracy plateaus or starts a steady decline, overfitting happens and the training is halted. The model version with the best performance on the validation set is selected. In other words, we use the validation set as the test set during training to select the model with the best generalization capability.

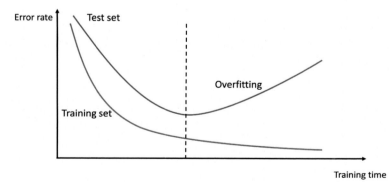

Figure A.1 Overfitting occurs during training: past the dashed line, the error rate of the model drops on the training set but rises on the test set.

Appendix B: Deep learning basics

As a promising artificial intelligence research branch, deep learning has made numerous breakthroughs in recent years. In many tasks including vision, speech, and text, deep learning greatly outperforms traditional models. The majority of current machine reading comprehension (MRC) models are based on deep learning. This section introduces the basics of deep learning used in MRC, which provides the foundation for many MRC models.

B.1 Neural network

The cornerstone of deep learning is the **neural network**. A neural network can complete the entire process for MRC: read articles and questions, analyze the semantics, and produce answers. This section describes the definition, computation, and optimization of neural network models.

B.1.1 Definition

The neural network is a computational model simulating the neuron network in human brains. Similar to human neurons, the basic component of a neural network is a **neuron**, also called a **perceptron**, which can process input information and generate the output. Neurons are connected through weighted connections to transmit information.

B.1.1.1 Neuron

A neuron maps the input of n values to one output value. Suppose the neuron's input is $\boldsymbol{x} = (x_1, x_2, \ldots, x_n)$, which is transmitted into the neuron via n connections. The weights of these connections are denoted by the parameters $\boldsymbol{w} = (w_1, w_2, \ldots, w_n)$. The neuron first calculates a weighted sum of the inputs:

$$U(\boldsymbol{x}; \boldsymbol{w}) = w_1 x_1 + w_2 x_2 + \cdots + w_n x_n = \sum_{i=1}^{n} w_i x_i = \boldsymbol{w}^T \boldsymbol{x}$$

Usually, it also adds an bias parameter b:

$$S(\boldsymbol{x}; \boldsymbol{w}, \boldsymbol{b}) = U(\boldsymbol{x}; \boldsymbol{w}) + b = \boldsymbol{w}^T \boldsymbol{x} + b$$

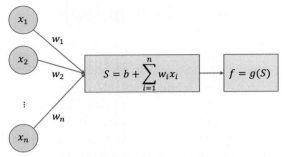

Figure B.1 Computation of a neuron, including the weighted sum S, the bias b, and the activation function g.

Thus $S(\boldsymbol{x}; \boldsymbol{w}, b)$ is a linear function of the input $(x_1, x_2, \ldots, x_n)$. Next, the neuron applies the **activation function** g on S to obtain the final output $f(\boldsymbol{x}; \boldsymbol{w}, b) = g(S(\boldsymbol{x}; \boldsymbol{w}, b))$. Fig. B.1 illustrates the computation of a single neuron.

The choice of the activation function is flexible, but it should satisfy the following properties:

1. the activation function should be a continuous and differentiable nonlinear function, which could be nondifferentiable on a constant number of points. In this way, it can be efficiently optimized by existing numerical methods;
2. the calculation of the activation function and its derivative should be simple and fast to make computation efficient, since activation functions are very frequently used in a neural network; and
3. since the chain rule is used in gradient computation, the range of the activation function's derivative should be reasonable to prevent gradients from being too large or too small.

Here, we introduce several common activation functions used in neural networks.

1. Sigmoid

The sigmoid function is $\sigma(x) = \frac{1}{1 + e^{-x}}$. Fig. B.2 illustrates its curve. As shown, sigmoid is an S-shaped function. It takes a value of 0.5 at $x = 0$ and goes to 1 quickly when $x \to +\infty$. The derivative of the sigmoid function is $\sigma'(x) = \sigma(x)(1 - \sigma(x))$, with a range of $(0, 0.25]$. The sigmoid function is continuously differentiable and simple to compute, satisfying the aforementioned properties. This makes it one of the most commonly used activation functions.

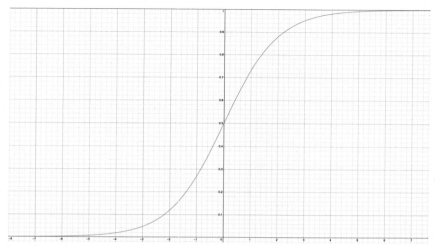

Figure B.2 The curve of sigmoid function.

Moreover, the sigmoid function is symmetric about the center point (0, 0.5):

$$0.5 * 2 - \sigma(0 - x) = 1 - \frac{1}{1 + e^{-(-x)}} = \frac{e^x}{1 + e^x} = \frac{1}{1 + e^{-x}} = \sigma(x)$$

It is worth noting that the sigmoid function is also used in Logistic Regression. In fact, a single neuron with the sigmoid activation function is equivalent to the Logistic Regression model.

2. Tanh

The *tanh* function is also known as the hyperbolic tangent function, that is, $tanh(x) = \frac{e^x - e^{-x}}{e^x + e^{-x}}$. Fig. B.3 illustrates its curve. As shown, the *tanh* function is an S-shaped function with range of $(-1, 1)$. It takes the value of 0 at $x = 0$, goes to 1 when $x \to +\infty$, and goes to -1 when $x \to -\infty$. The derivative of *tanh* function is $tanh'(x) = 1 - tanh^2(x)$, with a range of $(0, 1]$. Unlike the sigmoid function, the *tanh* function is symmetric about the origin, that is, it is zero-centered.

3. ReLU

The ReLU function is also known as the Rectified Linear Unit. It has a very simple form: the output is 0 when the input is less than 0, and the output is equal to the input when it is greater than or equal to 0:

$$\text{ReLU}(x) = \begin{cases} x, x \geq 0 \\ 0, x < 0 \end{cases} = \max(x, 0)$$

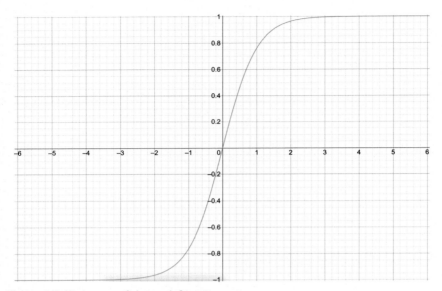

Figure B.3 The curve of the *tanh* function.

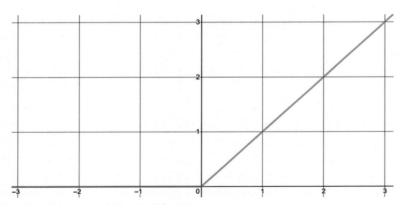

Figure B.4 The curve of the ReLU function.

Fig. B.4 illustrates the curve of the ReLU function.

One advantage of the ReLU function is that its derivative is always 1 when the input is greater than 0. In comparison, the derivatives of sigmoid and *tanh* functions both approach 0 when the input goes to infinity. Since many optimization algorithms adjust parameters based on the magnitude of the derivative (e.g., the gradient descent algorithm in Section B.1.3), a derivative away from the zero allows better regulation of the parameters. For example,

> The inputs to neuron are $x_1 = x_2 = 5$. The parameters are $w_1 = w_2 = 1$, $b = 0$. The weighted sum is $S = 5 + 5 = 10$.
> With ReLU as the activation function, the output is $f(x_1, x_2; \mathbf{w}, b) = ReLU(10) = 10$, with gradients $f'(W_1) = f'(W_2) = 5$.
> With sigmoid as the activation function, the output is $f(x_1, x_2; \mathbf{w}, b) = sigmoid(10) = \frac{1}{1 + e^{-10}} = 0.999954602$, with gradients $f'(W_1) = f'(W_2) = 0.00023$

One drawback of the ReLU function is that once the input is less than 0, its derivative becomes 0, making the optimizer unable to change the parameter value.

It can be demonstrated that with nonlinear activation functions, a two-layer neural network can approximate any complex functions arbitrarily well. Thus neural networks have a strong computational power.

B.1.1.2 Layer and network

Neurons can form layers, and the neurons in the same layers share their inputs. The output of a layer can be fed as input to the next layer. Thus each layer is connected by weighted connections to neighboring layers, forming the **feedforward neural network**.

In a feedforward neural network, the first layer is the input layer, consisting of n input values to the network. The last layer is the output layer. The layers between the input layer and the output layer are called hidden layers. All adjacent layers are connected by weighted connections. Fig. B.5 illustrates a feedforward neural network with three input values, two hidden layers, and an output layer of size 1.

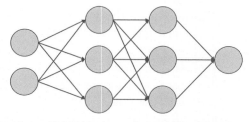

Input layer   First hidden layer   Second hidden layer   Output layer

Figure B.5 A feedforward neural network with two hidden layers.

The computation of the feedforward neural network is from the input layer to the output layer. Suppose the input layer has a_0 input values: $x_0 = (x_1, \ldots, x_{a_0})$. Then, the neurons in the first hidden layer compute their outputs $x_1 = (x_1, \ldots, x_{a_1})$. Similarly, the neurons in the second hidden layer output $x_2 = (x_1, \ldots, x_{a_2})$ and so on. Finally, the output layer generates $x_m = (x_1, \ldots, x_{a_m})$. This process is called the **forward pass**, which is from left to right in Fig. B.5.

In general, the number of neurons in each layer is different. Suppose the input layer contains a_0 neuron, the output layer contains a_m neurons, and the hidden layers contain $a_1, \ldots, a_{m-1}$ neurons. Then the number of parameters of the entire network is $\sum_{i=1}^{m} a_i * (1 + a_{i-1})$, because each neuron in a noninput layer has an bias parameter b. Therefore even for a fixed number of input values, one can design networks with varying sizes to adapt to different problem complexity and resource constraints. This makes the neural network one of the most flexible machine learning models.

B.1.2 Loss function

Given the input $x = x_0 = (x_1, \ldots, x_{a_0})$, the network's output $\hat{y} = x_m = (x_1, \ldots, x_{a_m})$ should match the ground truth y. As the network parameters are often randomly initialized, we need to adjust the parameters to improve the model's performance. One way is to compute the prediction error $y - \hat{y}$ and update the parameters according to their derivatives. However, it is often the case that $y - \hat{y}$ is not differentiable, such as classification accuracy. Thus in neural networks and many machine learning models, this prediction error is estimated by the **loss function**.

A loss function f is a function of all network parameters $\boldsymbol{\theta}$. It depicts the difference between the network output $\hat{y}$ and the expected output y. The loss function is not unique, even for the same problem. However, it should satisfy the following properties:

- a loss function should be differentiable for all network parameters; and
- a loss function should approximate the inaccuracy of the prediction, that is, the function in general takes a smaller value when the model accuracy is higher.

The second property means that, if the accuracy of the network with parameters $\boldsymbol{\theta}_1$ is higher than that with parameters $\boldsymbol{\theta}_2$, $f(\boldsymbol{\theta}_1)$ should be less than $f(\boldsymbol{\theta}_2)$ in most cases, but not guaranteed.

Take the binary classification problem as an example, where the model outputs 0 or 1 as the predicted category. Suppose the output layer produces the value $\hat{y}(x;\theta)\in[0,1]$. If $\hat{y}<0.5$, the model predicts 0, otherwise it predicts 1, that is, it predicts $I_{\hat{y}\geq0.5}$. This prediction is compared against the ground-truth answer $y\in\{0,1\}$. One possible loss function f can be:

$$f(\theta) = \frac{1}{2}\sum_{i=1}^{n}(\hat{y}(x_i;\theta)-y_i)^2$$

where the inputs are $\{x_i, y_i\}_{i=1}^{n}$. As the formula indicates, if the output value $\hat{y}$ is close to the ground-truth value y, the value of the loss function is small and the accuracy is high. However, we can find two particular sets of parameters such that this relation is reversed. For example,

```
Parameters θ₁ : ŷ(x₁ ; θ₁) = 0.49999, ŷ(x₂ ; θ₁) = 0.49999, ŷ(x₃ ; θ₁) =
    0.49999, ŷ(x₄ ; θ₁) = 1
Parameters θ₂ : ŷ(x₁ ; θ₂) = 0.5, ŷ(x₂ ; θ₂) = 0.5, ŷ(x₃ ; θ₂) = 0.5,
    ŷ (x₄ ; θ₂) = 0.5
Ground-truth: y₁ = y₂ = y₃ = y₄ = 1
With the parameters θ₁, the accuracy is 25%; with the parameters θ₂,
    the accuracy is higher, 100%. However, the loss function of θ₁ is
    smaller: f(θ₁) = ½(0.501² * 3) ≈ 0.375 < f(θ₂) = ½(0.5² * 4) = 0.5
```

In most cases, however, the loss function can be used as a reliable reference to compare two sets of parameters and facilitate the optimization process. We introduce two common loss functions in the next section.

B.1.2.1 Mean squared error
Mean Square Error (MSE) loss function computes the average of squares of prediction errors. MSE is suitable for regression problems, that is, given the input x, the model needs to predict a real value $\hat{y}$. House price prediction and stock price forecast are both regression problems. For these tasks, the output layer of the neural network has one neuron which produces $\hat{y}$. The MSE loss function is:

$$f_{MSE}(\theta) = \frac{1}{2}\sum_{i=1}^{n}(\hat{y}(x_i;\theta)-y_i)^2$$

One advantage of MSE loss function is that the two cases of $\hat{y}(x_i;\theta)<y_i$ and $\hat{y}(x_i;\theta)>y_i$ are symmetrically dealt with.

B.1.2.2 Cross entropy

Cross entropy loss function is usually employed in classification tasks, where the target value y is from a set of size K, for example, {apple, pear, peach}. The output layer of the neural network contains K neurons to predict the score for each class: $\hat{y}_1, \hat{y}_2, \ldots, \hat{y}_K$. The network selects the maximum score $\hat{y}_{k*}$ and predicts the corresponding category $k*$, that is, $k* = argmax_k \hat{y}_k$.

However, the accuracy of the argmax category $k*$ is nondifferentiable with respect to the network parameters. In other words, we cannot take derivatives w.r.t parameters θ for the accuracy function $I_{y=argmax_k \hat{y}_k}(\theta)$. Thus the **cross entropy** function is usually used as the loss function. It first normalizes the scores $\hat{y}_1, \hat{y}_2, \ldots, \hat{y}_K$ into probabilities by softmax:

$$softmax(\hat{y}_1, \hat{y}_2, \ldots, \hat{y}_K) = (p_1, p_2, \ldots, p_K) = \left(\frac{e^{\hat{y}_1}}{Z}, \frac{e^{\hat{y}_2}}{Z}, \ldots, \frac{e^{\hat{y}_K}}{Z}\right), Z = e^{\hat{y}_1} + e^{\hat{y}_2} + \cdots + e^{\hat{y}_K}$$

The goal is to maximize the probability for the ground-truth class y: p_y, which is equivalent to maximizing $log(p_y)$. Because the loss function should be minimized, it minimizes $-log(p_y)$. Thus given n training instances, the loss function takes a value of:

$$f_{cross\_entropy}(\theta) = -\sum_{i=1}^{n} log(p_{y_i}(x_i; \theta))$$

Since probability values range from 0 to 1, the cross entropy function always takes a nonnegative value. When the cross entropy is down to 0, the neural network accurately assigns a probability of 1 to the ground-truth label for each input.

Table B.1 showcases the cross entropy calculation for a three-class classification. As shown, when the ground-truth class ($y = 2$) is assigned a higher value $\hat{y}_2$, the cross entropy takes a smaller value.

Table B.1 Example of cross entropy, where $K = 3$ and $y = 2$.

$\hat{y}$		$p_i = softmax(\hat{y}_i)$		$-logp_i$	Ground-truth y	Cross entropy
$\hat{y}_1$	2.0	p_1	0.66	0.42		
$\hat{y}_2$	1.0	p_2	0.24	1.42	2	1.42
$\hat{y}_3$	0.1	p_3	0.10	2.3		
$\hat{y}_1$	0.1	p_1	0.00005	4.30		
$\hat{y}_2$	10	p_2	0.9999	0.0000434	2	0.0000434
$\hat{y}_3$	0.1	p_3	0.00005	4.30		

In particular, for binary classification, that is, $y_i \in \{0, 1\}$, the cross entropy can be formulated as:

$$f_{cross\_entropy}(\boldsymbol{\theta}) = -\sum_{i=1}^{n} y_i \log(p_{y_i}(\boldsymbol{x}_i; \boldsymbol{\theta})) + (1 - y_i)\log(1 - p_{y_i}(\boldsymbol{x}_i; \boldsymbol{\theta}))$$

B.1.3 Optimization

As the network parameters are randomly initialized, we need to systematically update the parameters to reduce the value of the loss function. One of the most commonly used optimization algorithm in neural networks is **gradient descent**.

Fig. B.6 illustrates the gradient descent of a 1D function $f(x)$. If the parameter x is initialized to x_1, we compute the derivative of f at $x = x_1$, that is, $f'(x)|_{x=x_1}$. As $f'(x)|_{x=x_1} > 0$ in the example, f increases when x is larger, around the point $x = x_1$. Therefore to reduce the value of f, x should be updated to a smaller value, that is, the opposite direction of the derivative.

For a multivariable function $f(\boldsymbol{x}) = f(x_1, x_2, \ldots, x_n)$, one can compute the derivative w.r.t each parameter: $\partial f/\partial x_i$. These derivatives form a vector $\nabla f(\boldsymbol{x})|_{x=(x_1,x_2,\ldots,x_n)} = [\partial f/\partial x_1, \partial f/\partial x_2, \ldots, \partial f/\partial x_n]$, also known as the **gradient**. Then, all parameters are updated in the opposite direction of their derivatives, and the rate of change is controlled by the **learning rate** α. In other words, x_i becomes $x_i - \alpha(\partial f/\partial x_i)$.

The core of gradient descent is to calculate the gradient of the function w.r.t the current parameters. Since neural networks are based on a multilayer structure, it is difficult to obtain a closed-form formula for all

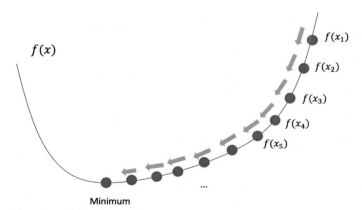

Figure B.6 Gradient descent for a 1D function.

the derivatives. One effective algorithm to compute the derivatives is **backpropagation**.

Backpropagation employs the chain rule to calculate the derivative:

Chain Rule

Suppose $f(g(x))$ is a composite function, i.e. f is a function of g and g is a function of x.

Then the derivative of f with respect to x is: $\frac{df(g(x))}{dx} = \frac{df(g)}{dg}\frac{dg(x)}{dx}$

For example, suppose $f(g) = g^2, g(x) = x^3$. Then $f(g(x)) = x^6$ and $\frac{df(g(x))}{dx} = 6x^5$. On the other hand, according to the chain rule, $\frac{df(g(x))}{dx} = \frac{df(g)}{dg}\frac{dg(x)}{dx} = 2g * 3x^2 = 6x^5$.

The chain rule can be used in the derivative computation of neural network parameters. The loss function is a function of neurons in the output layer, which are in turn functions of their connection weights. Thus the chain rule can be used to compute the derivatives of the loss function w.r.t the connection weights of the output layer. Following this method, we can calculate the derivatives of the connection weights in all previous layers. Code B-1 gives the details of the backpropagation algorithm.

When all derivatives are obtained, the parameters are updated in the opposite direction of the gradient. This process can reduce the value of loss function during training. We then periodically evaluate the model on the validation data to select the best version of the model.

Code B-1 Backpropagation algorithm

The neural network has $m+1$ layers. Denote the connection weight between the ith neuron in the lth layer and the jth neuron in the $(l-1)^{th}$ layer by $w^l_{i,j}$.

Suppose the ith neuron in the lth layer computes the weighted sum s^l_i of its inputs, with the bias parameter b^l_i. The weighted sum is then fed into the activation function g to obtain output o^l_i. The final loss function is denoted by $f(\hat{y})$ f.

The backpropagation algorithm proceeds as follows:

1. Compute the derivative of f w.r.t the output layer's neuron output o^{m+1}_i: $q^{m+1}_i = \frac{\partial f}{\partial o^{m+1}_i}$
2. Compute the derivative of f w.r.t the output layer's weighted sum s^{m+1}_i: $\frac{\partial f}{\partial s^{m+1}_i} = p^{m+1}_i = q^{m+1}_i \frac{\partial o^{m+1}_i}{\partial s^{m+1}_i} = q^{m+1}_i \frac{\partial g}{\partial s^{m+1}_i}$

(Continued)

(Continued)

3. As $s_i^{m+1} = \sum_j w_{j,i}^m o_j^m + b_j^{m+1}$, the derivatives of f w.r.t the connection weights and bias are:

$$\frac{\partial f}{\partial w_{j,i}^m} = p_i^{m+1} \frac{\partial s_i^{m+1}}{\partial w_{j,i}^m} = p_i^{m+1} o_j^m, \quad \frac{\partial f}{\partial b^{m+1}} = p_i^{m+1} \frac{\partial s_i^{m+1}}{\partial b_i^{m+1}} = p_i^{m+1}$$

4. Compute the derivative of f w.r.t the last hidden layer's neuron output o_j^m: $q_j^m = \sum_i p_i^{m+1} w_{j,i}^m$

5. Continue calculating the derivatives of other layers' connection weights and bias.

One problem with backpropagation is that, when the number of network layers increases, the absolute value of derivatives tends to become exceedingly large or small. This phenomenon is referred to as gradient explosion/vanishing. The reason is that the chain rule computes the product of many intermediate derivatives whose absolute value is away from 1. In the next section, we will introduce several techniques to alleviate this problem.

B.2 Common types of neural network in deep learning

The feedforward neural network in the previous section is the most basic network type. In the development of deep learning, networks of many distinct structures are proposed, which greatly alleviate the problems with feedforward neural networks, and enable effective application of deep learning in NLP, vision, speech, etc. This section introduces some common types of neural networks in deep learning, including convolutional neural network (CNN), recurrent neural network (RNN), and dropout. These networks are commonly used in MRC models.

B.2.1 Convolutional neural network

The feedforward neural network has connections between each pair of neurons in any two neighboring layers. So it is also called a fully connected network. However, in many deep learning models, a layer may contain a large number of neurons, so the size of the fully connected network can grow rapidly, which consumes massive memory and reduces computational efficiency. To alleviate this problem, one can use the **Convolutional Neural Network (CNN)**.

CNN was first applied in image processing. Researchers found that each image pixel is only closely related to its neighboring pixels in a small

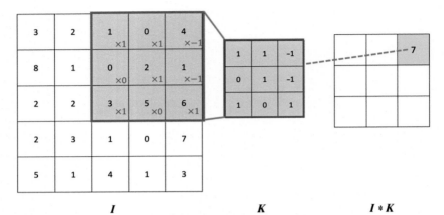

Figure B.7 An example of convolutional neural network. *I* is the input layer, *K* represents the connection weights, and *I*K* is the hidden layer. Each neuron in the hidden layer is only connected to $3 \times 3 = 9$ neurons in the input layer.

local area. Thus if each pixel is modeled by a neuron, it should be connected to only the neurons around it. Fig. B.7 illustrates a CNN, where I is the input layer, K represents the connection weights, and I^*K indicates the hidden layer. Each neuron in the hidden layer is only connected to $3 \times 3 = 9$ neurons in the input layer. If we sequentially highlight the input layer neurons connected to each hidden layer neuron, we will observe a 3×3 block moving in the input layer.

In the example above, there are 25 neurons in the input layer and nine neurons in the hidden layer. If a fully connected network is used, there will be $25 \times 9 = 225$ connection weights, that is, parameters. However, one can share the nine weights for each neuron in the hidden layer, that is, use the same K for all hidden layer neurons. This can significantly reduce the number of parameters to nine. Here, K is also called a **filter**. The resulting network is called a CNN since the process of multiplying K with different local areas in I is similar to the convolution operation in mathematics.

A CNN can also use more than one filters. For example, it can use two filters K_1 and K_2 to generate I^*K_1 and I^*K_2, which are referred to as two output channels. Similarly, if there are more than one input channel, for example, the three-channel RGB image, the CNN will compute the convolution of each input channel and each filter. Fig. B.8 illustrates a CNN with three input channels and two output channels. Each filter has three layers to convolve with each input channel, resulting in three

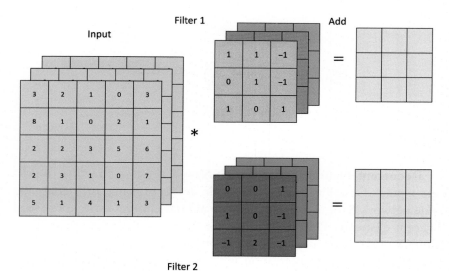

Figure B.8 A CNN with three input channels and two output channels.

matrices of size 3×3. These matrices are summed up. So the output contains two matrices of size 3×3, one from each filter.

In MRC models, CNN is commonly used for character embedding. Each word of length L is considered to be an image with $1 \times L$ pixels (characters). More details are described in Sections 3.1.2 and 4.2.2.

B.2.2 Recurrent neural network

In many deep learning problems, the input does not have a fixed length, for example, the length of the article in MRC. For these tasks, the corresponding embedding representations do not have a fixed shape. However, the structure and number of parameters of a neural network is predefined. Thus the aforementioned types of networks like feedforward neural network cannot process input of varying size.

One workaround is to predefine the maximum length L of the input text, and specifically design a network to take input of size L. If a sentence has fewer than L words, it will be padded to length L with special symbols. However, this solution wastes a lot of space when most of the input data is short. An alternative solution is to average the word vectors in the input to get a single vector representation. However, this ignores the word order in the input, and it is very difficult to compress the rich information within the text into one vector.

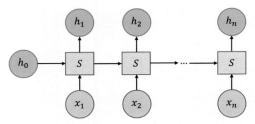

Figure B.9 Recurrent neural network.

Recurrent Neural Network (RNN) is a network structure to process inputs of varying lengths. The basic design principle is to apply the same network S for each input element and transmit information between adjacent elements. The advantage of this approach is that it can save the number of parameters and enable the processing of an input sequence of any length. Also, the information is shared between the input elements. Fig. B.9 shows the architecture of an RNN, where the input consists of the word vectors $\{x_t\}_{t=1}^n$, and information between elements is transmitted by RNN's hidden state vectors $\{h_t\}$. Because h_t contains the meaning of the tth word and the preceding words, it is also referred to as the contextualized vector or contextualized embedding.

Here, the network structure S should be able to both process each element and transmit the information. We introduce two commonly used RNN modules: **Gated Recurrent Unit, (GRU)** and **Long Short-Term Memory (LSTM)**.

B.2.2.1 Gated recurrent unit

The gated recurrent unit (GRU) [1] is an RNN module that receives two inputs: the previous hidden state h_{t-1} and the current input embedding x_t. The GRU then outputs the new hidden state h_t. To produce the output, a GRU module contains the sigmoid/*tanh* activation functions, a reset gate r_t to decide whether to ignore the previous hidden state, and an update gate z_t to decide whether to ignore the current input embedding. Thus the reset and update gates determine whether the semantics of the first t words, represented by h_t, depend more on the previous $t-1$ words or on the current input word x_t.

B.2.2.2 Long short-term memory

LSTM [2] is a more complex RNN network module compared with GRU. It conveys two kinds of information: cell state c_t and hidden state h_t.

The input to an LSTM module includes c_{t-1} and h_{t-1} from the previous step and the input embedding x_t. The LSTM module has a forget gate f_t, an input gate i_t and an output gate o_t to selective employ the input information and produce the new cell state c_t and the hidden state h_t.

GRU and LSTM can greatly alleviate the problem of gradient explosion/vanishing mentioned in Section B.1. The reason is that the average length of derivative chains for chain rule is shorter after using the gates in GRU and LSTM. Therefore it reduces the number of multiplying derivatives.

Because the meaning of a word is often related to its context from both sides, we can also use a bidirectional RNN. A bidirectional RNN consists of two unidirectional RNNs: one from left to right, and the other from right to left. The final state of each word is the concatenation of hidden states from the two unidirectional RNNs.

The output state of an RNN layer can be fed as input to the next RNN layer, forming a multilayer RNN network. In NLP, it has been shown that a multilayer RNN can extract higher levels of semantics from text and significantly boost the performance in many NLP tasks.

B.2.3 Dropout

A common problem in machine learning is **overfitting**, which refers to the phenomenon that the model performs very well on the training data but poorly on the test set. Overfitting can seriously impact a model's generalization capability on unseen data.

An important reason for overfitting is a high model complexity (e.g., too many parameters) combined with a small training set. Since it can adapt the model parameters to noises in the training data, this makes the model unable to be extended to cases other than the training data. As deep learning models usually have a high complexity, overfitting often occurs.

To solve this problem, we can enlarge the training data size, reduce the model complexity, use regularization, etc. Another popular solution is **dropout**.

Dropout [3] was proposed to reduce the model complexity without changing the model size. During training, in each step, the dropout mechanism randomly removes each neuron (and associated connections) in the hidden layers with probability p. The output, derivatives, and updates are then based on the remaining neurons and connections.

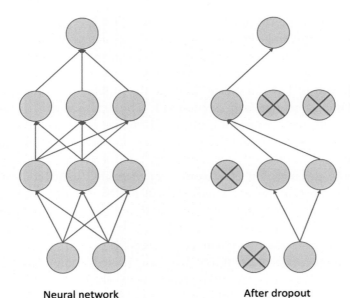

Neural network   **After dropout**

Figure B.10 How dropout works. During each batch, a random portion of neurons and their connections are removed.

Then, all neurons and connections are recovered before the next training step. Fig. B.10 illustrates an example of dropout.

During test, dropout is not used, that is, all neurons are kept. However, as each neuron only receives about $(1 - p)$ of the input connections during training, the input weighted sum is multiplied by $(1 - p)$ during test to fix the discrepancy. Another way is to divide the input weighted sum by $(1 - p)$ during training which requires no operation during test.

In practice, dropout can be used in either a network module or as a separate layer. A dropout layer sets each input element to 0 with probability p.

The advantage of dropout is that the network structure does not need to be changed. By randomly removing neurons in each training step, it is equivalent to reducing the network size. Dropout has been proved to be very effective in practice, and can be used in place of regularization to prevent overfitting. There is a lot of analysis on the reason for dropout's effectiveness. The prevailing views are:

First, dropout is equivalent to training many different models simultaneously and using the average of their outputs as the prediction result.

This aligns with concept of ensemble method in machine learning, which is effective in preventing overfitting.

Second, dropout prevents the coadaptation phenomenon between neurons. Coadaptation means that that a neuron highly depends on the outputs from certain other neurons, which is an important reason for overfitting. Since there is a probability that any two neurons do not cooccur, dropout strengthens the computational ability of each individual neuron.

B.3 The deep learning framework PyTorch

A deep learning framework abstracts commonly used network modules to achieve reusability. Also, it can enable automatic gradient computation, freeing developers from the burden of calculating derivatives for custom networks. Early deep learning frameworks were mostly developed in academia, such as Caffe, Torch, and Theano. Over time, frameworks from the industry become increasingly popular due to their high efficiency. Currently, the most popular deep learning frameworks are:

- TensorFlow by Google.
- PyTorch by Facebook.
- Keras, which is open source.

All these frameworks are written in Python. TensorFlow and PyTorch provide fine-grained control over the network structure and support almost all common network modules. In addition, these frameworks are constantly updated to enable developers to implement new networks, control optimization details, etc. While TensorFlow has been extensively optimized for large-scale deployment and computational efficiency, PyTorch is relatively simple to learn and use. Thus all code samples in this book are in PyTorch.

Unlike TensorFlow and PyTorch, Keras is an advanced API specification, which is compatible with different frameworks such as TensorFlow, CNTK, and Theano. Keras highly abstracts common network modules to simplify usage, especially for beginners (e.g., much shorter code), but lacks the agility to handle network details.

B.3.1 Installing PyTorch

PyTorch supports most operating systems including Linux, Mac, and Windows. To set up PyTorch, one needs to install Python first.

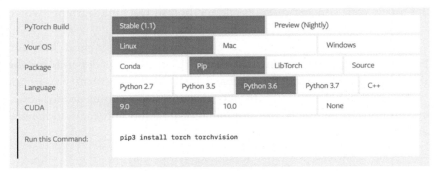

PyTorch Build	Stable (1.1)		Preview (Nightly)		
Your OS	Linux	Mac	Windows		
Package	Conda	Pip	LibTorch	Source	
Language	Python 2.7	Python 3.5	Python 3.6	Python 3.7	C++
CUDA	9.0	10.0	None		
Run this Command:	pip3 install torch torchvision				

Figure B.11 Install PyTorch.

If GPUs will be used for computation, the CUDA driver from Nvidia also need to be installed.

PyTorch can be downloaded from https://pytorch.org/ by selecting the operating system, Python version, CUDA version, etc. The website supports installation via conda, pip, libtorch, and source (Fig. B.11). After the installation is complete, one can enter the Python console and execute the command *import torch*. If there is no error message, it means that the installation has been successful. The version of installed PyTorch can be viewed by *torch.__version__*. In this book, we will use PyTorch 0.4.0.

B.3.2 Tensor

Tensor is a core concept in PyTorch. A tensor can be viewed as a multi-dimensional array to store data. Common types of tensors include FloatTensor and LongTensor, to store data and indices, respectively. A tensor can be initialized from an array or by random values. Here are some code examples of initializing tensors:

```
import torch
# a real-valued tensor of size 2 X 3 initialized from an array
a = torch.FloatTensor([[1.2, 3.4, 5],[3, 6, 7.4]])
# a real-valued tensor of size 5 X 6 where each element is drawn from
    the normal distribution N(0,1)
b = torch.randn(5, 6)
# change a single element in the tensor a
a[0, 2] = 4.0
```

Tensors can participate in computations such as adding and subtracting. Two 2D tensors *a* and *b* can be multiplied using *torch.mm (a, b)*, if the number of *a*'s columns is the same as that of *b*'s rows. *Torch.max (a, dim = d)* calculates the maximum value along the *d*th dimension of the tensor *a*. More tensor operations can be found in https://pytorch.org/docs/0.4.0/torch.html.

B.3.3 Gradient computation

The greatest advantage of a deep learning framework is that the computation graph can be dynamically generated based on the operations on tensors. This graph allows automatic differentiation so developers do not need to derive and write code for gradients.

In PyTorch, if we need to compute the gradient for a tensor, the *requires_grad* attribute of the tensor needs to be set to *True* (default value: *False*), for example, *a = torch.FloatTensor([[1,2], [3,5]], requires_grad = True)*. After a series of computations to get the result, PyTorch provides the *backward* function to automatically compute the gradient of each tensor via backpropagation and store it in the *grad* attribute. The tensor can be put into GPU for faster computation by the *cuda* function. Here is some example code for tensor differentiation.

```
import torch
a = torch.ones(1)          # 1D tensor
a = a.cuda()               # a is placed into the GPU
a.requires_grad            # False
a.requires_grad = True     # the gradient of a needs to be computed
b = torch.ones(1)
x = 3 * a + b              # x is the result
x.requires_grad            # True, as the gradient of a needs to be
                           #   computed
x.backward()              # compute the derivatives of all parameters
a.grad                    # tensor([ 3.]), i.e. the derivative is 3
```

B.3.4 Network layer

The PyTorch package *torch.nn* contains most common network structures, such as the fully connected layer, CNN, and RNN. It is worth noting that to speed up data processing in deep learning, the data is usually grouped in batches. A data batch consisting of multiple samples can be processed by the network simultaneously. Therefore in PyTorch most networks admit input tensors whose first dimension is by default the batch size.

B.3.4.1 Fully connected layer

The *nn.Linear* command initiates a fully connected layer with two layers of neurons. **nn.Linear (in_feature, out_feature, bias = True)** indicates that there are *in_feature* neurons in the previous layer and *out_feature* neurons in the next layer, and *bias* indicates whether the bias parameter is used (True by default). The resulting module has *in_feature* $\times$ *out_feature* + *out_feature* parameters, including the bias.

The input tensor to this network must have the last dimension as *in_feature*, and the last dimension of the output tensor is *out_features*. Here's an example code:

```
import torch
import torch.nn as nn
# a network consisting of four fully-connected layers
# input layer size is 30, two hidden layers have size 50 and 70, and
   the output layer size is 1
linear1 = nn.Linear(30, 50)
linear2 = nn.Linear(50, 70)
linear3 = nn.Linear(70, 1)
# one batch consisting of 10 input data samples, each a 30D tensor
x = torch.randn(10, 30)
# 10 outputs, each a 1D tensor
res = linear3(linear2(linear1(x)))
```

B.3.4.2 Dropout

The *nn.Dropout* command implements the dropout layer. **nn.Dropout (p = 0.3)** indicates that a dropout with a probability of 0.3 (default: 0.5) to set input elements to 0. The input tensor can be of any size. Here is an example code:

```
layer = nn.Dropout(0.1) # Dropout layer with a dropout probability
   of 0.1
input = torch.randn(5, 2)
output = layer(input) # the output tensor has size 5 X 2, with each
   element being 0 with a probability of 10%
```

B.3.4.3 Convolutional neural network

The *nn.Conv2d* command implements the CNN. **nn.Conv2d(in_channels, out_channels, kernel_size, bias = True)** indicates that there are *in_channels* input channels and *out_channels* output channels (more parameters of *nn.Conv2d* can be found at https://pytorch.org/docs/stable/nn.html). The filter size is *kernel_size × kernel_size* and *bias* indicates whether a bias parameter is used (true by default). The input tensor should be a tensor of size *batch × in_channels × height × width*, and the output tensor has a size of *batch × out_channels × height_out × width_out*. Here is an example code of CNN:

```
# a CNN with 1 input channel, 3 output channels and filters of size
  5×5
conv = nn.Conv2d(1, 3, 5)
# one batch consisting of 10 input data samples, each a single-
  channel tensor of size 32×32
x = torch.randn(10, 1, 32, 32)
# the output tensor has a size of 10×3×28×28: 10 data samples,
  each a 3-channel tensor of size 28×28 (28=32-5+1)
y = conv(x)
```

B.3.4.4 Recurrent neural network

The *nn.GRU* commands implements the GRU network, *nn.LSTM* implements the LSTM network. For example, **nn.GRU(input_size, hidden_size, num_layers = 1, bias = True, batch_first = False, dropout = 0, bidirectional = False)** indicates that each element x_t in the input sequence is a vector of size *input_size*, the hidden state h_t has a dimension of *hidden_size*, and there are *num_layers* RNN layers (1 by default). *Bias* indicates whether a bias parameter is used (True by default), and *batch_first* indicates whether the first dimension of the input tensor is the batch size (second dimension by default). *Dropout* specifies the dropout probability (0 by default), and *bidirectional* indicates whether the RNN is bidirectional (False by default).

The input to *nn.GRU* includes:
- *input*: all input elements. If *batch_first = False*, the input has a size of *seq_len × batch × input_size*, otherwise it has a size of *batch × seq_len × input_size*.
- *h0*: the initial hidden state of RNN, with a size of *(num_layers × num_directions) × batch × hidden_size*.

The output of *nn.GRU* includes:

- *output*: the hidden state of RNN's last layer. If *batch_first = False*, the output tensor has a size of *seq_len × batch × (num_directions × hidden_size)*, otherwise it has a size of *batch × seq_len × (num_directions × hidden_size)*.
- *hn*: the hidden state of the last input element, with a size of *(num_layers × num_directions) × batch × hidden_size*.

Here is an example code of a GRU-based RNN:

```
# 2-layer GRU with an input dimension of 10, and hidden state
   dimension of 20. The second dimension of the input tensor is the
   batch.
rnn = nn.GRU(10, 20, num_layers = 2)
# one batch contains 3 sequences of length 5. Each element is
   represented by a 10D embedding.
x = torch.randn(5, 3, 10)
# initial 20D hidden state for 3 sequences, 2 layers
h0 = torch.randn(2, 3, 20)
# output contains all RNN states in the last layer, of size 5 × 3 × 20
# hn contains the last element' s hidden state, of size 2 × 3 × 20
output, hn = rnn(x, h0)
```

B.3.5 Custom network

In PyTorch, we often need to customize a network structure, such as two fully connected layers with an RNN layer in between. To create a custom network in PyTorch, one can write the custom network as a class inheriting from the base class *nn.Module* and implement the constructor and forward functions. PyTorch will derive the network structure and conduct automatic backpropagation via the backward function.

B.3.5.1 Implement a custom network

In the following code example, we implement a simple network *FirstNet*, consisting of a fully connected layer, a dropout layer, and an RNN layer.

```
import torch
import torch.nn as nn
# the custom network class inherits from nn.Module
```

(Continued)

```
(Continued)
class FirstNet(nn.Module):
    # the constructor function
    # input_dim: dimension of input tensor
    # rnn_dim: input dimension of RNN
    # state_dim: dimension of RNN's hidden state
    def __init__(self, input_dim, rnn_dim, state_dim):
        # call the parent class's constructor function
        super(FirstNet, self).__init__()
        # fully connected layer with input dimension of input_dim and
            output dimension of rnn_dim
        self.linear = nn.Linear(input_dim, rnn_dim)
        # dropout layer with a dropout probability of 0.3
        self.dropout = nn.Dropout(0.3)
        # single-layer unidirectional GRU with input dimension of
            rnn_dim and hidden state dimension of state_dim
        self.rnn = nn.GRU(rnn_dim, state_dim, batch_first = True)
    # forward computation function
    # Input:
    # x: the input tensor. Size: batch × seq_len × input_dim
    # Output:
    # result tensor. Size: batch × 1 × state_dim
    def forward(self, x):
        # dropout the outputs from the fully connected layer. Size:
            batch × seq_len × rnn_dim
        rnn_input = self.dropout(self.linear(x))
        # the last hidden state of GRU. Size: 1 × batch × state_dim
        _, hn = self.rnn(rnn_input)
        # swap dim0 and dim1. Size: batch × 1 × state_dim
        return hn.transpose(0, 1)

net = FirstNet(10, 20, 15)    # instantiate the class
# first dimension is batch
# 3 sequences of five elements, each with a 10D embedding
x = torch.randn(3, 5, 10)
res = net(x)                  # Size: 3×1×15
```

B.3.5.2 Optimize a custom network

Based on the implemented *FirstNet* in the previous section, we add a regression task to predict a real number given a sequence. The loss function is MSE. There are n sequences in the training data with corresponding ground-truth values $\{y_1, \ldots, y_n\}$.

PyTorch automatically gets the dynamic computation graph based on the current batch and conducts differentiation, so there is no need to implement the *backward* function. Before gradient computation, the gradients of network parameters have to be manually set to zero via the function *zero_grad*, since PyTorch does not automatically clear the gradients from the previous batch. In addition, we can set the training/testing mode of network via the *train* and *eval* functions to handle operations like dropout differently according to the mode.

The following code shows how to optimize a network in PyTorch. In the code, the *torch.max* function obtains the maximum value along a certain dimension of a tensor and returns two outputs: the maximum value and where the value is located.

```
import torch.optim as optim    # the optimization package of PyTorch
net = FirstNet(10, 20, 15)
net.train()      # set FirstNet to training mode (dropout is used)
net.cuda()       # put the network into GPU (if GPU is available)
# randomly initialize the training data
# 30 input sequences, each with 5 elements represented by a 10D
   tensor
x = torch.randn(30, 5, 10)
# 30 ground-truth values
y = torch.randn(30, 1)
# stochastic gradient descent (SGD) optimizer with a learning rate
   of 0.01
optimizer = optim.SGD(net.parameters(), lr = 0.01)
for batch_id in range(10):
    # get the current data batch (batch_size = 3)
    x_now = x[ batch_id * 3: (batch_id + 1) * 3]
    y_now = y[ batch_id * 3: (batch_id + 1) * 3]
    res = net(x_now)                    # the result is of size 3 × 1 × 15
    y_hat, _ = torch.max(res, dim = 2)    # use max-pooling to predict
       y_hat. Size: 3 × 1
    # mean square error (MSE) loss function
    loss = torch.sum(((y_now - y_hat) ** 2.0)) / 3
    optimizer.zero_grad()        # clears gradients from previous
    batches
    loss.backward()             # automatic backpropagation
    optimizer.step()                  # the optimizer updates the para-
       meters in the opposite direction of derivatives
                                                          (Continued)
```

(Continued)

```
net.eval()          # set FirstNet to evaluation mode (dropout is not
   applied in this mode)
y_pred = net(x)     # get output in evaluation mode
```

References

[1] Chung J, Gulcehre C, Cho K, Bengio Y. Empirical evaluation of gated recurrent neural networks on sequence modeling. arXiv preprint arXiv 2014; 1412.3555.

[2] Hochreiter S, Schmidhuber J. Long short-term memory. Neural Comput 1997;9 (8):1735−80.

[3] Srivastava N, Hinton G, Krizhevsky A, Sutskever I, Salakhutdinov R. Dropout: a simple way to prevent neural networks from overfitting. J Mach Learn Res 2014;15 (1):1929−58.

Index

Note: Page numbers followed by "*f*" and "*t*" refer to figures and tables, respectively.

Printed in the United States
by Baker & Taylor Publisher Services